Finding Time
for Serenity

Finding Time
for Serenity

Every Woman's Book of Days

BARBARA CAWTHORNE CRAFTON

MOREHOUSE PUBLISHING
A Continuum imprint
HARRISBURG • LONDON • NEW YORK

First published in 1994 by Ballantine Books. Revised edition published in 2004 by: Morehouse Publishing, P.O. Box 1321, Harrisburg, PA 17105

Morehouse Publishing, The Tower Building, 11 York Road, London SE1 7NX

Morehouse Publishing is a Continuum imprint.

Library of Congress Cataloging-in-Publication Data

Crafton, Barbara Cawthorne.
  Finding time for serenity : every woman's book of days / Barbara Cawthorne Crafton.
      p. cm.
Originally published: New York : Ballantine Books, c1994.
  ISBN 0-8192-2121-X
  1. Women—Conduct of life. 2. Devotional calendars. I. Title.
  BJ1610.C74 2004
  242'.643—dc22
                                         2003026995

Printed in the United States of America
04 05 06 07 08 09   10 9 8 7 6 5 4 3 2 1

To Mary Fisher,
a busy woman and an inspiration to many

FOREWORD TO THIS SECOND EDITION

I am grateful to everyone who appears in this book. They number in the thousands: doctors, homeless people, my friends, members of my family, colleagues at work, famous artists and writers I've never met, seafarers, people I pass in the street and doubtless will never meet again. Some of them are alive and some are dead. I am indebted to all of them.

I'll never write another book, I told myself and anyone else who would listen after I had finished writing this book ten years ago. Since then, almost all my work has been precisely that. I keep forgetting that there are 365 days in a year.

But thanks to Morehouse for bringing it back, to Debra Farrington and Ryan Masteller. Enjoy these little essays: may they give you a little something to start your day, and may it be a little something you need.

B. C. C.

The Geranium Farm

2004

Finding Time
for Serenity

JANUARY 1

In Korea, the New Year is celebrated with a ritual of reverence for old people: The children make a ceremonial bow before their elders, kneeling all the way down until their foreheads touch the ground. Parents do the same before the grandparents; everybody bows to anyone who is older. And when the elder accepts the gesture of respect, the child is rewarded with a coin ... even if the child is all grown up.

I'm going to go on a diet, Americans say to ourselves on this day, *and get back to my pre-pregnancy weight once and for all.* Some of us have been saying that for twenty-five years now. But as we pull off the last page of last year's calendar, we say it again. *I'm going to do something so that I'll be like I was when I was young. Thin. Full of pep. Maybe this year I'll do something about these bags under my eyes.*

But do you really want to be what you were in those days? So you're fatter now—you're also smarter. More sure of yourself. You can't be those things when you're young and inexperienced; it takes time to learn from your mistakes. Wisdom takes time to accumulate. That's why the Koreans honor the old: wisdom lives in them. And it lives in us, too, more and more as the years pass. Stick around long enough and the errors of your youth can become the stuff of which good advice is made. You can be proud of the things you learned the hard way. They may have left a few scars, but they have made you wise.

JANUARY 2

"O brave new world, that has such people in 't!"
—THE TEMPEST, ACT V SCENE I

When we looked forward to the end of the twentieth century from the middle of it, we thought we'd have more things figured out than we do. If you grew up expecting to be a wife and mother in a fairly predictable way, you've already been surprised by how unpredictable that life turned out to be. If you grew up expecting the women's movement to have pretty much settled things by now, you've already been surprised at how *un*settled things still are.

So many things are possible for us now. We have choices we didn't have before. Great: now we have to be terrific in two worlds instead of one. We look at beautiful pictures of food in magazines and wish we had time to make dishes look and taste as lovely as that. Or we look at a list in another magazine of the ten hottest careers for women and notice that ours is not among them, and we feel just the tiniest bit judged.

Hotter than *what*? And according to *whom*? The career that's hot for you is the one that warms your heart. Maybe you do the work you do because you really love it. Or maybe you don't, and you do it because the people you love have to eat. Is one less strong and brave than the other? I don't think so. Who cares whether or not it's on somebody's hot list? Or beautiful enough to be in a magazine? Choices are supposed to make people *more* free, not less so.

So don't let the magazine pictures make you feel inadequate. Or the hot job lists, either. You can't do everything, and only a few things relating to any kind of work are glamorous. It's your *commitment* to what you do that makes it good for you.

JANUARY 3

"On the eleventh day of Christmas my true love gave to me, eleven pipers piping...." —THE TWELVE DAYS OF CHRISTMAS

By the way, Christmas is not over. You've got until the Feast of the Epiphany (January 6th) to do all the things you didn't get to before December 25th. That's what the Church calendar says, and I'm going by that. This has the following advantages:

1. You can send out your Christmas cards now, when they will be much more noticeable. You can also respond in an informed way to the news people sent you in their cards which arrived on time. That way you won't be sending Mr. and Mrs. cards to people who divorced during the year.

2. You can buy things on sale in a store that doesn't look and sound like the Commodities Exchange, and ... a salesperson will be around when you need one.

3. You don't have to take your tree down right away.

4. You can keep playing Christmas music on the stereo.

5. You can call people to wish them a Merry Christmas when they'll actually have time to talk to you.

6. You can space out some of the gifts you give to your children. They don't all have to come on the same day. It can be more like Chanukah. The benefits of this are enormous. No sensory overload. No present frenzy in which a gift is barely acknowledged before the next one is torn into. And your kids actually learn to wait.

With a little encouragement, people are at their best at this time of year. Let's not revert to our crabby selves too quickly. We've got all year.

JANUARY 4

"Where can I flee from your presence?" —PSALM 139:6

I got up this morning at five o'clock. I thought I would have some time to myself—two hours, maybe, in a silent house.

Looking forward to this delicious slice of privacy at the day's beginning, I went to the kitchen to make a pot of tea. And as I waited for the kettle to boil, I heard a noise outside the door. Oh, no. It was Rosie, eldest grandchild. Up early, just like me.

"It's too early for you to be up," I said severely. And then I looked at her and thought of what it was like when I was four years old and awakened to hear my grandmother in the kitchen. What was I making, Rosie wanted to know. Tea, I answered, and got her some juice.

I did regret my lost two hours, and yet I also think that four-year-olds have the right to expect their grandmothers to be glad to see them. I remember feeling exactly the same ambivalence when her mother got up at the crack of many a long-ago dawn and destroyed my quiet time. I needed it. But she also needed me. And I needed her. I didn't know then how short the time with her would seem when it was over. Hardly any time at all. And now? You talk about quiet.

Rosie's feet were bare. *Aren't your feet cold?* No, she said. I got her some socks anyway. She drank her juice and chattered happily on and on about her school and the cookies she and her mother made to take there for the Christmas party. She had no sense of having interrupted anything important. And she was right. She's a pretty important person. There'll be other mornings for me alone.

JANUARY 5

"Oh, how good and pleasant it is!" —PSALM 133:1

Radio playing nice music. House sort of clean. Laundry done. Candles on the table, ready to light. Table set. Food all ready to cook quickly. Recipe we both like. Even a nice dessert made.

I had the day off today, so I had time to make things really nice. I got all the house things done and still had five or six wonderful hours. I was alone all day. I could listen to the music I like without irritating anyone. Even the phone calls were all people I wanted to talk to. And there weren't all that many of them.

I am very aware of how nice this is: just to take care of the house and make a good dinner. So different from a normal, hectic day, with its appointments and interruptions, places to be on time, things to pick up on the way home, things to decide. We have to have take-out meals sometimes, or meals eaten at different times from everyone else because I get home so much later than my family. There are weeks in which I don't feel I see them very much, these people I love the most. A hurried good-bye in the morning and an evening in which we're too sleepy to interact much.

I leaf through a magazine. A psychologist writes that I should be having one meal a day which the whole family eats together. I don't always do that. But we do the best we can. We enjoy one another when we *are* together. And at least the phone calls are regular and frequent and satisfying. Full of love.

Don't worry if you can't do the best thing every time—you'll rob yourself of the enjoyment of the things you *can* do.

JANUARY 6

"What do you mean by coming in here at eighteen minutes past the hour?"
—SCROOGE, TO BOB CRATCHITT, *A CHRISTMAS CAROL*

You're late.

You're stuck in traffic and the minutes tick by. Only fifteen minutes before you're supposed to be there. Ten. Now you're supposed to be there. Now it's *after* the time you were supposed to be there. You are furious. What's the matter up there? Why isn't anybody moving? You feel your heart pounding.

They're wondering where you are. You wish you had a cell phone. Now they probably think you're a lightweight. Undependable. Where *is* she? Are you sure she knew when the meeting started? Somebody's probably calling your home.

Hold it. There are times when there is simply nothing you can do, and this is one of them. The traffic will unsnarl when it does, and heart palpitations won't speed things up. This is one of those things you cannot change. Move beyond it: it's lousy and it'll be over, but for now it's time to do some damage control. You'll have to apologize to those you've inconvenienced and explain what happened. If you're *always* late, you'll want to take a look at that. Leave earlier or something. But that's the future. For now, you're just stuck. And so ...

You now have some free time. Nobody can reach you and you can't do anything about it. But you *can* switch on the radio and calm yourself down. Think about what to make for dinner. Think about something nice. You'll get there. And you'll be better able to deal with the consequences of being late if you get a grip on yourself now.

"And the muscles of his brawny arms are strong as iron hands..."
—HENRY WADSWORTH LONGFELLOW

Today all the health clubs are running newspaper ads to cash in on people's New Year's resolutions. You and a guilty friend can sign up for the price of one person. Then you can get the kind of body you want, which is described in the ads as "hard."

This idea of women being hard is new. When I was young, we were supposed to be soft. I got to be very good at that, and have been extremely soft all my life. I am not sure hard is something I'm going to be able to manage at this late date. The doctor I'm seeing now has given me a group of exercises to do, like "as many situps as I can," which should eventually make my stomach hard. That will be a new experience. I also lie on the floor and tighten my buttocks and stay that way for ten seconds, so I guess my bottom will one day be hard as well. All of these hard muscles I'm developing are going to hold my spine in the right position, I hear, and then my back won't hurt. "How long should I keep doing them," I ask. *"For the rest of your life,"* he says.

In the train station today I saw a whole shelf of magazines about getting hard. Improbably-muscled men and women held each other like footballs, their blood vessels standing out like cords on their arms and chests because they have no fat at all. I can't say they're attractive exactly, but they certainly are hard. They work out for hours each day to get that way, and once they've gotten hard they can never stop. It'll all turn to fat if they do. Just imagine the poor things if that happened: enormous, doughy mountains of soft flesh staring sadly at faded muscle magazine covers to remind them of their glory days, back when they were hard.

You won't be seeing me on one of those magazine covers in a leotard, with my blood vessels standing out like cords. I'll be satisfied if I can make my back stop hurting. As I already feel better when I do these exercises than I do when I don't, they must work. I'll never be hard. But maybe I can be strong.

JANUARY 8

"Life is unfair." —JOHN FITZGERALD KENNEDY

Unemployed for over a year, my friend finally landed a short-term job. *I'll take it,* she says; *in this market you can't be choosy. Besides, its nice to have my professional expertise recognized for a change. This job search business is a little hard on the ego.*

Wouldn't you know: the Saturday before the first training weekend, she lands in the hospital with diverticulitis, a painful inflammation of the intestinal wall. She's had it before, but this time it's really bad. Her roommate tells me they're probably going to have to operate and she doesn't quite know how to break it to Brooke. Oh, no, I say: what about the job? Of all times for something like this to happen.

I am not going to miss this training weekend, Brooke tells the doctor. Sure enough, she goes home. A nurse comes to show her how to give herself intravenous antibiotics. *This is better anyway,* she says; *we'll destroy the infection with this stuff, then I can have the operation after it's cleared up. It's simpler this way.* But there's hardly anything she can eat. *I don't care,* she says, *I needed to lose weight. In fact, I would go to this training dead if I had to.* And at the end of the week, with an IV lock in her arm but very much alive, she gets on the train for the first weekend workshop.

She's a determined woman. She's kept herself in good spirits, going out on interview after interview, but it's been brutal. She knows she's part of the recession, that this is about the economy, not about her. But so what? *Sure, it helps to know you're not alone,* she quips, *just not all that much. What really helps unemployed people is getting work.*

JANUARY 9

"*Give us, outside sleep, serenity.*" —GIORGOS SEFERIADES

I don't know why I can't sleep, but I'm very grateful. I know I'm going to regret it tomorrow, when I have to plod through a long day without adequate rest, but I need this time to work. It is unusual for me to be able to work at night; usually I'm too tired. The difference today is that I'm keyed up about a deadline I have to make and the host of distractions which will crowd between me and it this week. How will I get everything done? I don't know the answer to that yet. I just *will.* I have to. I will make my insomnia part of the war effort. Why lie awake in bed fretting when I can be awake working?

I said yes to some social engagements I ought to have refused these last two weeks. I need the time to work. When it came time to go off on one of these junkets, I have felt both guilty and angry in all kinds of ways. Guilty about not working. Guilty if I canceled or postponed a date. Angry at whoever asked me to have a few hours of innocent fun, as if such an invitation were a deliberate act of sabotage. Angry that I can't have a social life when I have a deadline. Angry at myself, really, because I didn't space out my work better: I could have avoided this bottleneck by working more steadily. I rebuke myself sharply. *Why don't you ever plan ahead?*

But I am always like this with a project. I must be one of those people who needs pressure in order to perform. I wish I were otherwise, but we are the way we are. I would not want to live this way all the time, but I must say I'm impressed with the old girl. I can still respond to a shot of adrenaline when I have to.

JANUARY 10

I'm home, Corinna says when she calls at about one in the afternoon. *Madeline got sick at school again.* Her male boss, who has never had to miss work because of a sick child, is not above heaving an exasperated sigh, as if she had done this deliberately. *He's not a bad guy ordinarily. I guess people just forget sometimes what it can be like.* People who've never been single parents forget especially well, I find.

If she's not better tomorrow I'll see if I can move some things around in my schedule and watch Madeline. My mother would have done the same for me. But often I can't manage that, so Corinna's left to struggle through another childcare nightmare on her own. Corinna and a lot of other people. I wish it were easier.

I remember lying to an employer when one of my children got sick, telling him it was I who was ill. I knew he would question my commitment to the job if I didn't, and I was right. That was degrading; I felt guilty for doing it, as if taking care of my kids was wrong. But that's the message: be serious about your work or be a mother. You can't be both.

Except that more than half of all American mothers *are* both. There is some evidence that things are improving: Corinna doesn't lie about her kids being sick, and she doesn't feel as guilty as I did. Her boss may sigh noisily, but he doesn't do much else. And there are men at work who sometimes find themselves in the same boat. But it's so hard. I hope your kids are well and in school today. If they're not, I hope they can go back tomorrow, and that nobody says anything thoughtless and cruel to you about it if they can't. Or, if someone does, that you've got a withering response all picked out, and the guts to use it.

JANUARY 11

Jenny is an old cat. She has had a hard life. We got her from the pound. She had a litter of kittens, and then she had a cat hysterectomy. Her tail has never worked: it's paralyzed, sort of, and droops over to one side. For a number of years she was frightened of people; she would scuttle away from us to be by herself. Not much personality, we all felt. Something of a non-cat.

One of the other cats, sensing her vulnerability, took to tormenting Jenny. He'd wait beside the feeding bowl, growling menacingly, and attack her if she tried to come near it. He'd jump her in the middle of the night, and we'd all be awakened by their howls. Jenny took to hiding under the china cupboard during the day. She grew thin, because she could never get near the food.

She was rescued by my husband. He built a tall tripod out of logs and put it in a corner of the living room. Every morning he would carry Jenny over to it and install her safely on the shelf at the top. Richard brought her food and water, and carried her to the cat box. Jenny began to get fatter. She became calm and serene, a Buddha-like presence at the top of the cat tree, watching benignly over the family's comings and goings. Her life became that of a normal old cat again.

But Jenny has not forgotten Richard's role in her deliverance. Many nights she goes all the way up to the very top of our tall Victorian house, the very roof-pole, and calls for him to come and get her. Her day is not complete unless Richard has gotten her down from some high place. Jenny has a rescue fantasy about my husband.

I guess love just comes to some of us late in life.

<hr />

JANUARY 12

<hr />

"Love well that which thou must lose ere long." —SHAKESPEARE, SONNET 73

W e visit my husband's uncle. He has been battling lung cancer for about a year now. Now he is in hospice care at home, with an oxygen tank downstairs and another in the bedroom. A nurse comes every day, and neighbors drop in now and then so his wife can go shopping.

Our visit is quiet: we join them for dinner in their kitchen. The next day we go for a drive with them in their car. John has a holster in which he packs a portable oxygen tank, so he can go out for short distances. We see their church, and the main street of their little town. I take a picture of John and my husband standing in front of the church.

John first suspected something was wrong when he noticed that he was winded after one set of tennis. His doctor didn't take it too seriously at first; *You're seventy-nine, John, what do you expect?* Now he misses tennis, and the long walks he used to take with Jane. He has a hard time enjoying food, and he misses that. But they are so glad they can spend these last weeks of their fifty years together at home. At the moment they are working on a jigsaw puzzle one of their sons sent his dad: hundreds of little cartoon tennis players, whacking at the ball and bumping into one another.

When we leave, I look into Jane's eyes. Their cozy little home in upstate New York is just right for the two of them. I imagine her living here alone soon. *It meant a lot to us that you came,* she tells my husband. *John has always thought so much of you.*

Richard is quiet for the first half hour or so as we drive away from his uncle and from the scenery of his childhood. *It meant a lot to me to come here,* he says after a while.

JANUARY 13

"Silence gives the proper grace to women."

I walk into the seafarers' club early on a weekday afternoon. A man is on the pay phone. A few of the old guys are in there, shooting pool, watching TV, drinking coffee. They've got all the time in the world. I go into the kitchen to clean the grill. Then I do a few other things around the building, maybe another twenty minutes' worth, and come back into the club.

The guy's still on the phone. He finishes his call and hands me the cup of soup he's been holding in his hand all this time. Could I warm it up in the microwave? It got cold while he was talking. I laugh at him.

And they say women talk a lot, I tell him. *You were on the phone for half an hour at least. You could have starved to death.* He throws both hands up in the air, as if he were being taken prisoner. *Help, she's picking on me,* he tells one of the other guys, and one of the big talkers begins a rambling speech about the differences between men and women.

Most of the seafarers love to play this game of war between the sexes. We do it all the time. These old men have lived their lives on ships. They observe normal human interactions from a certain distance; they have not always had them. They are eager to connect. They love to tell me sea stories. Some of the stories are even true.

Retired from the sea now, they drink coffee and trade their stories all day, still feeling more comfortable with one another than with anyone else. The world of the ship is still their world, even though the ship is long gone.

You spend most of your life working, whatever you do. Even when you're finished forever, that world will shape you. What you have done is part of who you are.

JANUARY 14

"He plants trees to benefit another generation." —CAECILIUS STATIUS

Out of the blue, an old friend calls. *You sound wonderful,* she says. I *am* wonderful, I tell her. We marvel over the ages of our children; the toddler boy I remember is now driving a car, and his sister is graduating from college next month. I counter with my daughter's new house. She can't believe my other daughter is in college already. Her husband's stopped smoking. Great. Mine isn't retiring again this year. Great.

We lived through some hard times together in the old days. We were among the first women ordained as priests in the Episcopal Church, and it was rough sledding sometimes. There were fifty or so of us then, sprinkled throughout the country. Now there are almost two thousand women priests, out of a total contingent of ten thousand men and women. I have an old picture of us, with another friend: we're sitting in our clerical attire, and we're each wearing a long, gray, beard. If you can't lick 'em, join 'em, I remember one of us saying as we put the beards on, and we hooted with laughter. But there was pain behind the foolery. Those were not easy times.

Things are better now for women in the ministry. Not perfect, but they are better. Another friend is a Roman Catholic nun who feels a vocation to ordained ministry. The struggle through which we lived and laughed and cried has been denied her so far. She hangs in there.

We were brave in those early days. We still are, I guess: maybe a little tired, but still brave. It is also brave to carry on when you can't have what you very much want.

JANUARY 15

"Tis the gift to be simple". —"SIMPLE GIFTS," SHAKER HYMN

In New York, there is a manicurist on every corner. They are usually on the second floor of retail buildings, identified by a small neon sign in the window: NAILS. Or sometimes just NAIL—many of the manicurists are people for whom English is a second language, and it sometimes shows in their marketing technique, like the shop somewhere up in the East Seventies called CONFETTI OF NAIL. Such a festive name; what, exactly, does it mean?

I am an amateur manicurist. I love to do people's nails. I did my mother's nails when she was alive. I do my friends' nails. My own, too, of course, although I also love having someone else do mine. There was a period in my professional life when I did nails at lunchtime in the office. People used to come in and get their nails done, and we'd have a gab fest while they were waiting for them to dry. Then they'd have me fish a subway token out of their purses so they wouldn't smudge and off they'd go.

Often, especially when people came in alone, important things were said over the beautiful little bottles of nail polish. People would sit down, take off their rings and start talking. Something about having someone performing such a service for you opens the heart. *You must care about me,* the recipient of a manicure thinks, or *you wouldn't be doing this. I can trust you with my thoughts.*

I have never read anything in any article about professional demeanor in the office or appropriate behavior in the workplace that suggested that it is all right to do people's nails. I imagine the verdict would be the opposite: maintain an appropriate distance, do not go beyond a careful friendliness. Look the part. Don't do silly, things.

I guess I'm guilty. I do silly things all the time. Most of the people I know and like do silly things at work, too, and some of the most delicious times in the work week are the silly times.

The nail thing was also a subtle statement from the women's counterculture. Women groom each other. Men don't. Sometimes a man would come around and want his nails done too, thinking he was brave and funny for asking. And so he was. I would oblige with a quick coat of clear and ten minutes of uproariousness with whatever women happened to be around so he could see what it was like, and then he would pad happily back to his office, waving his wet fingers in the air.

JANUARY 16

"What do you want to be when you grow up?"

The universal adult question upon meeting a child. We grow up knowing we have to be something; it's not okay to answer "nothing" to that question, although you may be able to get away with "I don't know yet" if you don't mind being pressed further. *"Well, then, what do you like best in school?"* It is somehow very important to get the child's future settled right then and there. I wanted to be a ballet dancer, an orchestra conductor, an archaeologist, a teacher, a lawyer, and an actress when I was young. I wanted to be all of them, but I wanted some more seriously than others. Like most people, what I ultimately became was not any of the things I dreamed of as a child. Usually circumstances combine with talent and effort to produce our adult professional selves, and that's okay with most of us.

But many people still carry their dreams with them. They want to sing, or they want to write, and dream of doing it "someday." But they are busy earning a living, and someday never comes. This is too bad. Dreams are important. If you've carried one with you all this way, it must be an important part of who you are.

Don't postpone writing or painting until you can be "a writer" or "a painter": someone who earns her living from her art. A writer is just a person who writes. So if you want to write, start writing. If you want to be a singer, sing. Learn about it. Read about it. Ask professionals in the field about it. But most important, *do* it. Maybe you'll do it for a living some day. Maybe you won't. But we live a lot longer today than people used to, and life is not over until it's over. So just do it. Grandma Moses didn't even *start* painting until she was ninety. It's never too late.

JANUARY 17

"That which would be hateful to you, do not do to another." —HILLEL

At a meeting, the speaker is a woman who wears braces on both her legs as the result of a childhood bout with polio. I have known her for years.

She tells a story about receiving communion in a church. When the priest handed her the wafer, she stroked her cheek in a gentle way. My friend was deeply angered by that gesture, even though she knew the woman thought she was being kind. *She was treating me like a child. I am not a child. I don't need people to pat me! I will ask if I want to be touched. Please don't touch me without my asking for it. I know you mean it well, but it's patronizing. I fight hard, sometimes, just to get up in the morning. I want credit, not pity.*

Ouch. No, the priest in question wasn't me, but I'm afraid it could just as well have been. I believe that I have sometimes used touch in a motherly, tender way when it wasn't appropriate to do so. I admire my friend for pointing it out, because she has to be thorny to do so. Everybody likes disabled people a lot more if they're sweet. *Maybe,* she says, *but things don't change if you're just sweet. I want things to be better for people like me.*

You know, she goes on, *I'm disabled, but you all are "temporarily abled." I'm in a wheelchair now, but most of you will be in one sooner or later. My reality is going to be yours someday—mine or a variation of it. That's life. I know it now, but you're going to know it eventually. I don't just want life to be better for me. I want it to be better for you.*

JANUARY 18

"It's not the case that I don't understand. I understand perfectly. I just disagree."

My classmate leans back against his chair, hard. He is frustrated at the way our discussion is going. There has just been a disagreement between him and the professor, and one of the other students has suggested that he may not have understood what the professor was saying. *When a person of color disagrees with someone in authority,* he says, *white people say he doesn't understand. Well, I do understand. I just disagree. White people can't imagine that someone could see what they see and reach conclusions different from theirs.*

All the white students are uncomfortable. Do I really do that? Jerome is brave in our class. He does not shrink from observations like that, even though he knows they are painful for us to face. Our small group of diverse people struggles with things like this all the time. We hope that it will make us more sensitive leaders, and I expect it will. It often makes us mad, but it's worth it.

People who come from different cultures are—well, different. There are profound differences in how we see the world. It used to be that liberal people would say we're all the same inside. But we're not. Men and women, black and white, Asian and Western: we are different. It's hard for us to hear each other. It takes a lot of work.

Most of our neighborhoods are segregated, still. So is most of our social life. Even most of our churches. But the workplace has become the most diverse area of American life. We need to learn to communicate with one another. It's hard: if it's not hard for you, check it out. Like some exercises, you can only tell you're doing it right if it hurts.

JANUARY 19

"Exercise is a nervous disorder." —ROBERT BENCHLEY

I have learned that my father, who is eighty-three and missing part of one foot, has taken to riding fifteen minutes a day on an exercise bike. That's pretty inspiring. I also read this week about a young man who completed a marathon race in a wheelchair.

I feel so good after I have skied for twenty minutes on the Nordic Track. I feel good all day, virtuous about what I have done. It seems that I can feel the blood flowing more freely through arteries that are clearer. I even feel more energy after I've done Nordic Track. I truly feel all these things.

And yet I lie in bed and postpone putting on my sneakers. It's not the reality of exercise I hate. It's the *thought*. I hate the very thought of exercise. I hate the thought of being tired. I hate the thought of sweating. I hate the thought of being imprisoned by the slow passage of minutes. I hate people who talk about how good it makes them feel. I hate myself for sometimes being one of them. From my bedroom I can just make out the shape of the Nordic Track in the living room. In the first light of the day it looks like a large, stupid animal. I dread going out there. I lie in my lovely warm bed, hating the thought, until I am sure it's too late for me to begin exercising. Then I get dressed and slink guiltily out the door to go to work.

Why do I avoid something that makes me feel so good? Shouldn't I be enjoying this by now? My husband jumps on the thing every day. Now I think I hate him, too. I turn the radio up so I won't have to listen to the reproachful swish of the runners on the Nordic Track. I'll ski tonight. I promise.

JANUARY 20

"No one was strong enough to master him." —MARK 5:4

Something comes in the mail from Mothers Against Drunk Driving. They want support for their lobbying effort, and they enclose their platform: mandatory revocation of licenses for drunken drivers, mandatory revocation of registration, and a few other sanctions designed to keep drunks off the road. But not a thing about helping them get sober.

Alcoholism is a disease. Some people get angry when they hear that: they think it means that the drunk's behavior is somehow "excused" by his illness, that he isn't responsible because he's sick. That's not it at all. Accepting the disease concept is what enables the alcoholic to *become* responsible. It enables him to say, "I can't control my drinking. It controls me," and begin the steps toward managing a life without alcohol. It enables him to go to the meetings that help him get through the day without drinking. It enables him to acknowledge the character defects that he used to drink away. It enables him to admit how his drinking has caused him to hurt himself and others, and to make amends where that is possible.

Drunks who don't admit they're sick don't get better. It doesn't just "go away." The drunk can't resolve it away by himself. He needs help, and he needs to understand that it is a matter of life and death that he get help. Life and death for him. And life and death for the innocent children he encounters when he's behind the wheel. Just taking his license away won't protect them from him; he'll drive anyway, if he wants to. Only his sobriety can save the children.

JANUARY 21

"A teacher affects eternity." —HENRY BROOKS ADAMS

Anna calls from school. A friend from high school has told her that her favorite teacher is terribly ill and not expected to live. I am shocked to hear it. I'll find out where she is, I tell Anna, and see if I can go see her. *If you do see her tell her*—Anna falters, and I say I'll tell her.

What a tremendous teacher she is, I think as I hang up the phone. She taught English, and she and another teacher directed the school plays. Fabulous musicals, they did; they'd get sixty kids up on stage tap-dancing like it was nothing. Dozens of talented young professionals got their start with her. I remember her extra attention to a troubled lonely boy I was also working with, how she would stay after school to talk with him and encourage him. There were a lot of kids like that. I remember her with my kids. Ina Schlein could be tough. But she was the best.

Teachers ought to be the ones with the six-figure salaries, not CEOs. They are the most influential people in America, bar none, and the most taken for granted. I think of my children growing up, how important certain teachers were, and I know I owe them a debt I can never repay. I think of myself as a young person, and I remember how dearly I loved some of my teachers. It's a remarkable relationship. We don't raise our kids alone. We have a lot of help.

JANUARY 22

"Be it ever so humble, there's no place like home." —JOHN HOWARD PAYNE

The first biographer of novelist Jane Austen—her nephew—remembered that she used to sit at a little table by the window to write. If somebody came into the room, she would slide the paper she was working on into the desktop, out of sight. She took a great deal of pleasure in her family and its life. It was easy for them to love her as a daughter, a sister, an aunt. Those aspects of her were primary to them, not her genius as a writer. It is not even mentioned in the inscription they put on her tombstone.

That is true for us still. Your children don't love the accountant; they love Mom. Your mother's primary experience of you is not as the physician, but as the daughter. You may be a construction worker, but your husband's primary experience of you is as his wife. Home is about home. Work is about the outside world. This separation is most obvious to those who try to work at home. We have a hard time setting enough boundaries around ourselves to get it done. Our family doesn't know us as workers. They know us another way.

Women are sometimes annoyed because their families don't respect the commitment of energy their work requires. We come home exhausted and we're still supposed to be Mother of the Year and Playmate of the Month. Don't let them expect that. They can probably get along with less in terms of glowing performance if we give them a lot in terms of presence. There's nothing terribly wrong with an exhausted Mommy cuddling her child after a dinner that came out of a can. The cuddle will be remembered. The can will be forgotten.

JANUARY 23

"As I in hoary winter night stood shivering in the snow..." —ROBERT SOUTHWELL

Snow. Six inches in our backyard last night. Richard is still recovering from the flu. While he is in the shower, I leap into my boots and go outside in my bathrobe to shovel out the car. I want to get as much done as I can before he catches me and takes over. In my opinion, Richard over-shovels; paths to the car and to the garage, paths to the garbage cans. Certainly this is no job for a flu patient.

I can't find the shovel. It is buried under the snow somewhere. So I get a broom and sweep off the steps. I decided to take a chance and see if I can move the car without shoveling it out first. This works better than I deserve, and I cruise easily right to the door. Now the car is warm inside, and not stuck right next to the steps, which are clean. That ought to be enough. We don't need a path to the garbage cans this red-hot minute. I go back inside.

But now Richard is downstairs, bundled up like somebody Jack London would write about. He is horrified at my décolletage—I was in a hurry, I tell him—and deaf to my pleas that he not go out there. He is a stubborn man. When I emerge fifteen minutes later, showered and ready for the drive to the train, the yard is criss-crossed with his dumb paths.

You shouldn't be out there and you know it, I say. I am really angry. *You never listen to me.*

15

You don't listen to me, he counters, *out there in the snow with nothing on,* and all the way to the train station we argue in this desultory way. The truth is that neither of us trusts the other to know what's best for him or her. Each only wants to spare the other, but we each feel controlled by the other when we try.

JANUARY 24

"However plain you be, I'll love you." —GILBERT AND SULLIVAN,
PIRATES OF PENZANCE

It is impossible to grow up female and not get the message that being loved is intimately tied up with being pretty. Tiny little girls worry about whether they are pretty or not, encouraged to do so by the things they see on television. Teenaged girls admire fashion models, people whose job it is to be beautiful, people whom you never hear utter a word. Young women fear that they will not find love if they are not pretty enough; older women fear that the loss of youthful beauty will prevent them from finding love again.

Their mothers—or their friends—tell them that anyone who can't see beyond the package is not a person worth bothering about anyway. Besides, they say, you look just fine. "Just fine" is not what they want to hear. *You're just saying that because you're my mom, or because you're my friend and you love me. I'll probably never find someone.*

We look at pictures of people who are older than we are but look twenty years younger. We forget that they are paid to look that way, that they spend six hours or more each day maintaining that appearance. And we also forget that their lives don't seem any happier than ours; they, too, have unhappy relationships and divorces. Maybe more than unglamorous people have, because it is necessary for them to focus so singlemindedly on externals. Mom was right: it *is* what's inside that counts. Maybe you find someone and maybe you don't. Whether you do or not, you still have to live with yourself, and you are the one who decides how interesting a companion that self will be.

JANUARY 25

"You've come a long way..."

I have taken the day off today to go to a meeting of my women's club. You might think it is a consciousness-raising group or a political action group, but you would be wrong. This club is not about that. It was founded just before the turn of the century, and improvement of the mind was what it was for: women got together and studied something interesting, at a time when there were not as many places for an alert and interested female mind to go as there are today.

The basics of how we do things haven't changed all that much in a hundred years: we each prepare a paper on some agreed-upon theme, and two women read theirs at each meeting. We dress up; some members recall that after one woman appeared hatless at a meeting in the early seventies, nobody ever wore a hat again. The meetings are in member's homes, and women get out their silver tea and coffee services and their best china. None of this is going to change the world. But it makes for a pleasant and stimulating afternoon, and most of us feel we've earned a few of those.

The minutes of old meetings show that the first members of the club discussed what today would be called women's issues, with much the same rueful humor we use in talking about them now. I picture them at one of our meetings, these older sisters of the club, sitting among us in their large hats and long skirts. How would they feel about the white wine we had at the opening luncheon, I wonder. Our traditions nourish us, but we cannot be the women of the 1890s. We must be ourselves, both in the ways we are different from our foremothers and in the ways we are the same.

JANUARY 26

"As a white candle in a holy place, so is the beauty of an aged face."
—JOSEPH CAMPBELL

Will this twenty-dollar pot of cream that weighs just a little more than a letter really eliminate the dark circles under my eyes? That seems hard to believe. It also purports to minimize what it kindly refers to as "tiny lines," and it reduces puffiness. The description of how it will do this relies on my understanding of how something called "liposomes" work. I don't think that's really a word.

Like most women, I've spent a lot of time in front of a mirror. I know my face. I've watched it change. I remember my eyes when I was young. They're still a nice color, but the smooth skin around them is gone. And some of the lines at the corners are not "tiny." The puffiness underneath them sometimes makes me look like I've been crying when I haven't.

No liposomes are going to give me back my young skin. I remember pictures of Mae West when she was in her eighties, caked with makeup, her eyes fringed with thick false eyelashes. Trying to look young. It is grotesque to try to look young when you are old. But she tried—she didn't have a model of beauty other than that of youth. Youth *is* beautiful. But age has its own beauty as well. Jessica Tandy. Helen Hayes. Katharine Hepburn. None of them has tried to look twenty-five. They were old. And dignified. And beautiful.

"Pains of love be sweeter far than all other pleasures are." —JOHN DRYDEN

I understand that eating chocolate causes the release into the blood of the same enzyme which is released when one falls in love. This no doubt accounts for the practice of giving each other chocolate with Valentine's Day, a partnership which existed long before we knew about the enzyme, of course; we must have figured it out in our collective subconscious. It also explains why chocolate lovers often express their craving in fairly graphic sexual terms: they talk about chocolate orgies, about the seductiveness of chocolate, about being powerless to resist it, about being ravished by chocolate against their will. The Empire Diner in New York City serves something called a "Brownie All the Way." I remember the phrase "all the way" from my girlhood; it meant something quite different from anything you could do in a diner, even in New York.

The other thing that seems to go with chocolate is, surprisingly, death. Restaurants serve desserts like Death by Chocolate and Chocolate Suicide. This isn't as far removed from the romantic imagery as it seems at first, though: the message is simply that anything that spectacularly enjoyable must be sinful and will be punished. Which brings me to the third category of chocolate associations:

Mud. Mississippi Mud Cake. Chocolate Mud Pie. Or sometimes, just Chocolate Mud. Nothing is as wonderful as sinking your bare feet into some deep, wet, brown mud. It's even okay with shoes on—good in a different way, but still pretty darn good. And nothing is as sure to get you killed when you get home as having done that. Kids know this. But then they see a mud hole as they're walking home and they find themselves unable to resist. Pure sensual delight. Followed by punishment. We come to expect this. A lot of us think it's a fair trade for chocolate. Or mud. Or love.

JANUARY 28

"Because of deep love, one is courageous." —LAO-TZU

A thirty-something friend and her husband have been trying for years to have a baby. Everything: the drugs that make you have multiple births, tests about her Fallopian tubes and ovaries and everything else inside her, hormones that give her wild mood swings. *We make love as if it were homework,* she says, and laughs. But it is a bitter laugh. *This whole thing is the most degrading experience I could imagine.*

They've put some ads in the paper about private adoption. Desperate young women answer the ads, then call back to say they've changed their minds. They've talked to parents who have gone to other countries—to Peru, to Rumania. She's haunted by the idea that the mothers there are so poor they sell their babies. *I could never give mine up*, she tells herself. *But maybe we should go to Peru.*

She thinks a hundred times a day about how ironic it is: so many people want babies and so many other people have babies they don't want. Each horrible story in the paper about child abuse burns into her like a brand, makes her long to enter into the story; travel back in time, find the mother, stop the abuse: *Don't hurt the baby!* she dreams of bursting into the room and saying. *Give him to me.*

Maybe this is just not going to happen, she says. *But then we hear about something new they've come up with, and after all we've been through it seems crazy not to try this last thing that might be the thing that works.*

I tell her I think she's very brave. *Or very stupid*, she says, and laughs again. She's anything but stupid. They'll be good parents. There's got to be a baby for them somewhere.

JANUARY 29

"I'd call you back dear love, from the world below..." —EURIPIDES

I call my daughters. They seem well. Grandchildren okay. I call my dad to see how he's doing. He seems okay. My stepmother is okay.

Still I'm restless. I know that this is because the person I really want to talk to can't talk to me. I miss calling my mom. I miss her picking up the phone; "Hi, Honey" she would say. Only now I can't remember exactly the sound of her voice. And I'm not really sure, now that I think harder, that it was actually "Hi, Honey" that she said. Maybe it was just "helloo" in that funny kind of sing-song voice that she sometimes used. I can no longer say for sure.

I cut off a lock of her hair when she died. It smelled like her. I used to sniff it, sometimes, in the months after she died, filling my nostrils with the scent I loved. I can't remember now quite what it was like; after a while, the lock of hair lost its smell. Now it doesn't smell like anything much at all.

Our place in the world closes up after we leave it. After a while, nobody can see the place where we were anymore, not even those who loved us best. I can still know that she was kind and funny and smart. I can still remember things she said and did. But she herself is gone from our midst. Which is what hurts about death.

I'm always telling my husband I like his smell. Not his shaving soap, not his shampoo: just him. When he is away I sometimes wear his nightshirt just to get that nice smell. You must be crazy, he says, but I can tell he is pleased. I open the closet to hang up some shirts and his clothes smell like him. I love it. I hate the thought of its fading away some day.

"Death borders upon our birth..." —JOSEPH HALL

My husband brings me a sheet of paper he picked up at a conference. *Take a look at this.* A colleague's husband has written *The Grim Reaper's Book of Days*, which lists 366 different weird ways people have died, one for each day of the year. I read the blurb. Somebody in Dusseldorf was impaled on a six-foot icicle on January 10, 1951. On December 27, 1969, a circus performer fell off a trampoline into the mouth of a hippopotamus who happened to be standing nearby, and that was the end of him.

Good Lord.

I wonder what the author is like. Interesting sense of humor. When did he research this book? How long did it take? How did he pitch it to the publisher: *I'd like to propose a humorous 365-page book about exotic ways in which people have died?* Maybe he enlisted all his friends into the search for bizarre fatalities of history, and he'd get notes on Christmas cards that said things like, *"Don't forget William Rufus, the second Norman king of England, who got so fat that he exploded. Love to Laurie and the kids."*

A strange book to write. I can't help but laugh at the examples, until I stop and think that they really happened. Then I feel like a monster: these were real people, and here we are tittering at their last moments as if they were cartoons. People often do laugh at death, though; we try to find ways to domesticate our old enemy by making him funny, as if we could gain some immunity by our laughter.

"Brother, Can You Spare a Dime?"

The public radio station to which I listen is having its fundraising drive. This happens a few times a year; the rest of the time the station doesn't have commercials at all. But you pay for it during the fund drive: the radio announcers pay for it, too, in the humiliation of having to leave their usual scholarly mien and nag their loyal listeners to send money for something they can get for nothing just by turning the radio on. They tell us how selfish and shallow we would be if we just turned the radio on and *didn't* send any money, and they are right. But I can tell they hate doing this.

Listening to them reminds me of how many people make their living selling. It often means talking people into buying something they didn't know they wanted. Some people are incredibly good at this and enjoy it. Others would rather die.

Sales-oriented people think nothing of depending on a commission for their livelihood. They treat this dead-serious business as if it were a game, and love the thrill of a direct hit when they succeed in getting one. When they don't, there's always next time. This seems so brave to me; I can't imagine that kind of selfconfidence. I would be a nervous wreck.

If you make your living selling something, my hat would be off to you. If I had a hat. In no other way of making a living is what you earn so directly a result of how good you are at what you do. People on salary have a bad week here and there and yet the checks keep coming in. People who sell for a living sell or they get no paycheck. If that's you, you've got guts.

FEBRUARY 1

"...hurrying shapes met face to face..." —THOMAS BAILEY ALDRICH

It is eight o'clock in the morning, but the 6:56 train has not yet arrived. We all stand on the platform like sheep. Every ten minutes or so the loudspeaker crackles an unintelligible apology for the delay. The 6:56 arrives; only one door will open. Several hundred people move like a centipede to the end of the platform to board. The train can't take us all. We wait for the next one, and it stops all the way down at the other end. The centipede pivots and shuffles back the way it came, so that the first in line are now the last to board. Oh, well.

Getting to work has been such a comedy of errors this morning that people are past being angry about it any more. The train ahead of ours experiences repeated breakdowns. Our engineer gets on the loudspeaker to inform us about each one: by the time he begins his third such announcement, the whole train erupts in laughter and loud applause. We are like schoolchildren whose teacher has not appeared to start the class, unable to leave but enjoying an unexpected respite from our routine. People with cellular phones call their offices to move things around in their schedules. Other people get out their laptops and get down to work. But most people do neither of these things. They just goof off.

I am inconvenienced by this, but there's not a thing I can do about it and it's not my fault. The immediate significance of this delay is that I now have some unexpected free time. Eventually we're going to get there, and all those urgent things I'm missing will begin their clamor for my attention. Until then, I'm going to goof off, too.

"...to care for the healthy to keep them well..." —HIPPOCRATES

On a day when I have: 1) a deadline to meet; 2) four long exams written by seminary students to read; 3) a dozen phone calls to return; 4) a house that really needs to be cleaned; and 5) grandchildren coming for the weekend, my husband tells me he feels a little dizzy. I ask him some questions: any tingling in your arms? any headache? any nausea? *No, no,* and *no.* I look at his eyes; a few tiny red capillaries; are there more than usual? I listen to his heart: regular, sixty or so beats a minute. He doesn't want to call the doctor. He feels stupid calling to say he's dizzy. Wonderful, I say, you want to wait until you have a massive stroke and then call. Great idea.

I'm frightened. I also feel guilty, because here I am wondering how I'm going to get all this work done when my husband may have something seriously wrong with him. I must be a monster to even think about work if my husband is ill.

We call the doctor. The nurse asks him the same questions I did. She sounds very calm. Should we come in? No, they'll call, she says. Later in the morning, Richard begins to feel better. By the time the doctor calls, the dizziness is gone. Whew.

If something had been seriously wrong, all bets would have been off. They'd have had to find somebody else to read those exams and the deadline would just have had to wait. That's all.

But the truth is this: when someone gets sick, it's not just scary; it's also a pain in the neck. I feel guilty even thinking this, but it's true. So if caring for someone you love who is ill is part of your life right now, you've got a heavy load. Give yourself what breaks you can. Because the illness may be the main thing in your life, but it is not the only thing.

FEBRUARY 3

"Crocodile tears." —ROBERT BURTON, *THE ANATOMY OF MELANCHOLY*

We *may have to cancel the conference,* my colleague says on the phone. *I'll let you know by four tomorrow afternoon.*

The worst snow in a hundred years has hit New York City like Grant through Richmond. Nothing moves. My colleague calls me later, at another conference where I've been all weekend. I've been planning to go straight from one conference to another, without even going home in between. He says he doesn't want to cancel. He and I have worked hard on the program. Rescheduling will be a real pain. I tell him I hope we don't have to, either, and we hang up.

I am lying.

I would *love* it if we had to cancel. Then I could go home for two days, instead of dashing from one gig right into another. It's not that I don't think the conference is important, because I do. We did work hard on it. I would have gone and worked hard some more, and I would have done it cheerfully. But I'm tired and overcommitted, and I don't think it will hurt any of us to have a few unscheduled days off.

But there are no flights into Newark Airport at all tomorrow, so we're stuck here in Baton Rouge until Monday. Stuck. Can't even go home. This is a terrible shame. We will have no choice but to go back to that Cajun dance place tonight.

I'm just sick about the whole thing.

FEBRUARY 4

"Music ... ministers to human welfare." —HERBERT SPENCER

We are delayed in the airport. Only one runway is open in Newark, they tell us over the loudspeaker, so it's going to be a couple of hours behind schedule all the way around, at least. Everyone lumbers back off the plane dejectedly, to sit around in the waiting room until we can get back on. Nobody wants to wander too far away; we might miss the re-boarding when it occurs.

A young man takes out his viola and begins to play. A Vivaldi sonata, first, and then the viola part to an orchestral piece I can't quite place. It is soothing to hear this music while we wait out the air traffic control delay, all of us trapped here, our postponed commitments piling up urgently for us at our various destinations.

The sound of his music floats through the airline terminal, music from a time when there was plenty of time, when people didn't travel thousands of miles in a few hours. It floats through the terminal, past the neon signs advertising different kinds of beer, past the moving computer-generated signs that spell out messages as you watch them. It's music from a time when there were no neon lights, only candles and lanterns and the sun and the moon.

There is no other way to play a musical instrument beautifully than by practicing for long hours every day for many years. There's no way to speed it up. It is not done differently today than it was when Vivaldi was alive. A computer can't play a viola; it can simulate the sound perfectly, but it remains a simulation. It can't play.

We live fast lives. But not everything can be fast. We listen to the young musician practice in the airline terminal. Some things have to be slow.

"The north wind doth blow and we shall have snow."

I've been hearing the *scrape-scrape* of snow shovels outside. Is that somebody shoveling already, I ask my sleeping spouse. He grunts and I look at the clock to confirm that yes, somebody on the block is shoveling the walk at six in the morning.

They've been talking about snow for weeks and we haven't had any. Now today it's finally here. Although snow holds nothing for me now except difficulty in traveling, I still can't help being excited by it when I first look out the window. I remember the ecstasy in finding out that a day was a snow day when I was little, how my brothers and I would listen to the school closings on the radio and shriek when we heard our county mentioned among the fortunate. That was a free day, fallen straight from heaven. We did unusual things on snow days: cooked things, made clay out of flour and salt, made forts in the living room. Generally messed up the house. And played outside until we were so cold we had to come in.

You only have snow days in places where it snows but they don't know how to deal with it. You never have them in Florida, where it never snows, but you also never have them in Minnesota, where it snows all the time. You can't. Nothing would ever be open if you did.

My friend makes beef stew when it snows. *My kids don't really like beef stew that much*, she says, *I just like to make it on a snow day*. She's right. You should do something you don't always do on a bonus day.

Sometimes adult meetings are canceled when it snows. If you live in an area where they have snow days, I hope that happens to you some time this winter. If it does, do something unusual.

FEBRUARY 6

"True love's the gift..." —SIR WALTER SCOTT

My friend's husband has just taken all the money he received for Christmas and used it to buy her a ticket to Hawaii to visit her grandmother. She is stunned. A recurring theme in their marriage is her conviction that he doesn't value her contribution to the family as chief caregiver for their two boys. *He is clueless*, she always says, *he has no idea what I do all day*, and then she's off into a very funny parody of his latest insensitivity to women's reality. And now here he is with this ticket, and he says he's going to take care of the boys for a week while she enjoys herself.

She's scared to death. She's doing up laundry in advance so he won't have to wash clothes while she's gone. She's cooking and baking and freezing things.

What if they get sick, she worries. If they get sick, he'll deal with it. *But I go in there every night and look at them when they're asleep. I can't believe I'm actually going to do this, to go away.*

So she's wrong: he actually does value what she does. And I imagine he'll value it a lot more after having done it for a week himself. It will also be important for her to get on that plane. She's never been away from her family for that long. He hasn't had to do the things she does, and so the conviction has grown in her that he cannot. But he can. People figure out how to do the things they need to do, and he's a smart guy. He'll be fine.

FEBRUARY 7

"How great a matter a little fire kindleth!" —JAMES 3:5

Early in the Clinton administration, there was trouble finding a female appointee for Attorney General who could survive an inquiry into her childcare arrangements. Eminently qualified women were bowing out of the process right and left because of their "Zoe Baird factors": they'd used undocumented aliens as childcare workers.

What this showed was: 1) there's a childcare crisis in America; 2) women who work long hours and have the money to hire live-in help can't find documented workers to take care of their children; and 3) women are asked about this stuff and men aren't.

There's something really wrong when *not to have done something* becomes a qualification. I thought what we have done was more important than what we haven't. Particularly in the baby boomer generation, it's going to be hard to find people who *have not done* a lot of things: smoked pot; hired someone illegally. Other, spicier things, too, which used to be politely ignored and are now on the front page. We're going to have to find a way to acknowledge people's errors of judgment without discarding the entire person, or we'll be left with a leadership composed entirely of the negatively qualified: people who haven't done things. There's more to leadership than not having done something.

There's also more to the undocumented worker problem than a fussy obsession with rules: we have those laws so that workers will be paid fairly and so they can participate in the Social Security system. They have a moral basis. When they're broken, restitution should be made. But then life should go on.

FEBRUARY 8

"Because of frugality, one is generous." —LAO-TZU

Anyone would think I was thrifty, the way I wring every last bit of life out of a turkey. It is darkest February, cold as the dickens outside. I have pulled two plastic containers of the turkey soup I made from the Thanksgiving carcass out of the freezer and I'm heating it up for our supper. It smells wonderful.

Actually, I am anything but thrifty. I throw all kinds of things away. My husband follows me around, picking things I have discarded out of the trash: a spent tube of toothpaste with "plenty left in there if you just roll it up from the bottom," old envelopes ("you know I use these for lists of things to remember"), the last few shreds of cooked vegetables ("hey, I can use this for my salad at lunch").

So the soup is a little out of character for me. It is soul-satisfying, though. I may not be thrifty, but I am as vulnerable to the mystique of our pioneer foremothers as anyone else. They saved everything. Made their own soap out of animal fat, I believe, something I have not yet tried. Most of the things they did are too time-consuming for me. But anybody can throw a chicken carcass into a pot of water, turn the fire on low and walk away. It's a quick and easy way to get in touch with my grandmother. She was one of those superb home-makers of yesteryear, made jellies, pickles, wonderful things that I don't make. But she also made soup out of the chicken carcass, always commenting darkly on what a sin it was to waste food.

She was right. She'd be horrified at my profligate ways with leftover vegetables, so I hope she's taking note of the beautiful smell of the soup, rising toward heaven like incense. It's for her as much as it's for me.

FEBRUARY 9

"If women be educated for dependence ... where are we to stop?"
—MARY WOLLSTONECRAFT

Funny: there's very little water pressure when I turn on the tap. Corinna and the kids come in. *What's all that water out in the yard?* she asks, and I come out to see: sure enough, a torrent of water is gushing right out of the side of the house, like it gushed out of the rock in the wilderness. Oh, no. I hobble down to the basement and see that the pipe has burst, It sounds like Victoria Falls down here.

I know that you're supposed to turn off the water to the house when this happens. The problem is that I don't know how. I look at the tangle of pipes that crisscross the basement ceiling. Nothing looks like anything you could turn. They obviously haven't moved for years. The water continues to rush. I call the plumber. I also call the police. Both of them arrive at about the same time. The policemen leave while the plumber starts to make some real money.

I'm telling you this so you'll know: the valve is a flat plastic thing, shaped rather like a tongue depressor. It is probably red in color. It's probably near your water meter. Just push it down and the water into the house cuts off.

Make somebody show you where it is and how to shut it off. Maybe it's different in your house; maybe it's not red, I don't know. But whatever you have that brings water into your house, make somebody show you if you don't know.

Neither my husband nor I are plumbers. Yet he seems to know about valves and stuff. I don't. *Why did you call the police,* he asks me later that night. *We wanted to have a couple of men tell us everything was going to be all right,* says Corinna, and we all laugh.

But I feel like a fool. Never again, I vow. Never again.

FEBRUARY 10

"A man may grow old in body, but never in mind." —CICERO

My husband had lunch with a colleague the other day. *We talked about men and women,* he told me at dinner. *We decided that girls turn into women when they grow up but boys don't turn into anything. They remain boys, even when they're old.*

I didn't think men had conversations like that with each other. They have such a bad reputation: uncommunicative, unaware of their feelings, unable to talk about the things that bother them. And now here is an account of two middle-aged guys having a conversation that sounds like one two women might have.

Do I think that's true, he wants to know. *About women being women and men being large boys?* He does not have the feeling of having changed much inside since boyhood. How about me? I ponder this. I remember the girl: I recall that she had a lot of free time at her disposal, that she worried a great deal about herself and the impression she was making on others. And has she changed?

Yes, profoundly. The woman can do so much more. She is so much more sure of herself. She can do many things at once. She worries about other people all the time. She is wise now, sort of. She was not wise when she was a girl.

But don't you feel the same about yourself, I ask him? You are so competent at fixing things, at knowing which kind of glue to use when things break, at caring for plants, and you have so much expertise in your profession. The boy must also have changed, no?

We have been unable to answer this question yet. But surely the very fact of having asked it was manly, not boyish.

FEBRUARY 11

"Thinking nothing done while anything remained to be done..." —LUCAN

It is eleven degrees outside, the coldest day of the winter, so far. Richard goes thundering up the attic stairs and lets out a bellow. *Who opened the attic window,* he wants to know. *We're heating the whole outdoors.*

I'm sure I don't know. Maybe he left it open by mistake on one of his cat rescue missions. Just to be a team player, though, I get up and check the storm windows in our bedroom. I see they've never been pulled down. It's February: we've spent half the winter protected from the cold by nothing more than a wire screen. I thought he was going to take care of that. Actually, I guess the truth is that I didn't think of it at all. I would have made a great princess, I think as I struggle with the storm window. No head for detail.

The deal was that I would be spending a lot more time at home, writing. Surely I would have more time to keep the house running smoothly. But I am working against an important deadline, and I can't deal with the dust that has gathered in the corners right now. It's just going to have to wait. I'm afraid this happens all the time. How much money did we waste because of the storm windows? However much it was, it's too much. I'm going to have to keep up with things a little better.

I have a friend whose house is always perfect. Nothing is ever broken or forgotten. They don't let anything go. How do they do it? Do they stay up late at night, cleaning things? Get up early in the morning? Polish the silver instead of making love? I'm afraid to ask.

FEBRUARY 12

"The story's about you." —HORACE

You *have so many antiques,* a visitor says. My husband looks up, thinking she means him, then returns to his book. But she's talking about the furniture.

What we have are hand-me-downs. Some of them are unusual, like the curlicued wrought-iron coat rack in the hall, so weird-looking that we once lent it to a theater company. Richard's parents' bed is another wonder: four massive posts and of such a forgotten size that an ordinary mattress won't fit it. We have the rocking chair I used when my kids were little, the ends of the rockers gnawed almost completely away by the dog. We have my grand-mother's bed from when she was little; it was also my mother's, and mine, and my daughter's. We had a hideous Chinese umbrella stand that Richard's uncle dragged home from the Orient in the 1920s, but we gave it away.

This stuff was all somebody's new furniture once. Richard's uncle thought that umbrella stand beautiful enough to lug across the Pacific and through the

Panama Canal; the thing weighed about forty pounds. My grandmother's bed is nothing special; it's just a hundred years old, sanctified much more by its longtime membership in the family and its faithful cradling of the women I have loved most than by any particular excellence of design.

So, to our visitor, everything looks like an "antique" and seems valuable. The truth is that if we hang in there long enough we'll *all* be antiques, venerable and wise. Let enough time intervene between us and the crazy things we did when we were young, and those things will become sources of wisdom and even honor—not for their own excellence, but because of what they have caused us to become.

FEBRUARY 13

"...and stay in bed for the rest of the week."

That's a good one. Where has this guy been, I wonder ... Mars? Since when does any woman stay in bed for a week with anything short of cholera? Everyone I know crawls back in to work after a couple of days out, pale as a sheet of paper and half dead.

I remember a doctor telling me once to keep my feet up. My youngest was two at the time. I realized that he just didn't get it. Okay, thanks, I said and took the prescription he gave me. Why alienate the man?

I wonder how many women don't follow their doctors' instructions about things like staying in bed and keeping their feet up; just about all of us, I imagine. What you learn as you go through life accumulating obligations is that just about everything is negotiable: when the doctor says rest for a week, you negotiate it down to two days. You need eight hours of sleep, but you negotiate it down to six and hope to pick up some extra hours on the weekend. You read earnest magazine articles about the dangers of accumulating a sleep deficit, and you believe them. But your health needs are on the table with all the other competing claims on you, like so many special interest groups, and they don't always win.

Sometimes they do, though. When I was struck by a car and badly injured, part of the trauma was losing my power to negotiate with my body. I couldn't just ignore it and keep walking like I always did. For a while, I couldn't walk at all. My broken bones refused to be ignored. I've never been so furious in my entire life. But it did teach me that my body, like everyone else at the table, has a bottom line. There are times when the most important of other important things must yield to it.

"Oh, you beautiful doll..."

Valentine's Day has always been kind of big at our house. My daughters used to get heart-shaped boxes of candy with plastic dolls placed on top. So did I, when I was little. My kids were not as careful about those dolls as I was in my youth. A few days after Valentine's Day, I'd step on one of the dolls' heads, left in the middle of the living room floor. Or I'd come upon a legless torso in the bathtub. They just didn't get it about the dolls.

In my day, I saved those dolls to make elaborate literary displays on a shelf in my bedroom, which was my own personal museum. The exhibits changed from time to time: sometimes the dolls were famous women in history, sometimes they were women in my favorite books, sometimes they were characters in fairy tales. They had one plastic horse—a palomino—to share among them. One horse was enough, since all he could do was stand there: neither his legs nor theirs could move. But he could stand as if ready to be mounted, in the Western saddle he came with or blanketed with a bright hanky or tinfoil armor (if he had to be a medieval or Renaissance horse).

My memory of my doll museum is that it was perfectly splendid. Both my mother and my grandmother are dead, so I can't check this out. But it may be that it only looked that way to me. I know my mother gave the dolls away when I got older, so they may not have appeared as special as I remember their being.

So maybe my kids weren't total philistines. Maybe they did appreciate the dolls. Maybe they were doing something wonderful with them in a different way that I just couldn't see.

"Virtue is not left to stand alone. He who practices it will have neighbors."
—CONFUCIUS

Somebody came over while we were in the city and shoveled the snow off our sidewalk—front and back. I assumed it was my daughter's boyfriend, when he came to pick up his car parked in the driveway, but he was big enough to admit that it wasn't. What a nice thing for whomever it was to do.

I read in a magazine that more middle-aged men die of heart attacks shoveling snow than during any other activity. Oh, no. Richard dashes out at the first flake, and shovels intricate networks of pathways to every landscape feature in the yard. He is very thorough. I beg him to take it easy every time it snows, remind him about the middle-aged men in the magazine article.

I also remind him about skin cancer, and ask him about once a week when he has to see the dermatologist again. And scold him for not refrigerating food. And for straining his back lifting heavy things. Don't you want to live a long time, I ask him? He says he does. He says he's doing his best.

I worry about everyone I love. I call my kids just about every night, just to see how they are. I nag them about medicine if they happen to be taking any. When everyone spends the night—a very rare occurrence these days—I feel so completely safe that I realize I'm always just the tiniest bit on edge if they're not with me. Even after all these years. But when we are all under one roof, when nobody is out on the road and Richard is not out courting death with the snow shovel, when I can go from room to room and see everybody asleep, I am at peace.

FEBRUARY 16

"Why stand we here idle?" —PATRICK HENRY

My granddaughters are eager to get outside and make a snowman. They know from books what he's supposed to look like, and are disappointed that we don't feel able to let him wear our antique top hat for more than one brief moment. But he has a muffler, like Frosty, and a cork on a stick that looks sort of like a pipe.

I had forgotten what a mess it is after kids play in the snow. Everything is dripping wet, and water sits in little pools on the floor. The girls look beautiful with their pink cheeks, like children in a picture book. I am afraid of delivering them to their mother with colds, so I make them wrap up in a blanket for a little while.

When they are both warm, I set them to making things at the kitchen table. What they seem to want to do, though, is play school. Rosie has Madeline reciting things; Madeline is three, and only dimly aware of what is expected, but Rosie rewards her answers with a teacherly "Very good!" and pats her on the head. They remind me of little executives catching up on their business reading on vacation, unwilling to get out of the saddle altogether, even on a holiday. It's afternoon. They know they're supposed to be in school.

It's hard to get away even when you *are* away. I call in all the time when I'm on vacation; I can't enjoy myself unless I know that things are okay at work. Things are always okay when I call; they don't need to hear from me. The need to keep one foot in the workplace while the rest of me is out of it comes from within, not from the job itself. It's hard to let go of something as big a part of me as my work. We forget who we are if we're not working.

FEBRUARY 17

"Love is not love, that alters when it alteration finds." —SHAKESPEARE, *OTHELLO*

My husband and I seem to be changing shape. His stomach, which he has begun referring to as "the corporation," sticks out. For the first time in my life, so does mine; I've always had big hips, but this stomach thing is new. I imagine we would be a fairly grotesque pair to the disinterested observer who chanced upon the two of us unclothed. Fortunately, there is no disinterested observer. There's just us.

The remarkable thing is this: he still thinks I'm pretty. And I still think he's great-looking. This, even though we are both aware of these changes for the worse in each other and in ourselves. What does he see when he looks at me, I wonder. Does he see me the way I was when we first met? Maybe. He says he also sometimes sees me the way I looked when I was a little girl. And he didn't even know me when I was a little girl.

I have some pictures of him taken when he was a boy. One at seven, another at about thirteen, one at eighteen. One when he was in the Army. I wasn't even *born* then. But I look at those pictures, and I know him. And then I look at him, and I see all his former selves in his nice face.

We've started to work on getting our old shapes back. We're eating right and exercising. I hope it works. But it's nice to know that love doesn't depend on things remaining the way they are.

FEBRUARY 18

"As one comforted by her mother, I will comfort you." —ISAIAH 66:13

On a recent morning I needed to connect in New York with a bus to a town halfway upstate. The train was late. I missed my bus by four minutes. There was not another bus for two hours—now I was going to be late to the conference. Carrying my overnight bag while trying to hurry made my injured back hurt; before long I was blinking back tears of frustration and pain. I called home—I don't know why. What could anybody there do? Anna answered. My tears overflowed as I told her about the late train and the bus and my back. She murmured soothing things to me, told me not to worry, just to wait for the next bus and everything would be okay. All the things I would have said to her.

It was a little startling to hear myself crying into the phone to my own daughter. She used to come crying to me. Still sniffling, but unwilling to continue the role reversal, I pulled myself together and reminded her to take her medicine, the first motherly admonition I could think of.

But it was she who had mothered me. And I had needed it. I was young on the phone, and she treated me tenderly. I'm sorry for crying like that, I told her, that's not like me. *That's okay, Mommy, you can cry to me any time,* she said.

Perhaps there is no such thing as time. We mother our children and then they mother us. Usually both things happen at once, according to each of our needs. People who have been well-nurtured are good nurturers. The world into which we go forth every morning is a hard one. We can all use a little mothering now and then, from our own moms or from someone else.

FEBRUARY 19

"Whom neither shape of danger can dismay, nor thought of tender happiness betray." —WILLIAM WORDSWORTH

You can't pick up a newspaper this week without reading about a horrible incident in New Jersey: four members of a high school football team in a suburban town lured a twenty-one-year-old retarded girl into a basement and sexually assaulted her with, among other things, a broom and a baseball bat. Her parents have filed rape charges. The defense insists that she was a willing participant. Mentally, the girl is eight years old.

A particularly sad moment in the testimony came when the young woman was asked why she had cooperated. She told the lawyer that she had hoped one of the boys would ask her out on a date if she did what they wanted. I wonder what it was like for her mother to hear that. To have a differently-abled child is to say good-bye to many of the rosy dreams of what it will be like to have a daughter: the fun, the dates, the parties, the growing independence of American adolescence. To love such a child, and then to see those out-of-reach dreams dangled cruelly before her by people who wish to do her harm: it must be a bitter thing. Parents of such children have to work hard to arrange pleasures for them that come easily to other children: they have to help them have friends, help them live satisfying lives in a world that mom and dad have tried to make welcoming and safe. All that love, all that work—and the world turns out to be anything but safe.

The girl went on to tell the lawyer that she liked those boys. They were her friends.

FEBRUARY 20

"I shall not die, but live."

Nighttime after a big snowfall. The snow is too new to have been plowed away or trampled upon; it is pristine and undisturbed. Everything looks different under its blanket of white. The snow does strange things to the houses which surround our house: they seem smaller and oddly unreal, as if our neighborhood were a model train layout. It does something different to the night sky, too: it is bright outside. The reflected light of the moon bounces back off the snow, I suppose, so that at midnight it looks like late afternoon.

Underneath the snow, down in the dark ground, the bulbs of daffodils and tulips and crocuses and hyacinths are quietly gathering strength. The cold winter is an important part of their life, part of the series of signals which will lead to the first brave blossoms of spring in only a few weeks. If it were never cold and dark, the flowers would never bloom.

That is why these flowers—all different kinds of lilies—are the ones which centuries of tradition have used to symbolize resurrection. All flowers come out of the ground, but not all are entombed like the lilies, relying on their deathlike sleep to gather strength for their new life in the spring. The bulbs which sleep in the ground look dead. They are dull and brown, dry as bones. But appearances can be deceiving. They are not dead. They are alive.

In your life, and in mine, there are times when hope seems dead like that. For whatever reason—lost love, lost health, lost security—life seems insupportable. But time passes; the winter turns to spring. Miraculously, life and strength you didn't know you had spring up.

FEBRUARY 21

"All passes. Art alone enduring stays to us..." —HENRY DOBSON

A remarkable exhibit closes tomorrow at the Museum of Modern Art in New York City: a complete retrospective of the work of Henri Matisse. It is full of paintings most Americans have only seen in pictures, if at all; many of them are from the Hermitage in St. Petersburg, for instance, where I have never been and do not expect to go anytime soon.

Matisse began painting when he was twenty-one. His mom gave him a set of colors to help him pass the time while recovering from appendicitis. He went back to his job as a law clerk when he got better, but his heart wasn't in it. Within a couple of years he had turned his back on the law and was painting full-time.

Besides being a giant of twentieth-century art, Matisse was supremely happy as a painter. There's a photograph of him shortly before his death; he is lying in bed, holding a long stick with a charcoal pencil affixed to the end. The old man is drawing a picture. On the wall beside his bed.

Good old Mom Matisse. Anybody who has longed to make a career change and follow a dream knows what a gift she gave her son. I wonder if she and Papa were nervous when their son decided to be a painter instead of a lawyer. Probably; what parent wouldn't be? They probably had to subsidize that decision at first. That took some guts.

Fortunately for Matisse—and for the rest of the world—they were willing to take the chance.

FEBRUARY 22

"Neither snow, nor rain, nor heat, nor gloom of night stays these couriers from the swift completion of their appointed rounds."
—CARDINAL DE RICHELIEU

*G*usty, *southeast winds ... snow changing to rain later tonight ... a high of about thirty degrees ...* it's good to be inside hearing this weather on the radio instead of walking around in it. The snow which has already fallen is the wet, heavy kind that sits on the branches in great clumps. The change to rain has already begun, and soon the snow will turn to slush.

We seldom have a white Christmas anymore, it seems, but we usually have a white February. And then a slushy February. Everybody has the flu or a cold. Nobody wants to be outside.

I hear the mailman come up on the porch, pause long enough to put the mail in the basket and then retreat. What a hard job in weather like this, I think in my snug house. I remember that I haven't cleared a path for him, and wish I had gone out with the snow shovel so he had a straight shot to the door.

They must be in very good health, mail carriers. I don't think I've ever seen one who was overweight. All that steady walking is good exercise. But I wonder if they groan inwardly on a day like this, long to pull the covers back up over their heads and go back to sleep. My daughter calls me from her office. *Just about everybody is out today because of the snow,* she says,

Mail carriers don't do that very often. They put on their gray ponchos and keep moving, heroes all of them.

FEBRUARY 23

"Not with a bang, but a whimper." —T. S. ELIOT

I think I'm going to be fired, says a middle-aged woman who has come to see me. *We've got a new boss, and he's announced some major staff restructuring in the next few months. I'm not being invited to meetings I would have been in before, and projects seem to be happening all around me without any reference to me.*

She may be right. That certainly sounds like the corporate preamble to getting canned. It's a cruel thing, and she's in agony. Nothing is more dispiriting than seeing oneself become unessential in an organization in which one was once important. *I'm used to being a key figure at work,* the woman tells me. *It's awful knowing I don't matter there anymore. I gave that outfit some good years. I understand the staff restructuring, and I have to say that objectively, I even agree with it. The changes he's proposing make good sense. I just hate it that I'll probably be one of the people asked to leave.*

Of course, what she wants is for her new boss to say, "I'm making some changes but I'd never be foolish enough to let you go." She wants to stay. But if she can't stay, she wants some acknowledgment of what her good years there have meant, and she wants some confirmation of the fact that she is good at what she does. *I even want to know if I'm not any good*, she says. *If there's something wrong with my performance, I want to know*. Fair enough.

Meanwhile, my job is to try and help her move with energy into an uncertain future which she didn't choose. Being middleaged and unemployed is a scary thing. Fortunately, she has scores of people in her industry who think highly of her. She really is good at what she does. So she'll have to pull those forces together in her own behalf now, make sure they know she's looking, get their advice. She can even use this reversal of fortunes to explore a career change: she's thought of going to work in another sector of her industry before, and never pursued it. Maybe now is the time.

She is wise to begin looking and networking now, before her boss drops the other shoe. Nothing can make getting fired fun. But she can have a lot to do with making it bearable. And something good, maybe something very good, can come out of it.

FEBRUARY 24

"I hear my ill-spirit sob in each blood cell..." —ROBERT LOWELL

My friend has been sick for three days. *I couldn't even read*, she says, *I just lay on the couch and slept*. She's back at work today, but her energy level is low.

She feels guilty for missing three days of work, as if she were to blame for catching the virus that has had half the Eastern seaboard in bed for the last six weeks. When she is ill, she has the feeling that she is somehow not measuring up, that she is revealed as inadequate to the task of her life. *I feel I ought to be able just to ignore it and do my work*—she said this to me on the phone while running a 102° fever—*but I just can't seem to do anything but sleep*. In a way that makes absolutely no sense but which sounds all too familiar, she feels as if she were malingering.

A strong sense of duty is a good thing, but it can get out of hand. I wrestle with this in myself: I don't want to become an irresponsible child, but I'd like to be able to turn down the volume of my overactive conscience when I need to. Yet I seem not to have an off button.

My daughter parked her car in the parking garage yesterday and went to work. She noticed some strange noises when she turned it off. Twenty minutes later the guys from the garage called: the car was still trying to run, even though the ignition was off, coughing and backfiring and filling all five levels with smoke. It just couldn't stop.

Poor car. I know how it feels. My friend who feels guilty about getting sick knows. We all know.

"When are you coming home, Mommy?"

I remember driving home from work at night when my children were little. The babysitter and I had an agreed-upon time for my appearance. I usually made it. But sometimes there would be a traffic jam or something, and then I would race against the dashboard clock. I thought of them waiting for me, my little girls. Imagining their small faces looking out the window for me in vain, I would feel my chest begin to tighten and my heart begin to pound. Sometimes I would even cry: tears of love and guilt. What kind of a mother are you, I would ask myself fiercely.

When I burst through the door, there they would be, drawing or watching television or playing records. Often they didn't even know I was late (although the babysitter certainly did!). The rest of the evening would be as it always was, that familiar blend of love and exhaustion that was our family on a weeknight. But I will never forget the anxiety of not being with them when I was supposed to be. It's a built-in feeling, I suppose, so that the human race will do the right thing by its young. That's a good thing. But it doesn't make life easy.

FEBRUARY 26

"From winter plague and pestilence, Good Lord, deliver us!" —THOMAS NASHE

What do you have for the flu, I ask the pharmacist. *You just have to let it run its course*, he says, *although you can treat some of the symptoms. Take aspirin for the aches.* What about the gland in my throat that feels like a golfball? *Maybe an antihistamine will help.* I choose one that you mix with hot water to make a hot lemon drink and hurry home. Richard looks like Marley's ghost when I get there, with his neck wrapped in a woolen scarf. He's got the flu, too.

Corinna sounds terrible on the phone. She's trying to have the flu with two small children underfoot. They're bored and fretful; she's wretched. She's worried about work—*everybody was out yesterday*, she says. *They're going to be mad.* Well, you can't help having the flu, I tell her. They should thank their lucky stars you came in yesterday.

If I can move tomorrow and she can't, I'll go and get the kids. Then she can sleep. If I'm still awful, I can't. *This is awful*, we keep telling each other. *Awful*, we answer.

Actually, we're lucky. This flu of ours is just awful. Another strain of it killed more people during the First World War than gunshot wounds. People caught it and died within hours—children, mothers, whole families. I don't know why that doesn't happen today, since the treatment for flu is still basically to do whatever you can to make yourself feel better and wait until it goes away. No more than they could do in 1918. So it's awful, all right.

But it sure could be worse.

FEBRUARY 27

"Remember that you are dust, and to dust you will return."
—LITURGY FOR ASH WEDNESDAY

I pound the charred remains of last year's palm leaves to a fine powder and pour them carefully into an abalone shell. Throughout the day I will use it to smudge a cross on people's foreheads as they come in and out of the church, beginning the season of Lent with a sober reminder of their mortality.

I like Ash Wednesday. It is not morbid, in my view: it is simply accurate. We *are* going to die someday, so we'd better make this day count. We don't know how many more like it we will have. Especially now, when so much of people's efforts go into accumulating things, it is easy to come to believe that it is the accumulation of things that gives meaning to life. *I'd really be happy,* we think, *if I could get that vacation home, that new car, that stereo system, that Persian rug.* But then along comes a day like today, and we remember that we're not taking any of those things with us when we go. *I was dust, and I will be again someday.*

Bruno shuffles into the church and takes off his cap with difficulty. He has Lou Gehrig's disease, and his hands are of less and less use every day. Zipping a zipper, buttoning a button, signing his name: these are all hard for Bruno to do. He has begun to have trouble swallowing. He will eventually cease to speak, and then to breathe.

I don't want to speak the traditional words as I smudge his forehead—*remember that you are dust, and to dust you will return*—but I do. Maybe this is his last Ash Wednesday. I see that he is thinking the same thing. *Thank you,* he says quietly, and we walk out together into the bright sunshine.

FEBRUARY 28

"Did I wake you?"

I can understand why my caller sounds surprised at my sleepy voice. It's only eight o'clock in the evening. Other adults are reading the paper or watching television or going to malls. I go to bed earlier than anyone else I have ever known. Six o'clock seems like an excellent bedtime to me, if I can swing it. Eight is good, too. I have trouble concentrating if I'm up past nine; whatever it is that wants to keep me awake had better be pretty darned interesting. I've slept through the second acts of most of the major operas and through the most exciting parts of many films. I have never seen "The Tonight Show." I tried to watch "Saturday Night Live" *once*, but I couldn't stay awake. I resist invitations to attend evening performances of plays unless I'm in them; then I'll go. Only that kind of adrenaline producing situation seems to keep me awake. Otherwise, it's a wasted ticket.

Of course, I often get up at four in the morning, which is the time when I do my best writing. The house is silent and nobody calls. I'm well rested, having been asleep for eight good hours, and ready to go. Everybody has a rhythm with respect to the time of day, a peak time. I don't try to buck that. I do what I have to do when I'm in the best shape to do it. I apologize for the rest, and hope that the world will call back when I'm awake.

FEBRUARY 29

WARNING: DO NOT READ THIS IF THIS IS NOT A LEAP YEAR. YOU WILL LOSE YOUR PLACE.

For astronomical reasons which I understood in the fifth grade but cannot now explain, February has an extra day every four years. For centuries, people have felt entitled to be a little offbeat on that day. Women could propose marriage to men, for instance, or ask them to a dance in the days before that was commonplace, as it is alleged to be now.

This was a terrific custom, and it is now time to stage a modest comeback. Let this be a day upon which you do something that inverts—just a little bit—the power structure in which we all live and move. You could call a man "honey"—no, on second thought, don't do that. Just tell him he looks pretty today. Ask your children for money before they have a chance to ask you. Call a doctor by his first name after he uses yours.

People are always slightly shaken when a power they possess but do not acknowledge is assumed by someone else. It's good for them to be shaken that way, for not all the pecking orders we have are good ones. But we have them, nonetheless, and they change slowly. A sly custom like that associated with leap year exposes the power system we all take for granted by turning it upside down. It may even make the powerful more sensitive to the way they are perceived by others. It can't hurt. It might even help change some things that need changing.

Which is probably the *real* reason why they only have it every four years.

MARCH 1

Both of us are longing for something sweet after dinner. We are trying to be good, so we do not mosey over to the coffee shop in town for something rich and chocolatey. We have fruit instead. I wish I could tell you that this does the trick, but it does not. What we had in mind is something about five times as intense as the pears we are eating.

I am especially immature about these things. I have to distract myself from my cravings as if I were my own child, consoling myself with some other treat, one of the non-food variety. There are people, I am told, for whom food is just food. I cannot imagine what that must be like.

In Italy, you usually don't eat something heavy and sweet after dinner. Of course, the Italians are famous for their wonderful sweets, but they prefer to have them as a treat, maybe in the late afternoon. Fruits there are fattened to a sweet perfection by the sun, until they are better than anything we have here, and you really do feel you've done dessert when you've eaten a luscious Italian peach or a couple of fresh Italian figs.

Italians won't eat things that are not properly ripened. Maybe one of the reasons I'm so childish about sweet desserts—and I am not alone in this—is the insubstantial blandness of the fruits that are sold in American markets: they look good, but often they have no taste at all. Just "shelf life," a phrase that probably has no Italian equivalent.

The fruits in the market look so good here. But looks aren't everything. It's not enough for something just to *look like* what it's supposed to be. It's got to *be* what it's supposed to be, too.

MARCH 2

"If we do meet again, why, we shall smile..." —*JULIUS CAESAR*, ACT V SCENE I

Is this the Trenton train?
Yeah.
Hey, I saw you on the train this morning!
I knew this to be true, for I remembered his black leather jacket with a Girl Scout pin in the lapel—I had wondered how he came by the pin—and his shoulder-length hair. *Yeah, you're right,* he said, kindly affecting surprised recognition, although I knew he did not remember me from among the crowd of middle-aged women he saw this morning. What a nice young man.

I am so surprised when I run into someone I know in New York. Yet just this evening I came across my friend Leslie in the subway. That's twice in one day. I feel I have to exclaim over it when I recognize someone, as if it were

40

important to commemorate the occasion of breaking the anonymity in which people come and go.

When I go to a restaurant in the New Jersey town in which we spend much of our time and don't see someone I know, I feel a little offended. This is my town, I think, as if I owned it: where is everybody? Who are these people? Are there this many people I don't know here?

If we know each other, we will help each other. If we don't, we may not. Remember Kitty Genovese, the young woman who was stabbed to death while hundreds of neighbors listened to her screams? Her name became a watchword for urban callousness. When reporters asked why nobody came to her aid, the neighbors all said they didn't want to get involved.

I look into people's eyes when I see them. I want to remember them. And I want them to remember me.

MARCH 3

"...work like madness in the brain..." —SAMUEL TAYLOR COLERIDGE

The woman at my dentist's office calls. They've just received the fifth rejection notice from the insurance company for the crown my dentist installed five months ago. No, make that nine months ago. Can't I do something?

I begin what will end up being an hour of telephoning and being put on hold, during which I explain my problem again and again. Everybody agrees with everybody else that I am covered. But the computer has missed this, somehow: it spits me out like an olive pit each time.

Each insurance company has a different form. Each policy covers different things. This dentist has several women employees who do nothing but process these things, generating mountains and mountains of paper. I felt myself going mad toward the end of the hour I spent chasing down my own claim. I can only imagine their condition by the end of the day, and I marvel at my caller's good humor and patience while we are talking on the phone.

Somebody has to pay her salary and benefits, and those of her colleagues who do the same work. That's why medical charges are so outlandishly high: look at what it takes for these doctors to get their money. If I did a job for someone and didn't get paid for nine months, I'd be livid. There's got to be a better way.

I know people who are remaining in jobs they detest because they need the medical benefits. I also know people who are remaining on welfare for the same reason. And I know people who have been dropped from coverage because they developed a chronic illness. Something that costs so much and drives us all so crazy has got to change.

41

MARCH 4

"This life's dim windows of the soul..." —WILLIAM BLAKE

I love the way windows look when they're clean. If I wash a window every day, all the windows in the house will be clean in three weeks. So I get out some window cleaner and begin the window of the day. I clean inside first and then go out with a stepladder to do the outside. Then I come back in and look out. There is a film on the window now; the yard looks like an old photograph through it. Objectively, I'd have to say that it looks substantially worse than it did before I washed it. And then I remember that I have never done a good job washing windows. There is always a film on them when I finish. I have gotten lots of hints about window-washing over the years: *you should use white vinegar to wash windows*, a friend from seminary told me; a kid in the youth group at my first church told me to use newspaper. He said you don't get streaks if you use newspaper. I've done all those things and a number of others. The place ends up smelling like a salad from the vinegar, my hands are black with newspaper ink, and the windows still look like hell when I'm through.

I guess I'm just not cut out to wash windows. So I think I'm not going to wash a window every day and get them all done in three weeks, after all. I think I'll call somebody and find out how much it would cost to have him come in and do them all in one day. Somebody who does it right and doesn't leave streaks.

MARCH 5

"Can I help cook?"

Rosie always wants to help me make bread. So does her little sister, although her hands are not really big enough yet to knead the dough. They stand on kitchen stools to help me. *Pat the flour*, I tell them, and they pat the flour on the countertop, sending up huge clouds, coating their hands so that they won't stick to the dough. Then we flatten and fold, flatten and fold, until the dough has been folded in upon itself dozens of times. It is light and elastic, full of the air we have trapped between the folds. We know that it's going to rise beautifully once we've shaped it.

I tell them that you can make braided bread. Sometimes they have braids in their *hair*, so they roar little-girl belly laughs at the idea of braiding bread. We make long snakes out of the dough and group them in threes, ready to braid. I would like to tell you that the little girls watching admiringly as I braid the first loaf, and then beg to learn how. That we have a mystical sort of moment over the bread, a wonderful women-bonding-with-one-another sort of moment. The truth, however, is that they come to the end of their attention spans right about then and go outside to play. I finish the braids myself.

Well, so it goes. Sometimes we start to share our wisdom with the kids we love and their eyes glaze over. I remember cooking with my grandmother; I have an image of the two of us in the big kitchen at home, making raspberry jam that filled the house with its intoxicating smell, making cakes and cookies, grating carrots and chopping cabbage for coleslaw, cooking for hours. The raspberry jam was real; so were the cakes and cookies and the slaw. And it did take hours; that I know for a fact. What probably really happened, though, was that *she* would cook for hours while I popped in and out, sticking round for the fascinating parts and disappearing when I got bored. That is not part of my rosy memory, and I'm not about to change it at this late date. Grandma is dead, so she'll never tell. I probably didn't go the distance with her then. But I do now. And a new generation begs to help. And then skips out to play.

MARCH 6

"He is now fast rising from affluence to poverty." —MARK TWAIN

Deposed Wall Street junk bond king Michael Milken is finishing up the prison sentence he earned for his role in the insider trading scandal that symbolized the greed of the Eighties. Recent photographs of him reveal the embarrassing distance he has fallen from his former power: they don't let people wear hairpieces in prison, so Milken, who always looked so young and vigorous with his luxuriant head of hair, has been revealed to be almost completely bald.

My guess is that he couldn't care less about whether anybody knows he's bald. He's lost a lot more than his hair. Of course, he's still got more money than most of us can even imagine. It will be interesting to see what he and the other Eighties robber barons do when they get out of prison. My guess is that they will do good things with their money and their considerable talent. They know that what they did was wrong, and they've paid heavily for it. I think they will want to redeem themselves. They've certainly got what it takes to do that.

Don't sneer. I knew a man who spent time in jail for embezzling public funds; he went on to found one of the largest service agencies for homeless people in New York City. The same wit and energy he had put into fleecing the public now were spent on creating a program that became a model for cities throughout the country. He died last year, respected and sincerely mourned, remembered not for his sin but for his achievement.

Everybody has things in his or her past to regret. Some of us have really big ones. But people can change. And *nobody* is beyond redemption.

"It was involuntary. They sank my boat." —JOHN FITZGERALD KENNEDY

This was Kennedy's response when someone asked him how he had become a hero. He was a very young officer when PT-109 went down. Doing what he had been trained to do, he commanded the crew in the water as he had done on board. In saving his shipmates, he permanently injured his back, but he discharged the duty his office forced upon him. As was the case for many other presidents, Kennedy's wartime experience was a major factor in shaping his outlook on life and on the world. It was so important to a generation shaped by the Second World War that it is hard for some of them to imagine political leaders being formed in any other way but on the field of battle, as if there were no heroism worth considering besides the obvious heroism of war.

But, of course, there have been other presidents who were not soldiers. Thomas Jefferson was not. Neither was Abraham Lincoln. And, looking into the future, neither were most of the very strong women whose ranks will probably supply us with our first female president. So it's hard to buy into the idea that a person who hasn't been a soldier could never have what it takes to be the president.

There are lots of different kinds of heroes. And heroines. Something very like heroism is summoned by most of us, at one time or another during the length of our lives, when we must deal with something that seems impossible. I think of people I have known who struggled to get through school, who struggled to care for a terminally ill family member, who struggle to support their families, who struggle daily in recovery from addiction. I call them heroes. We could do worse than to have such a person as a leader—and we often have.

MARCH 8

"Comparisons are odious." —JOHN FORTESCUE

The nineteenth-century novelist George Sand wrote thirty pages a day. Every day, no matter what. People who we remember as extraordinarily gifted were indeed that, but they also worked hard.

I don't write thirty pages a day myself. I think I'm doing really well if I manage ten. But George Sand probably didn't always do thirty pages either, at least not at first. She probably worked up to it. People like George Sand are like body-builders: they work their way up to their high level of productivity.

It's always a little risky to compare yourself to other people. An inspirational example is one thing, but an act that's impossible to follow is nothing but discouraging. The only person it makes any sense to compete with is yourself. Just do more than you did yesterday, and you're growing. Just master something that used to be beyond you, and you win.

I met a young woman who did not learn to read until she was in her thirties. School had discouraged and frustrated her, and so she had dropped out at fifteen. Working with the Literacy Volunteers of America, she learned to read, to write, to compose essays. Her image of herself grew and changed as well: she is well-groomed and smartly dressed, like any other young professional woman.

She has attempted the high school equivalency exam several times and has yet to pass. She knows that she *will* pass if she keeps studying. She knows that because she used to be unable to read, and now she can.

Now *that* is a star.

MARCH 9

"Make a virtue of necessity." —ROBERT BURTON

It is seven-thirty, and the train is full. Everybody is tired, but few people are asleep. The evening train is different from the morning one in that way: there are many slumberers in the morning, but most of the evening crowd is awake, chatting with seatmates, rereading the paper or a magazine. Some people read Bibles. Some work on the crossword puzzle. A woman knits. The conductor comes through jovially, exchanging good-natured insults with some of the regulars. You can tell that this is something they do every day.

Everybody on the train wishes his or her commute were shorter. But it's not. And so they all use the time as a kind of debriefing session for themselves, so that they can unwind from their pressured days before arriving home for the second shift. Most of these people will not find their slippers and a hot dinner waiting for them: they'll have to make that dinner, put in a load of laundry, open the mail, and interact with children who have missed them and want attention.

Many of them use this time well. They feel more rested when they get off the train than they did when they got on, and are more able to summon good humor for the family than they were an hour ago when they ran out of the office. The evening train is a good example of making the best of things you can't do anything about.

MARCH 10

"Nothing is too late..." —HENRY WADSWORTH LONGFELLOW

I had an appointment at 6:30. It is now seven o'clock, and there has been no phone call. I'm sure I've got the date right. Probably I'll find a message asking to reschedule when I get into the office tomorrow.

I am never, ever angry when someone misses an appointment. Quite the contrary: I am thrilled. It means I have a spare hour. A bonus. I can catch up on something I need to do, and I always need to catch up on something because I'm always behind schedule. Invariably, the person who stood me up calls later on with profuse apologies. I graciously accept; it's really okay, I say; I just used the time to catch up on a few things. The person who stood me up thinks I'm an extraordinarily kind and understanding woman.

This time, when my six-thirty appointment is about forty minutes late, he suddenly appears. He is full of apologies about the subway delay. I do not tell him I'm disappointed to see him. That would be so rude. I do say that we've got to push our agenda a little, that we have less time than we would have had, and so we get down to work immediately.

Ah, well. I didn't get away scot-free. But I still got forty minutes to myself I wouldn't otherwise have had, so I can't complain. Flexibility with regard to schedule is important to my peace of mind. I can spare myself a fair amount of indigestion by looking at a missed appointment as extra time: it's dropped straight from heaven right into my lap.

MARCH 11

"Where there is much desire to learn, there of necessity will be much arguing..."
—JOHN MILTON

Some people are distressed by the presence of disagreement. *Let's not talk about religion or politics,* they plead when it looks like there may be a discussion brewing, *you just start trouble.* But is a difference of opinion about something that matters necessarily trouble? I don't know that it is. If a person is so committed to her opinion that she's afraid even to *hear* another view, how sure of it can she be? Our opinions ought to be strong enough to stand up to an argument, and people who talk about them are not attacking one another, they're just *talking.*

We each believe what we believe for a reason. I may not buy your reasons, but I should be able to understand them. I should at least come to know how you got where you are. So much more goes into a passionately held conviction than mere facts: a person's whole life experience leads her to her beliefs. That's

46

why it feels like a personal attack when she or he is questioned about them. But it is not.

Take any group of people and drop a hot issue on them: abortion, or gay rights, or racism. You're going to get a spectrum of opinions. Some of them will surprise you. The people in the group may be very much alike, but they each have had a different life, and their different lives will have brought them to different beliefs.

So go ahead and talk about the tough ones. Just one thing, though: a conversation is when two or more people talk. If only one voice is heard, that is not a conversation: it's a speech. Few are enlightened by speechifying. So talk. But listen too.

MARCH 12

"Let her own works praise her in the gates." —PROVERBS 31:31

Martha Stewart* puts out a magazine that's all about herself. In the front there's a calendar—Martha's Calendar, it's called—in which you can see when she's going to be on the "Today" show and when she's going to plant her sweet peas and when she's giving a lecture in Pensacola. Yet there are a lot of blank days on Martha's Calendar, and I suspect we are not being told the whole truth here. Martha is editor-in-chief of a national magazine, the author of several books, and a one-woman retail empire; I'm not sure how many blank days she has just to kick back and smell the sweet peas.

Which brings me to what is wrong with Martha Stewart, Inc. We are being shown a life replete with delicious meals and gorgeous rooms as if they all happened by magic. A spotless, smiling Martha plumps a pillow here, adjusts a branch there, unmolds a soufflé. Nothing is frantic or pressured. Her enormous house with its five pristine bathrooms is a source of deep satisfaction to Martha, Inc., and she wants us all to have similar deep joys. But you never hear about what goes into keeping it that way.

I don't mind the beauty. Or the size. What I object to is the apparent effortlessness. *It's just not the truth.* Don't tell us everything can be perfect and it won't be any work. It makes us feel inferior when we work like hell and everything is *still* a mess; this happens *a lot.* I like things to look nice, too. But it *is* a lot of work. Messy work, sometimes. Just tell the truth, Martha, Inc. We can take it.

---

*Ten years ago, when I wrote this essay, Martha was at the top of her game. Life has changed for all of us. I include it just as it was though. For old time's sake.

MARCH 13

"You shall no longer give the people straw to make bricks..." —EXODUS 5:7

I've never quite gotten what the Hebrews needed straw for when they made bricks, but not having it sure slowed down their work. That was dumb. If Pharaoh really wanted them to get that pyramid up on schedule, he should have given them some straw.

Don't we have a paper folder, I ask a colleague. She is folding six hundred letters to fit into business envelopes. By hand. I tell her a folding machine could tri-fold those letters in about ten minutes. We used to have one at my old place, and it was great. *Well, we don't have one here*, she says grimly, and folds another sheet.

I take a stack of papers and begin folding. We talk, as we fold, about a bit of business we need to settle, and the folding is done in half the time it would have taken her by herself. But it still took too long. It's a waste of your time to do it this way, I tell her. Why don't we look into what it would cost to get one of those folding machines? It can't be all that expensive.

I don't know how much a folding machine costs. But, unlike embroidery or oil painting, folding letters is not better if done by hand. It doesn't make a damn bit of difference, and it's so much faster with the machine, Her boss should get her the tools she needs to do her job efficiently. She won't feel ripped off or angry. She'll be and feel more valuable because she'll be spending her time on things that *do* require hands-on attention.

MARCH 14

"The greatest reverence is due the young." —JUVENAL

People make tremendous sacrifices for their children: work two or even three jobs, and do without new clothes and restaurant meals to pay for the things they need. In my experience, very few parents resent the sacrifices that they make. They're just glad they can find a way to care for their kids, however much it takes out of them. Nobody is a perfect parent, but my observation is that most people are pretty good and almost all of them do their best. The love they are able to show their children is the most unselfish love they are likely to show anyone.

That is why it's so upsetting to us when we read terrible stories in the newspaper about parents who are deliberately cruel to their kids. We feel a natural reverence for children—anybody's children, not just ours. They have a special claim on our compassion. They have a special meaning for us: hope for the future is what they represent to us, and instinctively we want to protect this. We feel outraged when this hope is violated. We know our kids deserve everything we can give them. Every time one of these horrors surfaces, we ask ourselves how anyone could do this. We shake with anger at the abusive parent.

Almost all abusive parents were themselves abused as children. It's not an excuse—there is no excuse for child abuse or neglect—but it is a reason. For good or ill, people tend to replicate their upbringing. Good news for most, terrible news for some. But still: we may not be responsible for where we find ourselves, but we *are* responsible for where we go from there.

MARCH 15

"Watch over your servant as her days increase..."
—THE BOOK OF COMMON PRAYER

My friend leaves the Saturday night service without staying for the potluck supper afterward. Not sick, I hope, I ask when I call her the next day. *No, no, I'm fine*, she says. But she had a panic attack in church and just had to get home: her mom's in the hospital again, and she gets nervous if she's away from the phone for too long.

I remember that. It was more than a year after my mother died before I could hear the phone ring late at night without a spasm of fear. The repeated crises of the chronically ill tether everyone who loves them to the phone. When they recover everyone breathes a sigh of relief. Until the next time.

They come so close to death so often. They seem possessed of an odd immortality. Choking on the fluid in her lungs, unable to draw breath, my mom would go to the hospital critically ill. A few weeks later she would emerge, weak but breathing without a rattle in her chest, so happy to be feeling better. It seemed that it would always be so: she would almost die and the doctors would always bring her back. And then, one day, it didn't work. She had come so close to death so many times and lived; it was a shock when she came close to death and then just went on into it.

Leslie's mother is five hours away. An hour by plane. Leslie may not be there when the time comes, for no one knows when that will be. This time? Next time? It feels like never, but it will not be never. So she stays near the phone, bound by love and worry. *Thanks for calling*, she says; *I thought you might be my sister when the phone rang*. Yeah, I know, I say, and I tell her that I will pray for her mom.

MARCH 16

"New things are made familiar, and familiar things are made new."
—SAMUEL JOHNSON

People who work together are a social unit: they may be an effective one or an ineffective one, but they are a social unit. They do things together that are not, strictly speaking, part of the work, like going out to lunch together and having office parties. They do these things to enhance their social bond. They spend more time interacting with one another than they do with their own families—a terrible thought, but it's true. So they ought at least to enjoy each other as best they can. Off they go, to retreat houses in the woods, to Holiday Inns, off on Outward Bound experiences in which they all get back to nature, these people who are not blood relatives and who mostly didn't choose one another.

If I can just *get* myself to an out-of-town conference, I always find it valuable. But it never fails: when it is time to get ready and go to one, I resent having to go. It interrupts my routine. I have to travel there, and that takes valuable time. I'm busy enough as it is, and I don't need to lose two days' work. The retreat that looked like a good idea three months ago now seems like a huge waste of time. Why did I ever say I'd do this?

But once I'm there, I get it. That's why conferences really have to be held somewhere *else* to be successful; they have to be held some place you don't go to every day. You need the newness, the slight disorientation of being in a strange place; it does something good for your concentration. It makes you see your colleagues differently. And, of course, it prevents day-to-day concerns from siphoning away your energy. They all will still be there, along with a stack of phone messages, when you get back.

MARCH 17

"We have seen the enemy, and he is us." —POGO

Every Saint Patrick's Day for the last few years there's been a fight in New York about whether or not a gay and lesbian Irish group can march in the parade. The parade's sponsors, wonderfully named The Ancient Order of Hibernians, have been adamant in their refusal to allow ILGO (the Irish Lesbian and Gay Organization) to participate. This year was a real free-for-all. The city government waded into the melee and tried to withhold a parade permit from the Hibernians. Political wheelers and dealers issued public statements about whether they would march or boycott. Church people talked about freedom of religion and about family values.

This is America: people *are* free to believe as they choose. And any religion worthy of the name *should* care about family values. I cannot help but wonder about that, though. Nobody has said much about what actually goes on at this parade every year. Here is what happens: people drink enormous quantities of green beer and get very drunk. And then they get very sick. The streets are a mess afterward. Many of the revelers are teenaged boys. Some of them drove into the city to come to the festivities, and must drive home again. They could easily kill themselves or others.

While we are talking about family values, let's remember that alcohol abuse has broken the hearts of more families than gay people ever did. The parade organizers were incensed at the city about the permit; this is a religious festival, they fumed, so stay out of it. I'm just not sure the Saint Patrick's Day parade is the best advertisement religion ever had.

MARCH 18

"For the means of grace, and for the hope of glory..."
—THE BOOK OF COMMON PRAYER

I wanted to be a famous ballet dancer when I was little. Accordingly, my mother saw to it that I had lessons. I studied for many years, and I can still do amazing things with my legs.

In those days, I imagined myself floating across the stage as if airborne, light as a feather. The reality of me was somewhat different from that picture: I was a large child, tall for my age and chunky. I didn't float anywhere except in a swimming pool. Although I got to be a pretty good dancer, I eventually had to come to terms with the fact that mine would never be a dancer's body. So I taught dance to young children, and I choreographed dances for other people. I know that my training as a dancer made a very tall woman much more graceful than she might otherwise have been, and I am sure that my disciplined muscles snapped back faster from my recent injury than another person's might have. But my ballerina dream was not to be.

I remember how very important that dream was to me. It just *had* to come true. I watched with growing dread as I grew taller and taller; I willed my growth to slow down and stop, all in vain. Was it possible that this thing I wanted so much was not to be? I had made no other plans. But it sure was possible, and that's exactly what happened.

I was not crushed by this realization on one dark day that I remembered ever afterward. It *dawned* on me. That was good—I had time to prepare, time to develop the well-okay-let's-try-something-else reflex that everyone had better have in good working order. Not every dream can come true. But you don't die from it. You just dream a new dream.

"Rome was not built in one day." —JOHN HEYWOOD

People look forward to weekends a little unrealistically. *I'll clean the house from top to bottom. We'll have a romantic dinner and maybe see a movie. I'll sleep late. I'll do the recycling and those errands I've been putting off and finish that book and pay some bills. And six or seven other things.*

Then it's Saturday morning and somehow you just don't leap out of bed and start, the way you were going to. Before you know it, it's eleven o'clock and all you've done is get up and have breakfast. By late afternoon, when you've gotten through the recycling and the errands, you begin to suspect that you won't be getting to all the things you thought you would when the weekend began. The romantic dinner now seems like rather more trouble than it would be worth. You choose the book over the movie and go to bed early, thinking vague thoughts about cleaning the house on Sunday afternoon. And the next afternoon you *do* clean it. Sort of. By Sunday evening, you've only done about three quarters of what you'd planned.

Was this weekend a failure? Nah. Stand firm: the main purpose of a weekend is to escape from overstructured days and nights. You're on a schedule all week long. It's relaxing just to let one thing lead to another. Unplanned time is not wasted, for you need it to unwind.

So don't be too hard on yourself if you don't get everything done this weekend. It will all still be there for you to get to when you can. The most important thing you can do is rest and refresh yourself.

MARCH 20

"Lullabye, and good night."

I saw it in an antiques store window and wanted it immediately: a small cast-iron bench that looked like a little bed. It *was* a bed, I found out. It used to have chains strung around the posts to keep a baby from falling out. Then, when he became old enough, the chains came off so that he could get in and out of bed by himself.

When I thought it was just a bench, I wanted it in a purely materialistic way. Something about it changed for me, though, when I learned it was really a crib. I felt vaguely sad looking at the little holes where the chains had been strung when the baby was tiny, a little sad thinking about those parents picking it out for their little one. It had clearly belonged to a wealthy family; simpler folk would have had a wooden cradle, This one is a tiny version of elegant Empire furniture, a bed suitably fashionable for the child of fashionable parents.

But the little body that lay in that bed is gone, grown up and gone. Maybe not even grown up—so many children died young in those days. But gone, for sure: the child who slept in that bed has been dead at least a hundred years. I think of the parents' tenderness with him, their longing for his arrival, their desire that he have the best of everything. Can they have been so different from me? Surely they, too, were often engulfed by love for their little one so intense that it almost hurt. And now all of them are gone. Only the little iron bed remains. Once it stood, empty and hopeful, awaiting the arrival of its small occupant. Now it is empty again.

I do not buy the little bed. It's too expensive. And somehow I don't want to see it become just a bench.

MARCH 21

"...until we are parted by death." —THE MARRIAGE OFFICE,
THE BOOK OF COMMON PRAYER

I could use a supportive community right now, my friend says. I'm fifty years old, getting a divorce, trying to sell a house. I'm working my tail off. My kids are angry with me about all the changes in our lives. She is full of all kinds of feelings: fear of being single again, doubt about her attractiveness, lonely for the companionship of someone who loves her, exhausted from the demands of making a one-salary living.

She came into all of this late in life. The marriage now ending is twenty-seven years old. She began her career after her children were in high school, when she went to school to get the credentials she would need. She's successful in her profession now, and so she knows herself to be capable of making it on her own.

I've seen her wedding pictures: handsome, open-faced young people all in a row, self-conscious in their special wedding clothes. Happy, all of them, as the bride and groom began their prescribed walk through life. They had a community then, scores of people to wish them well. Neither of them meant for it to end. But neither did they have any idea then of what that walk would be like. What they were bringing to it. How it would change them. What they would become.

Everybody loves a wedding. Everybody wants to be close to the bride, to shake hands with the groom. Divorce is different. Not everyone wants to come so close. But the bad times are when you really need somebody there. Be tender with yourself if your marriage has failed, or with someone you know who's going through a divorce. Nobody chooses this kind of pain. But sometimes it happens anyway.

"...I thought I'd die laughing."

One of the most popular television shows in America is one which shows home videos people have sent in. The show receives hundreds of entries each week, but claims to select only the funniest to broadcast. One of the clips which runs every week with the program credits shows a young man ironing. He sets the iron down to answer the phone, then absentmindedly picks it up by the hot part. Shocked by the pain, he drops the iron on his foot. Then he immediately picks it up, only to burn his hand again. He is clearly in agony. The audience howls.

Wait a minute. Since when did it become funny to watch somebody burn himself badly? Why is the person who was filming this guy ironing not putting his video camera down to come and help? And why is the audience laughing at this?

I remember seeing cartoon shows on the television when I was little. Lots of them were like this video clip: some cute little furry animal kept having terrible accidents caused by the hidden agency of another cute furry animal. He would emerge from explosions with his fur smoking, or he would burst through the back wall of a house, leaving behind him a hole in the wall shaped just like him running. Somehow these cartoon animals never died. They just kept having impossible accidents and walking away from them.

Have we come to think that life is a cartoon, that the things which happen to people aren't real? That's not what you'd call a step forward. Literature has long encouraged us to applaud when the deeds of the wicked catch up with them. That's hardly the same as watching an innocent person burn himself and laughing at the sight.

MARCH 23

"Waste not, want not." —POOR RICHARD'S ALMANAC

What happened to that plastic container of rice I was saving?

My husband is frowning into the refrigerator. *I'm afraid I threw it out,* I tell him. *I'm sorry. It was old.*

He is furious. *Old? You wanna see old? I'll show you old!* He pulls out a roasted pepper from before Christmas, two or three jars of rotting gravy, and a teaspoon or two of Thanksgiving cranberry sauce. *There,* he says. *That's old.*

But I would never have eaten those. I was afraid you were going to eat the rice and get sick, I tell him, smelling defeat. I also smell the putrid chicken soup he has just fished out from the very back of the refrigerator. Horrible.

I don't know why I'm keeping food I know we're not going to eat. My mother always used to tell me it's a sin to throw food away, but I know she didn't mean that I should let tiny amounts of food sit in the icebox for months.

We should go through the refrigerator every week and this'll never happen, he says, handing me a jar of soybean spread from a Korean houseguest we had in 1989. We should do a lot of things, I tell him silently. Aloud, I tell him this is a good idea and we'll do it.

We won't have weekly refrigerator summits, I can tell you that right now. Like so many other good intentions, this one is probably doomed. I am awash with admiration for people who keep their refrigerators up-to-date, but am unlikely to be one of them. Too many other things are ahead of that one in my lineup. I had no right to throw his ancient rice away. I'm in no position to criticize him on this score if I'm out of control myself.

MARCH 24

"Never put off until tomorrow what you can do today."

M y van died. She chose to end her life infront of Anna's boyfriend's house, so at least she was not alone. Now she's sitting there, waiting for me to find someone who can tow her away to wherever cars go when they've had enough.

This is a major inconvenience. I work all day every day, and the people who tow cars want you to stand around waiting for them all day. I can't do this. Neither can Anna's boyfriend. So Estelle—that's the van—has been sitting there for a long time now. The other day, Anna told me that the police want to tow Estelle away. Now I really feel like a deadbeat.

I want to go and tell the police how hard I work. I picture the reception I would get and decide against it. I want somebody besides me to handle this. I do not have time for this. But everybody works, and everybody else manages to get things done. Why do I put things off like this?

My friend took an expensive bedspread to the cleaner and left it there for a year. *Maybe longer,* she said, *I don't really remember.* Then she was embarrassed to go and get it, and she never did. I like that woman. Another time she took six of her husband's shirts to the laundry and sort of forgot about their being there. He kept asking her where the shirts were. *I guess I'll just have to tell him be can kiss those shirts good-bye,* she said. I think she was a little hostile; they're divorced now. The divorce was actually not about the shirts, but she never did get them back.

Still, I once picked up an entire truckload of perfectly good clothes from a dry cleaner to give to a shelter for the homeless. So many clothes, I said to the owner. Expensive things, some of them. *Yeah,* he said, *you'd be surprised at what people just leave here. They drop things off and I never see them again. I hold it for six months and that's it. Take all you want,* he said.

Cool. I'm not the only one. There are hundreds of other middle-class deadbeats out there. We don't mean to leave our stuff lying around. We're just too busy to do anything about it. I am aware that other people manage better than I do, and that some of them are probably busier than I am. Maybe. I try not to think about that too much. I will do better. I promise. But it is good to know that I am not alone.

MARCH 25

"The issue is in God's hands." —PINDAR

I heard on the radio today that you can fax prayers to Jerusalem to be inserted between the stones in the Wailing Wall. The service gets about two hundred faxes a day. In the evening, the proprietor sticks the folded pieces of paper into chinks in the wall. *I don't think there's anything wrong with it,* says a woman visitor to Jerusalem who was interviewed, *but you've got to do your part. I mean, a fax just isn't enough.*

Interesting. I wonder what "enough" is? Do you just pray and pray, doing it the right way and using the right words and then when God has had "enough," a bell rings and you get what you asked for? Centuries of the experience of the faithful suggests otherwise. People everywhere have longed for something with all their hearts and not gotten it, and it wasn't because they had not done "enough."

As hard as it is to accept, the truth about life is that bad things just happen. As far as I can tell, they happen at random, and there are no incantations we can mutter or journeys we can take or spells we can cast that will stop them from happening.

That they happen or don't happen is not really the point of prayer. Prayer is about you *in* the things that happen. What you are able to know and feel about God *in* the things that happen. There are as many different ways of praying as there are people doing it. We want very much to avoid pain and be granted our hearts' desires; if this cannot be, we want to find meaning in what we must endure. Finding this meaning, in the quiet of our own souls, is what prayer is for many people. The method is less important than the act.

MARCH 26

"Thy Lord hath decreed that ye worship none save Him, and that ye show kindness to parents..." —THE KORAN, 17:23

On the last day of Ramadan, the Khan family rises just after four to eat breakfast, as they have done every day for the past month. This is so they can finish the meal before sunrise, which will be about five-thirty today. Nobody in the family will eat or drink again until the sun goes down at a little after six o'clock this evening.

During the lunch break at school, the Khan children go to the library and do their homework so as not to be tempted by the smell of food. *This is the only bad part,* says the eldest boy, *not being with my friends at lunch like I usually am.* But he is proud of his self-discipline. *It's no big deal not to eat all day,* he says. I think of my kids and their after-school snacks. They would have thought it was a big deal.

Their mother comes home early from work to begin cooking the meal which will break their fast. Everybody is home and ready to sit down by the time it is officially sundown, ready to enjoy the food and each other, and the dining room becomes a sort of family paradise.

They feel close to God during their holiest of months, close to other Muslims. The rituals and fasts of my faith do the same thing for me. We are not all that far apart.

But hate crimes against American Muslims are more and more frequent. Tabloid newspapers encourage Americans to view all of them as terrorists. What is it in the human being that needs to scapegoat entire races of people? We just finished forty years of hating the Russians; are we going to spend the next forty hating Muslims?

MARCH 27

"Eat it. It's good for you."

There are Good Muffins in the double boiler, I tell Anna when she stumbles forth in the morning. *Oh, good,* she says, and gets out a plate. Good Muffins is her name for the kind I make. There is absolutely nothing special about them: they are plain muffins with no spices or raisins or anything else. They are always the same. I have been making them since my kids were babies, and my kids love them.

My husband, on the other hand, makes serious healthy muffins, They are full of wholegrain flour and raisins and corn meal. They are not very sweet. They contain no salt, and supply the minimum daily requirement of every vitamin known to humankind and a few we haven't discovered yet. In every respect, they are better than my Good Muffins.

Except that I'm not sure a muffin needs to be that educational. At least, not all muffins do. Anna likes Good Muffins because they connect her with her childhood. I like them because they taste good, they are fast, and I can make them without even thinking about it. And because I've been making them for the people I love for twenty-five years.

GOOD MUFFINS

Stir together: 2 c. flour, 1 tsp. baking powder, 1/2 tsp. salt, 1/4 c. sugar (or less). Melt 1/4 c. (half stick) butter; add 1 c. milk and one or two eggs—

depending on how rich you're feeling. Beat slightly. Pour milk-egg mixture into dry ingredients and stir only until blended. Fill greased muffin tins and bake at 400 degrees for about twenty minutes. Serve hot. Keep warm in top of double boiler if people eat in shifts. *Makes one dozen.*

MARCH 28

"For there is a music wherever there is a harmony, order or proportion."
—SIR THOMAS BROWNE

We are at a Cajun restaurant here in Baton Rouge. It's world-famous, apparently, and we walk past an autographed picture of Ronald Reagan dressed up like a cowboy as we enter the dining room. The cuisine is unfamiliar to me: delicious sauces, warmly spicy but not hot; crawfish, which we don't have at home; blends of flavors I can't quite place. There is also a Cajun band.

Immediately two couples start to dance. They are wearing simple clothes: jeans and plaid shirts on the men, sweaters on the women. They look like garden variety folks who have just come from work. Their dancing is relaxed and easy, but it's also fast. It's gentle, deceptively so, sort of like the food: this is really something, you think as you watch, but it seems like no big deal to them. The steps become more and more complex, yet the air of relaxed ease persists. *This is easy*, it says; *we do this every night.* The couples turn around and around in sweet spirals, catching each other's hands neatly without seeming to try, moving together and apart. It all fits together so well.

The people of the seventeenth century believed that the heavenly bodies were dancing, that the movements of the planets and stars were ordered to music. They thought that this music held things together in the universe, provided a sweet sense to the hole of reality. Watching the Cajuns dance, so intricate yet so relaxed, I am reminded of the music of the spheres, as this heavenly dance music was called. If they do dance in heaven, it's probably like this.

MARCH 29

"Welcome, happy morning, age to age shall say!"
—VENANTUNAS HONORIUS FORTUNATUS

Although there is still some snow on the ground, there is an encouraging lightness about the sky and a gentleness in the air these days: spring is coming. In the store windows along my walk home are crisp new outfits for Easter; one, a lacy white shell with a sheer navy blue skirt and white blazer, makes me wish for a moment that I wore something other than ecclesiastical robes on

Easter day. But I'm used to that. I pass my favorite children's store: little white straw hats with ribbons down the back, flowered dresses in beautiful colors, tiny white purses and tinier short white gloves sit in the window. Here is an indulgence I *can* enjoy, and I do. That is why we have grandchildren.

I remember those hats, those little confections of organdy, fake pearls, and lace. I thought mine was beautiful, and couldn't wait to wear it; halfway through the service, loathing the elastic band under my chin, I couldn't wait to get it off. I remember looking around the house for things to put in my little purse: crayons, nickels, a few jellybeans for the journey. I remember how the thin ankle socks we favored sometimes slipped down into our shoes at the heel. Looked bad and felt worse. I much prefer the white tights of today. Or the little socks with ruffles.

Something new to echo the newness all around. People come up to communion in their brightly colored finery, leaving their dull winter colors behind like discarded cocoons. A little girl points a patent-leather toe at me so that I can see and admire her new shoes, and I do. We all feel fresh and good-looking on this festival of redemption and new life, as if we'd wakened from long sleep. "Hell today is vanquished," we sing as the service ends, and we think it really is.

MARCH 30

"You trust in this broken reed..." —ISAIAH 36:6

A high cholesterol level in a routine blood test sent my husband on a rigid, lowfat diet. He's a good sport: he went on the diet, eating very carefully and not cheating ever. After two months of this, his cholesterol dropped a grand total of one point. His doctor put him on a drug that reduces cholesterol. In two weeks his level dropped a hundred points. That stuff really works.

Six months later the doctor left the area and turned his practice over to somebody else. This guy tells Richard that he doesn't think cholesterol is all that important, and besides, this magical drug he's been taking can have adverse side effects on the liver. What he really needs to do is take an aspirin every day. *So I guess I'll finish the drug bottle and then start taking aspirin,* Richard says.

I am distressed by this. If it's not important, what the heck was all that weighing and measuring for? How can one doctor think cholesterol is a killer and another think it's no big deal? Richard hates to be rude to doctors. He likes to do exactly what they say. But how can they be so far apart about what's important? I begin a campaign of strategic nagging, designed to make him get a third opinion. I encourage him to make noise, to be irritating, to ask questions. The squeaky wheel gets the grease, you know. I want there to be a final expert, a doctor whose opinion is beyond question.

Of course, there's nobody like that in *my* field. We all disagree with each other about important things all the time. Why should doctors be different? It bothers me when medical things are inconclusive, but that's the way things are sometimes. Medicine is a science like any other, continually revising its opinions in the light of new evidence. I want doctors to be gods. But they're just people.

MARCH 31

"I'm donating my body to science. They're coming for it on Monday."

My friend has had multiple sclerosis since she was seventeen. *Its onset is usually at a somewhat later age, but I was a precocious child,* she says. Today she is in her early fifties. When we first met a year ago, she was walking. Now she is in a wheelchair. But MS is characterized by sudden and dramatic remissions; she may wake up one day able to walk again. *So I haven't given away my roller skates.*

She really is donating her body to science on Monday. She goes every year to a research hospital, where scientists study her for three weeks. *They're really electricians,* she says, *they think it may be faulty wiring.*

In between her wisecracks, Catherine admits that the three weeks of research are unpleasant. Most of the tests are not painful—and when I hear that word *most,* I remember that she does not have to undergo *any* of this, that she is doing this as a volunteer—but the hospital is sterile and boring. She is always glad to get home. *So I won't be at tennis practice, but I'll see you in three weeks.*

Physically, Catherine is very beautiful: her face is delicate and fine-boned. I have seen a picture of the seventeen-year-old: she was a knockout. She is intelligent and artistic; the walls of her apartment are covered with paintings. She has a green thumb, and her plants soak in the sunlight at a window which looks out over the East River in lower Manhattan. The disease has robbed her of many things. She has been in and out of hospitals for more than thirty years. But she is a considerable person. She is often discouraged, but she uses humor to express the tragic facts of her life. This way, they become speakable.

APRIL 1

"Laugh and the world laughs with you..." —ELLA WHEELER WILCOX

We have just returned from a play at the theater department of the university where my husband teaches. It was a comedy: a young woman is in love with an army recruiting officer who is not her father's choice as a suitable husband for her. She disguises herself as a man and arranges to enlist. Various confusions ensue before she reveals her identity, her dad sees the light, and they all live happily ever after.

The play is almost three hundred years old. The audience roars at the jokes, joining them in spirit to the audience of the 1705 premiere, which also loved it. Lots of the humor here is bawdy and suggestive, just like on MTV.

Imagine the two audiences, so different and yet so much alike. They with no cars, no telephones, no penicillin, no nuclear weapons. We with no smallpox, no kings, no powdered wigs, no swords. But the ludicrousness of love and crossed signals, the ongoing duel between the sexes, the generation gap between parent and child: the citizens of both centuries know what those things are all about.

They are not dead. We're laughing at their jokes, so they are not dead. To laugh at ourselves is one of the things that makes us human. Animals don't do it. And enemies don't do it, either: if they start, they soon stop being enemies and become friends. It is the comedians, not the heads of state, who are the real agents of peace. To laugh together makes us one, regardless of the differences between us. People who are dead live again when we laugh together, as we call out from one century to another our human greeting of love and laughter.

APRIL 2

"And there are some who have no memorial, who have perished as though they had never been..." —ECCLESIASTICUS 44:9

Four young women have made a career of singing music that was used in the church during the Middle Ages. They have named themselves after an unknown folk hero of the music world, one of the many anonymous composers whose works have been catalogued by music historians so that they will have a way to refer to and distinguish between them. "Anonymous 4" is the richest of the sources in detail about the way music was played and heard in those days. *We sort of chose the name by accident, but it fits us,* explained one of the women. She doesn't bring it up, but the idea of a quartet of women singing this music under the name "Anonymous" reminds everyone of the invisible presence of women in the history of music.

The music was sung by women in their convent chapels, just as monks sang it in their monastery chapels. The men's choirs also performed music in non-monastic settings, like the king's chapel, for instance. Women didn't. *I think some women must have sneaked in there sometimes, though,* says one of the Anonymous Four, and they all laugh. *But really, men don't own this stuff. It was sung all over Europe by hundreds of women's choirs.* Some of those anonymous composers probably *were* women. When people think of ancient church music, they hear men's voices singing it. Or they gush about how fabulous boys' voices are, and insist that no one else can sound like that. *Actually you don't hear people who keep up with things say that much anymore,* says another woman, *because a number of first-rate mixed choirs record that kind of straight-tone singing today.* And because of the quiet good humor and thorough virtuosity of women like Anonymous Four.

APRIL 3

"We regret that we are unable to offer you a place..."

High school seniors are getting letters from colleges now. After months of alluring brochures from eager-to-please admissions departments, the shoe is suddenly on the other foot: *will the school I choose want me?* Then one day an envelope with a real address, not a label, sits on the dining room table until she comes home to open it. What's inside? I get home first. Ashamed of myself for doing so, I hold it up to the light. What I see is not good news.

I am crushed by this rejection, much more than I would be if it were my own, I notice. Can't they tell how wonderful she is? I guess not. I dread her homecoming. I don't want her to know about this. I don't want her *ever* to know. I hear the door. I watch as she opens the envelope and a stony expression settles on her face. I didn't ever want to see her face look like that.

But we go out to dinner. We talk about our anger and say some spiteful things about the school that make us both feel better. They'll be sorry someday, we tell each other. And then we talk about what people learn from failure. It's usually a lot more important than what they learn from success. You may lose a choice you counted on having, but that doesn't mean you don't have other choices, including some you may not even have thought of yet. So when you lose, go ahead and feel bad for awhile. Then take back your life. You're still you. And you're still *wonderful.*

APRIL 4

"So long as we love, we serve." —ROBERT LOUIS STEVENSON

My friend works in the largest public library in the world. The Lunatic Asylum, she calls it. She says it is truly insane there. Her staff of young people, most of whom are truly good kids, are run ragged every day. Some of that just goes with the size of the library and the huge number of readers. But some of it is unnecessary, she says: they're confused about procedures and schedules because management has lost sight of what the work looks like from the perspective of those who are doing it. *The poor kids get a different set of directions from upstairs every day. I've got to fight every day just to see that they are left alone long enough to stack the books. It's a miracle we get one book on one shelf! I'm like Mr. Roberts in between Jimmy Cagney and the crew.*

Sometimes she asks herself why she doesn't just leave. But she loves the stacks, love the books, loves to help scholars find the things they need for their research. She loves the young people who work for her, enjoys their company and their energy. Bureaucratic craziness aside, she believes the library is an important place. She worked her way through college there. *I was one of those kids once,* she says; *that place put me through school. I feel I owe it something.*

So she stays. *I don't really care much about advancement,* she says. *I'd hate to lose touch with the way our work is really done—become one of those people upstairs who make everybody crazy. I guess I could earn more somewhere else. But I think I'm supposed to be here. The library is who I am.*

APRIL 5

"Anger is a weed; hate is the tree." —AUGUSTINE OF HIPPO

A woman comes to see me. She is feeling angry at everyone and everything. *I think I must be going nuts,* she says. *I bit a co-worker's head off this morning when she asked me questions about a project we're doing. I don't know what got into me; she and I have been friends for years. Now she'll probably never trust me again.*

She's been angry at her husband lately, too. All of the things she used to love seem flat to her now. She used to love her work, *Now I don't care if it gets done or not,* she says, *I really don't care.* She used to love being with her family. Now it just seems like one demand after another. *I just don't have any joy left in me,* she says. *I used to. I don't know what happened to it.*

As we talk, she mentions that her mother died last fall. *Frankly, it was a relief* she says. *We never got along very well. She was always finding fault with everything I did. I just couldn't please her. I never felt supported or approved by her. I just don't think she liked me.* I see tears in her eyes as she says this, and I tell her so.

She was never able to have the kind of relationship with her mom that she longed for. And now, she never will. I wonder if that isn't what's behind her unaccustomed anger, and I ask her if maybe that's it. *I don't know,* she says. *Maybe it is, I don't know.* She talks on for a while about how it was with her mother, and she seems more relaxed after having done that.

You're not always mad about the thing that makes you jump all over someone. Sometimes you're really mad about something else. Especially if you find yourself getting angry all over the place, over and over again.

I don't like being an angry person, the woman says. *I've never been like that. I never thought it was really about Mom, but maybe it is.* Now she has something to work on. She'll figure it out, on her own or with a wise and caring therapist. She knows herself to be a good woman and a loving wife, mother and friend. Right now something is getting in the way of that. Whatever she needs to do to regain herself, she will do. And her life will belong to her again.

APRIL 6

"Young women of America: please don't worry about us. We are okay."
—MIDDLE-AGED WOMEN OF AMERICA

I remember, when I was young, feeling sorry for women the age I am now. I thought that they must have wished they were like me. I enjoyed my reflection in the mirror. I took my energy for granted and noticed that older people often had less. I thought that they must feel badly when they saw me, with my energy and my promising future. I thought it must hurt to acknowledge a shortening of time, a diminution in power. I see now that this was because I didn't know what power was, or how little I really had back then.

I am shocked now by the memory of how important being noticed was to me when I was young. I am shocked by how vulnerable I was to the admiration of men, how much I wanted it, how necessary an accessory to my intellect it seemed. I am shocked by how important it was that people listened to me. I have embarrassing memories of being overwhelmingly concerned with what kind of an impression I was making, which sometimes caused me to grandstand in a way that must have looked foolish to others: I though I was being smart and brave, but I must have looked so insecure. Ouch. We live and we learn.

I don't hold it against young women when they are like that, though, so I guess my seniors tolerated it in me as well. I now know how truly kind they were.

APRIL 7

"While I nodded, nearly napping..." —EDGAR ALLAN POE

The current bishop of New York excuses himself from lunch with twenty minutes to spare before his next meeting. He's going to take a nap. The people around him are used to this: he can lie down and fall asleep at once, waking up refreshed after ten or fifteen minutes. This is something he just has to do: he is not at his best if he doesn't give himself these ten minutes. His job is stressful: he oversees hundreds of clergy and parishes in which thousands of people live out their faith. The diocese is one of the largest in the church, part of one of the largest and most problem-ridden cities in the world, and the struggle to find the money to do the things it needs to do falls ultimately on him. A big job: the work never ends.

This guy is matter-of-fact about his naps. He notices the limits of his energy beginning to appear and does what he needs to do to get some more, just as he would pull off the road to get some gas if he began to run low.

I have a hard time falling asleep in the daytime myself. I just get droopy and stay that way until another shot of adrenaline comes along to lift my energy level. At night I'm exhausted—I've spent every bit of energy I had. I would feel absurdly guilty taking fifteen minutes out for a catnap, and I would be too wound up to fall asleep. Such an inhibition makes no sense at all: it constitutes a decision on my part to be inefficient. The bishop is right; being tired is not a moral failing.

Being too proud to do something about it may be, though.

APRIL 8

"Embrace, thou fool, a rest that knows no care..." —LUCRETIUS

Was there such a thing as burnout a hundred years ago? I don't think there was, at least not as a widespread social phenomenon as it is today. There were lonely eccentric geniuses who worked themselves into early graves. Artists and composers, most of them. But I don't know of any reports of the condition we have among large numbers of ordinary people: a beleaguered tiredness that makes a person depressed, bitter and angry about work she used to love.

Odd-people worked long hours back then, too, and a lot of the work was hard physical labor. Housework was harder, too, than it is today. Yet we burn out and they seem not to have done so. Or if they did, they didn't write about it.

Here is why I think this is: our increased capability to do work with technical ease has made us raise our expectations of the amount and quality of work we should be able to accomplish. Deals are accomplished in minutes; a hundred years ago, a lengthy exchange of letters would have done the same deal in three or four weeks. You can do more of them now, so now you *have* to. We've lost most of the limitations we used to have. We never feel like we've *finished*; there is always more we can do, always more to be done.

I don't think we can win an argument in which our minds, bodies, and spirits are all arrayed against us. When they say it's time to make some changes in your life, it's time to make some changes. Better listen. Some hard decisions may be ahead, but when your beleaguered self shrieks, "I can't take it anymore!" it knows whereof it speaks.

APRIL 9

"Decently and in order..." —THE BOOK OF COMMON PRAYER

Rosie loves to color. Her mother did, too, when she was little. She could amuse herself coloring pictures for hours; she still enjoys doing it with Rosie.

Isn't it better for them to draw, though, says a friend. *More creative? Don't you think it's confining to have to stay inside the lines?*

No. Not for a five-year-old. They're not stunted by learning to work within limits. By and large, kids like limits. They feel a sense of achievement when they know they have followed the rules well. Of course we want them to be independent thinkers, to see beyond what is to what might be. But people learn to do this by degrees. They first learn the rules for how things are ordinarily done. Then they learn in what circumstances and for what reasons to break them.

People often tell me they don't want to impose religious values on their children. *I want him to make up his own mind when he grows up.* So they don't teach them anything at all about religion. I think that's a mistake. He doesn't "make up his mind" when he grows up. He just remains ignorant; it never occurs to him, unless somebody tells him, that there's anything to "make up his mind" about.

So teach your children what you believe and show them that it matters to you, knowing that they may one day decide to do something else. At least give them something to reject. Then they will claim something they can make their own.

APRIL 10

"Pause a while from learning to be wise..." —SAMUEL JOHNSON

One of my husband's students was a high school teacher going back to school for another degree. *You know what you ought to do,* he said to my husband one day, *you ought to vary the class period by putting something in the middle of it: a song, maybe, or some pictures relevant to the day's subject. I do it with my kids. It breaks up the time and makes people concentrate better. Try it.*

He did. During the Jane Austen seminar, he played some music Jane used to play on the piano. During the satire class, he played a cassette by a political humorist. Then he would get back to the lecture. The students liked it. There seemed to be less nodding off halfway through the ninety minutes than was formerly the case.

It works with high school students. It works with college students. I've adopted it for myself, and I think it works for me, too: I write for only about thirty minutes at a stretch. Then I do something else: make a cup of tea, make a phone call, do my exercises. Take a walk. Anything that isn't writing. When I come back to the computer, I'm better able to think and compose.

People in previous centuries had more staying power at one activity than we seem to. Teachers never thought they had to vary students' activities; they just expected them to learn. And they did. But people in those days were much more tolerant of discomfort and inconvenience than we are, and I think we have to take the way we are into account when we plan our lives. We are easily bored. Whatever it takes to wake us up is probably worth doing.

APRIL 11

"Beauty is in the eye of the beholder." —MARGARET WOLFE HUNGERFORD

I used to love dusting and arranging things on my mother's dressertop when I was little. She had a jewelry box, with a little dancer inside who turned around when you opened the lid. She had a fancy comb and brush, and a round mirror. There were pots and bottles of perfume and face cream. She also had a photograph of herself that she kept there—four photographs, actually: different elevations of her face, placed side-by-side in a brown leather frame. I adored those pictures. My childhood memory is that my mother was a glamorous woman in them. Her hair was carefully marcelled, the sculpted waves hugging her cheeks in the fashion of the day. She wore a silk blouse with a softly-draped neckline, and a gold necklace. When I was unpacking things from the house after she died, I came across that series of four photos. These are going to deteriorate, I thought to myself, and took them out to be restored and preserved. Now they sit on my dresser in a new frame.

Looking at these old pictures now, I see that my mother was not really a glamorous woman when they were taken. She was only a young girl, sixteen or seventeen at most. Younger than my youngest child. That face seemed to have all the answers when I was little. Now, though, my mother at sixteen looks tentatively out at me from her new frame. Most of her life is in the future. She has not yet met my father. I myself am twenty years away.

I couldn't see her inexperience when I was little, could not even imagine a time when she didn't know everything. I could see only the mother I knew in those photographs, and so she looked older to me than she really was, competent and in charge. But now I see the shy young girl.

APRIL 12

"Keep it simple, stupid."

Most meetings go on far too long. This is a great truth. A second great truth is that this happens because people give speeches at meetings when they're supposed to be talking to each other. A speech and a conversation are not the same thing. I have to stop myself from drumming my fingers on the table when a colleague holds forth too long. What is it that makes some people do this? Low self-esteem, a fear that they won't be noticed if they come up for air? A dismissive attitude toward the possible contributions of others? Or just total unawareness of what they're doing? I have a catty observation to make, for which I have no documentation other than years of experience in meetings: I think it is primarily men who do this. Women are stereotyped as talking too much, but I don't think that's true. I think it's men. I just don't hear much speechifying from women in meetings. I hear a lot from men. Not all of them. But when someone holds forth, I think that someone is much more likely to be male than female. I'm sorry if I offend, but that's my observation. Correct me if I am wrong.

Real leadership and power are much more about listening than talking. I can't imagine a situation in a meeting which would require one person to talk continuously for longer than a minute or two, unless she's giving a report. I'm sure you never go on and on like that. I don't. If *nobody* did, meetings would be shorter and we'd all get more work done.

APRIL 13

"Friends share all things." —DIOGENES LAERTIUS

My father has a huge teddy bear named Joe. It was given to him when he had his coronary bypass: the massive wound to muscle and bone occasioned by opening the chest heals painfully, and clasping the bear to his chest countered the pressure on the sutures and made him feel better. When my mother had the same operation years ago, they handed her a pillow to hug. These days, though, it's bears. So nowadays you have a sizable group of otherwise-dignified older people who treasure large teddy bears, keeping them on their beds during the day (like my dad does) or on the dresser. After what they and the bears have been through together, they're not about to get rid of them.

What a good idea: something cuddly, something that puts a personal face on the painful process of healing, offering wordless, ursine comfort and kindness and compassion. When people are sick or in pain, no matter how old they are, they want their mothers. Or, more precisely, they want to *be* mothered, to be comforted and reassured. Shock and physical pain make us feel like children can: scared and sad and lonely. And so a nice armful of bear does for a wounded adult what it does for a child.

Good old Joe. He sits on the bed, his button eyes staring straight ahead, ready for a hug if one is needed. People physically recover from that kind of enormous surgery so quickly today: they're out walking the dog before you know it. But it's still a tremendous shock to the body and soul, one which is carried deep within forever. Joe was there through the worst of what was really a brush with death. So he sits all day, in his place of honor on the bed, silently reminding my dad that together they won.

APRIL 14

"I'm sorry we're not here to take your call...."

*I*t's awful when people don't have answering machines, my friend says as she tries a number and listens to it ring and ring. *You have to keep calling them. Such a waste of time.*

Of course, some people still won't talk to the machines. *I want a person,* they say, *and I'm not going to talk to a box.* Others are pioneers of a whole new style of human interaction: they'd rather talk to the machine than to the person. They can avoid someone for days with a well-strategized system of telephone tag; *Sorry we keep missing each other,* they say to the machine, not sounding very sorry at all.

My husband and I both work at home a lot. I use the machine to screen my calls: I listen to see who it is and break in if I want to talk to that person right then. Otherwise, I get back to him later. That seems a little rude to Richard; *You're right there,* he says accusingly. *Yeah, but I'm working,* I tell him. *If I were an engineer out on a construction site they couldn't call me, either. Just because I'm here doesn't mean I can talk right now.*

It takes two people to have a conversation. Because one wants to talk doesn't mean the other one has to. As electronics open more and more of our lives to the inspection and participation of other people, we deserve some boundaries if we want them. We need privacy, and the freedom to make our own decisions about how to spend our time. I really believe this. But a friend of mine is so tough it takes my breath away: she doesn't have a machine and doesn't answer the phone if she doesn't want to. *You mean you just let it ring without knowing who it is? Sure,* she says. *It's my phone. If I want to talk to someone, I'll call.*

APRIL 15

"For I am possessed of a cat surpassing in beauty, from whom I take occasion to bless Almighty God...." —CHRISTOPHER SMART

*S*omeone gave me a little coffee-table book called *Cats At Work.* In it are photographs of cats doing different cute things at their owners' places of business.

One of them, a gray tabby owned by a photographer, poses in the studio. Another cat, whose owner has a graphic arts studio, accidently copied her own rear end while napping on the copy machine. Darling.

It's about time the cats did some work around here. Mine never lift a paw. They wake us up early in the morning with their complaining. They want to be outside instead of inside. They want food in their bowl at five in the morning. They want separate bowls so they don't have to take turns.

They do sometimes catch something outside and bring it to us. A mouse, usually, or a large bug. Interesting that they don't eat it: cats are carnivores. But they usually don't eat what they catch; they contribute it to the family larder in a definite way, putting it carefully in front of the door so we'll see it when we come home.

This is an extremely kind gesture for them to make. Clearly, they are trying to help.

But they can't be said to work, however one views their offerings of dead moles and birds. Their role in a house is ornamental. And emotional—deeply satisfying, cats are, in a way that devotees of the more demonstrative dog can never understand. Cats behave as if they were doing us a favor by living with us. And they may be right. Nice work, if you can get it.

APRIL 16

"Remember the Sabbath day, to keep it holy." —THE TEN COMMANDMENTS

A friend of mine is an observant Jew. She works in a high pressure job, like so many other friends of mine. Her job requires a lot of tough negotiating skills and is full of competition. She's really good at it, and she puts in long hours. Yet every Friday she leaves work in time to make it home by sundown, in order to light the Sabbath candle. Sundown comes at a different time every week, of course, because of the tilt of the earth's axis or the shape of its orbit or something, and so my friend has a datebook which gives her the exact time for the sunset; it's printed right there in the Friday box of every week.

What happens if you're late, I ask her. She answers that she never is. *If I were, my family would light the candle and say the prayers without me. But I wouldn't be late. It's my job to start the Sabbath. I just make sure I'm there to do it.*

I think of my own Friday evenings, hurrying to get things wound up at the office so I can make the train, hurtling down the tracks in the dark with the other tired commuters. I picture myself standing up and telling people "I've got to go now" at three-thirty on a winter afternoon and then just leaving. Don't people get mad? *I explain what I'm doing if someone asks, she says. I schedule around it. Most people figure it out. Maybe they think I'm a fanatic or something, I don't know.* She smiles: she knows that the people she works with think she's brilliant. She's earned that reputation. But on Friday afternoons, she just stops. To light a peaceful candle and gather her family together. Monday will come soon enough.

"We live and learn."

My daughter answers her phone with a distracted "hello." I can tell by the way she speaks that single word that she's beleaguered and tired. She says that both girls have been awful since they got home. Now they've just gotten out of the bathtub, a good place to mellow them out a little.

I know how it can be when kids are tired and don't know it. When I'm tired, I just want to lie down. Little kids aren't like that, though: they seem to want to attempt impossible things when they are tired, and then to cry about their failure to accomplish them. I've never understood that.

Corinna is a better mother than I was. More patient, yet more sure of herself when she disciplines. I love seeing how well she manages her kids and her work. I don't even mind that she's got me beat, because I actually think I may be part of the reason why she's so good. Here is what I think: Corinna watched me juggle home and work all her life. I didn't always do it very well, and she saw that too. But she saw me do it, and so the idea of combining the two worlds was not the new thing to her that it was to me.

Just like the New York subway system: people from other cities are always telling us how much cleaner and nicer and quieter their undergrounds are than ours. Well, sure: ours was the first. You guys had our experience to work with, our mistakes to know about and avoid. So ours is a mess. It also moves seven million people around the city every day, and has done so for seventy years. Anyway, who's perfect?

My motherhood was like that: not perfect. But it was really amazing to do it all, I think. And the next generation learns from our experience. And will do it better.

APRIL 18

"Hi, Honey—I'm bringing a few people home after work...."

Three or four times a week, Susan's husband used to call her at about five o'clock to let her know that he was bringing a dozen people home with him for cocktails. Clients, they were, or prospective ones, plus his boss and his wife, and one or two colleagues and their wives. Three or four times *a week? Sure,* she says. *It was part of my job. I could do a cocktail party for twelve people in twenty minutes.*

That's incredible, I say. How did you do it? *I planned for emergencies,* she says. *I always had a supply of surefire fast things for all occasions.* She refers to her job title of those years in capital letters: Corporate Wife. They moved all over the country while he built his career. She administered each move, getting everybody into new schools and Scout troops, decorating each house so that her old furniture looked stylishly at home in its new surroundings. Within a week of arriving in town, she would be ready to do one of her instant cocktail parties. It makes my head spin to think of it, I tell her. She shrugs; *it was my job.*

In praise of, and as additional ammunition for, Corporate Wives and other busy women everywhere, here is Susan's recipe for:

CORPORATE WIFE DIP

1 cup sour cream	dash Cayenne pepper
1 cup mayonnaise	1 cup grated Cheddar cheese
1 cup chopped onion	

Combine ingredients in top of double boiler and heat until bubbly. Serve hot with crackers. People will think it's crabmeat.

Smile and say nothing.

APRIL 19

"Woman's work is never done."

My grandchildren were playing "Grown-Up Lady" the other day. Rosie, the older one, was telling her little sister about the computer work she had to do. She said she had so much work it went all the way up to the sky. Madeline looked up respectfully, to see how high into the sky Rosie's computer work went. She had her doll in the crook of her arm. She was a mommy and carrying her baby around was her work.

Madeline rarely turns loose of her doll. When she is tired, she cuddles it close and sucks her thumb. A few minutes of this makes her feel relaxed and she drifts off to sleep. It's hard for her to fall into a doll-less sleep.

Rosie is different. She does not cuddle herself to sleep with a doll. She usually likes an audience, somebody to listen as she chatters on and on, a stream-of-consciousness recitation of interesting facts and wild fantasies. She lies there and talks, subsiding only momentarily when somebody tells her to be quiet and go to sleep. On and on she talks, finally to drop off in mid-paragraph, flat out on her back, as if she could at any moment start up again.

I wonder what they will do when they grow up. Will Madeline be a homebody and Rosie a career woman? I remember my own kind of pretending when I was little: I used to stand at a sink full of soapy water, washing doll clothes and sighing noisily, as I had heard my mother do. Other times I chose to do more adventurous things, like be a knight. But whatever I was doing, it seemed important to do it *really hard.* And I am still that way, running myself ragged with the things I do.

APRIL 20

"Oh! How I hate to get up in the morning..." —IRVING BERLIN

T oday would be a good day to stay in bed.

A soft and steady tattoo of rain on the roof woke me. It is cool enough outside that I need the quilt, and I snuggle deliciously beneath it and listen to the rain. It would be lovely just to stay right here and read all day. I begin to think of how I might rearrange my schedule in order to bring this off. But then I remember a meeting that I really can't skip. It's right smack in the middle of the morning. I'll have to go in after all.

As unbearable as that thought seemed when I was under the covers, it's not so bad once I've begun my walk down the street. The mental exercise of making this a day off was, all by itself, refreshing. So it didn't actually work out; well, just the possibility was pleasant. And another day I'll be able to swing it.

What will it be like to retire, I wonder as I walk. Imagine not having to get up and go somewhere. But I notice that I don't often stay in bed when I do have the chance. I probably wouldn't have today, even if I could have stayed home. I get up and write or read the paper, or I get up and do things in the house. Whatever: I get up. Lots of the people I know who have already retired say that they continue the structure to which they'd become accustomed through years of working. They don't sleep 'til noon; they get up and do the things they want to do.

I don't think it's staying in bed that we really want. It's autonomy. You don't have much of that in the working years. No matter what you do for a living, your time is not your own.

But one of these days....

APRIL 21

"A man travels the world over in search of what he needs and returns home to find it." —HENRY VAN DYKE

I stayed in the city this evening to have dinner with a friend. The restaurant was full of people who were all doing the same thing: socializing after work.

For years I couldn't do much of that, because of the kids. I had to hurry home to take care of people. I would hear a single friend talk about stopping in at Macy's on her way home from work, and I would envy her her freedom. My homeward journey was a tense race with the dashboard clock, arriving home with my stomach in knots if a traffic jam had made me late. Life is so different now, with everyone grown up. I feel like an adult, instead of like an escaped convict: I can call my husband and just tell him I'll be late.

But what's amusing is the fact that I really don't do that very often. I wanted to go out in the evenings when I wasn't able to do so, but now that I can, I'd usually rather not. I like to come home. I like to be where it's quiet and I don't have to talk if I don't want to. I'm older than I once was, too, and don't have the energy in the evenings that I used to have.

I walk past a tavern on my way to the subway at about five-thirty. A group of thirty-somethings are in there having a good time with each other, drinking beer and laughing uproariously at something. They look happy. They're unwinding from their long day in their way, as I will shortly do in mine. It's nice to see people having fun, I think as I pass by, but I don't long to be among them. To each his or her own. I'll be glad to get home.

APRIL 22

"When wild in woods the noble savage ran..." —JOHN DRYDEN

The seasons do change in tropical places but they don't have the mad beauty of spring, like we have in places where the winters involve snow and freezing rain. Part of the appeal of spring is the resurrection aspect of it: seemingly dead trees bringing forth tiny leaves in a startling, sharp green against the black bark, little purple crocuses peeping out of the ground. Some of the days are warm—another bit of madness after all those frozen weeks—and people walk around outside just for fun at lunchtime for the first time in months.

It was this madness that always prompted my friends and me to rush the season a bit when we were little, to rummage through our drawers for shorts and summer tops and run around outside in them. There was a walnut tree behind our house that had a branch five feet above the ground, perfect for swinging courageously on. In our shorts and our bare-midriff tops, we leapt into the air and caught the branch, swinging our bodies out into the air and screaming at the top of our lungs. It was a delicious pagan moment. We were Wild Women of the Jungle.

The day after we played Wild Women of the Jungle, I would be in bed with a sore throat. The last thing my mother needed, I'm sure, on top of her other chores. *I'm not sorry for you,* she would say to me. *This is your own fault—out there screaming like a banshee with hardly a stitch on.*

I wasn't sorry for me, either, as I snuggled under the bedclothes and thought about the day before. You get what you pay for. Wild Women of the Jungle was worth it any day.

"In quiet conversation..."

There is a lot of ironing I've been meaning to get to. Maybe today's the day. A few months ago I decided I wasn't going to buy any more synthetic shirts. Just cotton from now on, I said. I'll iron them, like I used to do. Sure.

But today I will do them. I used to sit with my mother in the afternoon while she ironed. She ironed everything: sheets, my father's handkerchiefs, my brothers' jeans. My dresses with big full skirts and little puff sleeves. While she ironed, we would talk about things. We could introduce tender, sensitive subjects without having to look at each other steadily, and in discussing certain subjects that can be a good thing. She would studiously press a tiny ruffle while we talked. Steam and heat and my tentative approaches to things that bothered me hung in the air. I think we got more done that way than we would have by sitting down and gazing into one another's eyes, like people did on TV. To this day I find it easier to talk about my problems while I'm doing something with someone than I do while I am just sitting.

I think a lot of people feel the same. At the church, the kitchen is full of women. They are preparing food for a church dinner. Why do they come and do this, when their lives are so busy? Why cook there, when they have to spend so much time cooking at home? I think the talking is part of the attraction; they peel apples and mix pie dough, talking about their kids and politics and sex and everything under the sun. They wouldn't say as much just sitting there. The work brings it out.

APRIL 24

"...to write and read comes by nature." —MUCH ADO ABOUT NOTHING,
ACT III SCENE 3

A friend who is fluent in Spanish was approached by the woman who cleans his office; *Could he read her a letter she had received,* she wanted to know, *as she did not read English?* Sure, he said, and unfolded the letter. He saw that it was written in Spanish, the woman's native tongue. He was about to point out her mistake but stopped himself just in time as he realized that she was ashamed to tell him that she couldn't read at all.

Hearing my friend tell this story reminded me of Sandra. She was in my class for our first few years of elementary school. Sandra was small and thin. Her dresses were often limp and wrinkled, in those days when a crisply-turned-out little girl meant a considerable investment at the ironing board by someone at home. I remember that Sandra fainted one morning in school, and I remember that the principal took her to the kitchen, where the cafeteria ladies gave her some food.

On the last day of school in third grade, Sandra brought me her report card. Would I read it to her? I began, and was horrified as I read ahead and realized that Sandra was being held back. I was going to have to announce that fact out loud, in front of the knot of curious little girls in which we stood. And I did that. I can still see her discouraged little face. *Did I fail?* she asked numbly—that was how we put it in those days. I nodded, not knowing what to say, then mumbled something about how she should ask our teacher, that maybe it was a mistake. I have never forgotten my part in Sandra's humiliation, my clumsy attempt afterward to evade the awful truth. But I was only nine years old. That bit of news should never have been left to a child to decipher or another child to deliver.

I wonder if she ever learned to read. Adult illiteracy is a source of crippling hopelessness to many hardworking people. They feel stupid and ashamed. But they are not stupid. Shakespeare was wrong: reading doesn't come by nature. We are not born knowing how. Somebody has to teach us. And somebody has to make it possible for us to learn.

APRIL 25

"The best ideas are common property." —SENECA

When Nelson Mandela was ordered by his doctor to rest, the stock market in Johannesburg took a steep dive. The icon of the anti-apartheid movement and the probable first black president of South Africa was seventy-four years old. What would the African National Congress and South Africa itself be without him? People feared for the recent fragile gains in the destruction of this brutal system. They were so long in coming, and now they could all be lost.

But the ANC is an old organization. It was well established before Nelson Mandela was born, and it coordinated the long struggle against apartheid without him during the twenty-seven years of his incarceration. As important a symbol of his cause as Mandela is, the cause is more than any one person.

Some of the concern about a post-Mandela South Africa is racist, when you think about it: it suggests that there is only one person of color in South Africa who can guide this process, that black South Africans are so dumb and so easily led astray that they would lose what they have gained without Mandela's guidance.

Our imagination is always caught by a great individual. Some people are so commanding that it is hard for us to imagine their issues without them. But important social movements have a life of their own; they are never really about one person, even a major figure like Nelson Mandela. It is time, now, for majority rule in South Africa. Whatever happens to any one person, it's still going to happen. With or without Mandela, the transition will not be smooth. Nothing about human struggle is ever smooth.

APRIL 26

"Knowledge must come through action..." —SOPHOCLES

The Salvation Army officer at an interfaith conference believes that homosexual activity is wrong and that AIDS is a punishment for it. He organizes members of the Army, though, to visit persons with AIDS in the hospital. The representative from an organization working for recognition of the gay and lesbian experience within the Church thinks that homosexual love, like heterosexual love, is a gift from God, and he's involved in a similar hospital visitation program. He thinks condoms and sterile needles should be available to people free of charge. The Roman Catholic priest at the meeting opposes the use of condoms and believes homosexual activity is a sin, but doesn't think AIDS comes from God as a punishment for it; he, too, is deeply involved in medical care issues for AIDS patients. The African-American minister believes that AIDS is a form of warfare against minorities, and is also involved in compassionate service to persons with AIDS.

None of the people at this meeting agree completely about the nature of human sexuality and its many expressions, or about the place of illness in the way in which God works in the world. They don't think the same things, but they *do* the same things. Sick people in hospitals and at home are cared for better because of the things these people do. They also respect each other's work; they can't help it, it is so much alike.

We're not all going to agree about important things. But that doesn't have to stop us from working together to make the world a better place. It seems that work is a better glue for binding the human family together than talk. What really changes people is not argument but action.

APRIL 27

"The wrong way always seems the more reasonable." —GEORGE MOORE

People hardly batted an eye when Hillary Rodham Clinton quietly designated the White House a no-smoking area in the early days of the Clinton administration. Bill's allergic, it turns out, and she doesn't want the house to reek of tobacco. She also doesn't want to contribute to making people sick at the same time she's designing a blueprint for an affordable national health care system.

The people who make tobacco products used to get *doctors* to endorse their products. A magazine ad showing Dr. So-and-So smiling at a Lucky

Strike is a collector's item today. The Surgeon General's report which sounded the definitive alarm about a link between smoking and lung cancer appeared in the 1960s, but there were articles in medical journals about its dangers decades before that. Didn't Dr. So-and-So care about the dangers smoking posed to people's health?

You do not see those ads today. But you do see ads in which very healthy-looking young people do all manner of athletic things in the name of this or that cigarette. They always have very white teeth, psychologically refuting the evidence of our very own eyes: people who smoke have yellow teeth.

People do change their ways. The guy who posed for the Marlboro ads had a conversion of some sort and quit abruptly. He realized he was endorsing something that killed people, making it look rugged and American to smoke. That modeling job must have made a lot of money for that man, but he gave it up. It was not in his immediate interest to do so. But he knew it was in ours.

APRIL 28

"What would the world do without tea?" —SYDNEY SMITH

*W*hat we have in mind, says my husband to the waitress, *is tea. You want hot tea?* she asks uncertainly. *And could we perhaps have some muffins or something like that? Well, we usually have muffins at breakfast*, she says. *Maybe you have some left*, Richard suggests gently, and she goes off to see. We're not in England; we're in Louisiana, so the notion of tea in the afternoon does not click at first. But soon she's back with a lovely tray full of just what we want: individual pots of tea, lovely muffins, rolls with butter and jam, cream, sugar, slices of lemon. We eat our fill and we are wonderfully restored.

Unlike the cocktail hour, tea doesn't cloud one's thinking. While it really can't be said to be low in calories—at least, not the way *we* do it—it's no worse than the chips and cheeses which come with alcoholic drinks. We emerge feeling brisk but calm, able to imagine a productive early evening and a nice dinner later on.

I have a friend who energizes and relaxes herself with a taped book which she plays as she's driving home from work. Her head is spinning when she leaves her job each afternoon, and she likes nothing more than having someone read her a story on her way home. Another friend always walks home—it takes about an hour. She arrives home feeling healthy and relaxed.

It's good to punctuate the day with something pleasant before beginning the "second shift" of home stuff that awaits us when work is done. Everybody puts in a long day. Give yourself something fun at four or five o'clock and you won't feel martyred by eleven.

"An assembly of good fellows, meeting under certain conditions."
—SAMUEL JOHNSON

For a dozen years, I have belonged to a women's club that meets every other week to discuss research papers which the members prepare. The club is almost a hundred years old. Now, just this week, I've been invited to join a similar one—this one reads and discusses books—which is composed entirely of priests. This means that until recently it was all-male, It is a youngster in comparison to my other club, being only seventy-five.

The new club meets for dinner in the cathedral deanery, amid many-headed candelabra and fine silver. Dinner is prepared and served by the dean's superb cook. Excellent wine flows abundantly. My old club meets for tea; the members have to get home in time to prepare dinner for their families.

Both clubs began when men's and women's worlds had few points of intersection. My old club-which I will not leave in joining the new one-will never integrate to include men. We would be horrified at the thought. And yet this new club did just that, widening its membership to reflect a changed church, adding women and African-American men. Is my old club being unfair? I don't think so. It's still a man's world. Women still need to gather strength from one another and to learn from one another in the solidarity and affirmation that single-sex groups provide. I'm pleased to be invited to join the new club and delighted that this men's club widened to include us. They didn't have to do that. But I'm also pleased to have my other, women only club. There is a nourishment for women that only the company of women can provide.

APRIL 30

"I have lived long enough...." —SHAKESPEARE, *MACBETH*

Nobody wants to be a volunteer docent in the ship model gallery today, so I'm elected. Although being a docent would bore the socks off just about anybody—it consists of sitting in a chair and watching people look at ship models—it's perfect volunteer work for a writer. Nobody knows I'm here, so nobody can call me. None of the people who come in will want to talk; they just want to look at ship models. So I can be a friend to the cause and still get some work done.

Except that a man from the neighborhood whom I haven't seen in awhile drops in to take a look at the models and stays to talk. He has had some health problems this fall, and hasn't had anybody to talk to about them. So we talk about his blood pressure medicine and his struggles with his diet. *It's not that easy to stay on it, especially since I have to cook for myself. I was never much of a cook.* We talk about his degenerative disc and how the weather seems to affect it. We talk about loneliness and insomnia and how there isn't anything worth watching on TV. We talk about how he misses his wife, who died a couple of years ago. It is a long conversation, and in the end, I do not get much writing done.

But it was important to talk to him. Some of his sickness is just from being sad and lonely. I get so stressed out from my overloaded life that I forget how painful it can be to live on the other side. It is just as hard on a person whose life is too empty as it is on one whose life is too full.

MAY 1

"...the lovely April of her prime..." —SHAKESPEARE, SONNET 3

*D*o *you think you can compete with those women,* the announcer asks a former women's figure skating champion. She answers with a long discussion of the importance of age in her sport. *It's a real question,* she admits. She is already past her prime. She is twenty years old.

This is appalling to hear. I hadn't done a *tenth* of what I wanted to do when I was twenty. What does the rest of life look like when you know you can never again be as good at what you do as you were when you were sixteen? To be a has-been in your twenties?

I hope something else appears in the lives of these very young superstars to make them feel worthwhile. Coaching other athletes is what many of them do, of course. That must be fun, assuming they possess enough strength of character to rejoice sincerely at another's success. And listening to them critique one another's art, I hear no trace of envy in their voices. But it cannot be that they do not long for their day in the sun to come again. The same steely self-discipline with which they master their bodies can be brought to bear on their souls, I suppose, to keep them from succumbing to self-pity. They have to come to terms with the fact that everybody has a turn, and they've already had theirs.

Hardly anybody enjoys the kind of stardom that they've had. But many of us know what it's like to work hard to become really good at what we do and then, eventually, to be supplanted by someone younger. And to have to admit that she's very good. It takes as much of a different kind of strength to do that gracefully as it took to become the very best.

"You made your bed, and you can lie in it."

This is something people say when someone complains. It is based on the erroneous assumption that the fact of having chosen something means that you can never legitimately complain about it again. You're only allowed to be irritated by things you didn't choose, I guess. Stay-at-home mothers are never supposed to complain that they sometimes long to talk to someone over six. Mothers working outside the home are never supposed to complain about being pulled in five different exhausting directions at once. Childless women are never supposed to regret their childlessness.

But hardly any choices in life are between something that guarantees everlasting joy and happiness and something else that ensures nonstop suffering. I can't think of a single one. Just about every way we choose is mixed, containing some wonderful things and some not-so wonderful. So we want to complain about the not-so wonderfuls. What's wrong with that? It helps to complain, so long as you don't go overboard. It lets off some steam. And it sometimes garners a little sympathy, which we can all use now and then.

There is another message in you-made-your-bed-now-lie-in-it. It's usually said by someone who did something *other* than what you did. It suggests that, because your life is hard, you must have made the wrong choice. But life would still be hard if you'd taken a road different from the one you took. You can't win.

But you can complain. Keep it to five minutes, and be my guest.

"Thank you for not whining."

I had this saying made up into a stand-up sign for my desk. It has been in every office I've had for years. Its polite menace suits me perfectly.

Of course, in my line of work, people come and talk to me about their lives a lot. Somebody will sit down in the chair and begin talking. Pretty soon he'll catch sight of the sign, and say something about not wanting to whine. You're not whining, I'll say, go ahead. I'll tell you if you begin to whine, believe me.

Re-reading yesterday's impassioned defense of the right to complain made me realize that I might have unwittingly opened the floodgates to release a torrent of Awful Whining. That is the last thing I would want to do. As a public service, then, I offer the following Brief Guide to Distinguishing Between Legitimate Complaining and Awful Whining.

1. A complaint is stated once, or only repeated if it has not been understood. A whiner repeats the same thing over and over again.

2. A complainant will be glad to see the problem that caused the complaint fixed. A whiner won't; it deprives him or her of a chance to whine.

3. A whiner generalizes the problem ("Everyone is always doing—"). A complainant confines his or her complaint to a specific problem.

4. A whiner whines frequently. This is because the need to whine comes from within, and is not really about the content of the whine itself. A complainant complains infrequently. This is because her complaints really are about what they seem to be about.

That's it. I told you it would be brief. It is also the gospel truth. Thank you for allowing me to clear that up. I would hate to be misunderstood on this one.

MAY 4

"No one like one's mother ... ever lived." —ROBERT LOWELL

Today is the feast of St. Monica. She is best known for being the mother of St. Augustine, the principal architect of the Catholic doctrine of original sin. In fact, that's all she is known for. We would not remember her at all if it weren't for her famous son.

But we don't remember *all* the saints' mothers. Monica made the list because of her untiring efforts to convert her pagan son to the faith. Augustine was a handful. He had a long and circuitous journey, trying on all sorts of lifestyles and philosophies, and Monica followed patiently along behind him, continuing to tell him the truth as she saw it. Finally he came to Christianity in his own way. Before she died they had a few years of happy agreement.

Monica is the patron saint of mothers. She is also the patron saint of married women, so she holds down two jobs. But she is far from being the only woman in the world who has watched helplessly as a grown child messed up his life, longing to save him from the consequences of his foolishness and knowing that she cannot.

Augustine was intelligent and privileged; his family was wealthy. Then as now, it's just that kind of young person, one with lots of options, who can easily lose his way. The parents want to scream with frustration: *Look at all the advantages you've had*, they plead. *I never had half as much when I was your age.* The young adult listens and feels guilty, but that doesn't make him get his act together. Nobody can tell him. He has to learn it himself.

MAY 5

"It is more blessed to give than to receive." —THE BOOK OF COMMON PRAYER

I felt so badly today, Anna said at dinner. A man came up to her in the park and asked her about her shoes. He liked them—they are sneakers with enormous

82

platform soles. Expensive downtown chic shoes. *He was homeless, I guess,* she said, *at least, he looked like it. And when he asked how much they were and I told him, he tried to act like that wasn't a lot of money for a pair of shoes. But even I thought $85.00 was a lot. And he didn't have $85.00 for anything. I felt so awful. I wish I'd lied about how much they were.*

Just make sure you also do some good with your money, I tell her. Of course a young woman wants pretty things. And occasionally she overspends for them. But don't ignore that uncomfortable feeling you get when your own comfortable lifestyle is confronted by someone else's poverty. That discomfort has a function: you're not supposed to be awash in self-hatred and guilt because you have nice things, but you *are* supposed to reach out to people who don't. The two things are connected: of those to whom much is given, much is required. This is not just to ease a guilty conscience; it's no sin to enjoy the good things in life. But one of the good things is being able to give some of it away. People who volunteer among people in need invariably say that they get much more than they give. They're not being pious; they're just telling the truth. Doing good is part of the good life. And it feels *wonderful.*

MAY 6

What the Well-Dressed Woman Will Wear

I just leafed through a magazine and found an article about decorating do's and don'ts for the current year. I took a closer look to see how our place rates. As luck would have it, most of the don'ts have found a place in my decorating scheme. It seems that I should have used something bigger and flashier in the kitchen than the tiny print I like. A similar lack of pizzazz afflicts the dining room, painted in two shades of gray-blue that seems restful and serene to us, but then what do we know? And the white curtains I favor are nowhere to be seen among the do's; they are a don't thing, I guess.

My clothes are don'ts, too, I think, judging from another article in the same magazine. We're no longer supposed to wear these loose things I just bought, but I find that they do good things for a don't body like mine. Besides, they're not worn out yet.

I resent the do-don't concept: whatever happened to individual taste? One suspects a commercial motive: if we can be made to feel badly enough about the things we have, we will buy new ones. And somebody will make money.

Years ago I saw an exhibit of women's clothing at the Met. There were dresses which had belonged to women from all walks of life, queen to peasant. The peasant clothes changed the least in the three hundred years covered by the exhibit. They couldn't afford to change wardrobes every year. But *their* brightly colored clothing was the most beautiful in the collection. I also noticed that most of the peasant costumes were carefully patched in many places: under the arms where the fabric strains, at the waistline. Those women weren't about to throw out a dress.

MAY 7

"Once upon a time, there was a beautiful princess...."

When I was a little girl, I wanted to marry Prince Charles. I saw a picture of him in a kilt, and he looked like suitable husband material. Marrying him would also be the shortest route to my real goal, which was to be a princess. Now *that* seemed like my kind of work: wearing beautiful gowns and tiaras, giving people commands, ordering whatever I wanted for breakfast and getting it. Doing whatever I wanted to do.

Things didn't work out for Charles and me. I did meet his sister, though, a couple of times: once for the quickest of royal handshakes and another time for a more extended chat. I found her intelligent and droll, just as I had hoped she would be. No gown or tiara on either of these occasions, just two smashing suits on a body that wears clothes very well.

The first time I met her, she had six other appearances to make that day. She makes hundreds of visits a year, to charities and churches, to museums and hospitals, to orphanages and shelters. She must be interested and sympathetic with thousands of complete strangers, and she must travel several hours a day to do so. She apparently does *not* do whatever she pleases. What she does is work. And she works hard.

Princess Anne is very rich, of course. She lives in several splendid homes, and has rooms full of designer clothes in each of them. Most of us—and we also work hard—don't have these things. On the other hand, we have chosen our work, and we can choose to do something else if we want to. She didn't choose hers, and she is not free to change it for something else. I don't think I'd like that very much.

So it's probably just as well about Charles and me.

MAY 8

"But most of all, I remember Mama."

I miss my mother.

Fifteen years after her death, I still think about her every day. Not tearfully, as I did in the beginning. But I see something that reminds me of her and wish she were around to see it, too. Or I hear a song she loved and wish she could hear it. Or maybe I just feel lonely and out-of-sorts for some reason, and I wish she were here to tell me how terrific I am.

I usually call someone on the telephone when I feel that way. We have a nice conversation. But that was not what I wanted, I say to myself as I hang up. It wasn't my mother. Nobody ever is.

Long after your mother stops taking care of you, long after you make your own money and your own decisions, long after you live somewhere else, you still have someone in the world to whom your well-being is absolutely important—so long as she's still alive. One doesn't realize how lovely this is until it's gone. Husbands and lovers aren't the same; they're your peers, and your relationship with them is so various, so much what you both make it. Children aren't, either; your responsibility to them is as ultimate as your mother's was to you. But your mother is there for *you*, even when she can no longer really do things to help out. Even when you're the one who has to take care of *her*. That's what I miss: just having her *there*, the person she was, remembering together the things we both remembered.

MAY 9

"Who is my mother? Who are my brothers?" —MATTHEW 12:48

Frontier people used to spend their entire lives with their families. When they got married, it was to somebody local, and the new couple would settle down nearby. Parents and grown children saw each other just about every day. Grandparents were around. Children felt secure. Nobody got divorced.

Or so we like to tell ourselves. Actually, the families which settled the western part of the United States were lonely couples under a lot of stress, not the big happy clans we imagine. Months could go by without their seeing another living soul besides each other, let alone a passel of supportive relatives. It wasn't easy; some frontier couples didn't make it. The divorce capital of America at the turn of the century was not sinful New York City. It was Sioux Falls, South Dakota. TRUTH.

Our isolated families are not so different from theirs. To get by, we do what those people did: we sometimes make our own families. Different ones for different people, of course. Some of us choose neighbors. Some choose coworkers, or people with similar interests. Some of us really do have blood relatives around, and actually enjoy their company. Others don't.

But nobody has to be utterly alone. Let's not waste too much time bemoaning the decline of a family system which, for many people, never existed. Much better to look around us and make something beautiful with the people we *do* have than to be awash in self-pity about the ones we don't.

MAY 10

"No man is an island." —JOHN DONNE

My mother and I were having lunch a few days before my first child was due. She slid easily into the booth and I stuffed myself carefully into the one on the other side. *I thought this would be a good idea today,* she said; *after all, you'll never be a free agent again.*

What an enormous thought. Her words have stayed with me. They were the gospel truth. A door to part of my life was about to slam shut and lock behind me, and I would never go back through it again.

Not a door: a false floor. I crashed through a false floor in the little room of my life, the one that I had lived in all by myself, and found myself in another room I hadn't known about. I am not an island, making decisions for myself alone. We are responsible for each other. We can never live as if we had only ourselves to worry about. We are not alone.

Can only mothers know this, then, because that is how I myself found out about it? No, of course not. Anyone can know it. A whole scientific discipline has grown up around it: ecology knows that nothing happens by itself, that nothing can be seen or decided on or understood only on its own terms.

But this recognition is not forced on everybody the way it is forced on mothers. Others can pretend it isn't so, and they often do; mothers cannot. The evidence of our own bodies insists that we acknowledge it, and we are reminded throughout our lives that it is true. It was scary at first—*you will never be free*—until I realized that all of us are bound.

To each other.

MAY 11

"What are little girls made of? Sugar and spice and everything nice."

It's important to dress appropriately when you go to work. And it's important to be a team player—to let the other members of the staff know you'll be easy to work with. It's also important not to be a clock-watcher; put in the time it takes to do the job right, and people will notice.

That's all true. They *will* notice how good you are. But you may *still* earn less than a man in your position earns. Only you're not allowed to say so, or you'll lose even that. Yes?

No. You'll probably win in court if you challenge your company on an equal-pay-for-equal-work suit, if you have the proper documentation. Only you can know if you can afford the adventure. But if you can manage it, you'll probably win.

Yes, things are better for women than they were. Absolutely. Some of us remember a time when even the *suggestion* of maternity leave or equal pay for equal work would have been laughed out of the personnel office.

But we haven't *arrived* yet. The woman who makes noise is still vulnerable to criticism and retaliation. And someone unscrupulous enough to retaliate can probably get away with it, if he wants to. But there are ways to lobby for yourself short of the legal process, and some of them are successful. A valued employee who asks for more money or recognition as a condition of her staying will be heard by a rational company that wants to keep her, or wishes to avoid possible legal unpleasantness. It will try to "do something for her." The "something" may be something you can live with. At the least, it will probably be more than you had.

MAY 12

"Give me your tired, your poor...." —EMMA LAZARUS,
INSCRIPTION ON THE STATUE OF LIBERTY

A woman in a thin blouse who does not look like she's from around here pulls a flyer from the stack in her hand and holds it out to me. It is about a chiropractor who wants to give me a free estimate on my back. In any walk around New York City more than a block long, I accumulate a fistful of such paper: drugstores, foot doctors, skin specialists, computer stores. A man handing out flyers advertising a topless bar passes me by: he's been instructed to hand his flyers only to men.

The flyer people look weary and down at the heels. Most of them seem to be recent immigrants. I wonder what it is like to have come from so far away and find yourself handing out flyers to people who don't want them. Most people look at the pavement and push the proffered flyer away as they hurry past. A friend tells me that she never takes them: the practice of leafleting is environmentally irresponsible. I guess it is. The first trashcan you pass after you've walked by a flyer person is always brimming with his or her crumpled wares. They're handing us a piece of paper so we can throw it away. I've never seen anybody reading one of the flyers. Not once.

I always take them anyway. Maybe they shouldn't exist; they can't actually increase sales. And the flyers are a damned nuisance. But it's not the fault of the poor souls who stand on the street corner handing them out. So I always take a flyer and say, "Thank you." My first job was no winner, either.

MAY 13

"She walks in beauty." —LORD BYRON

Here is a picture of Delphine. It was part of an exhibit of portraits of homeless people in different settings. The exhibition attracted a lot of attention when it opened. The whole city was wrestling with its helplessness in the face of this intractable social problem. People would hurry by the piles of rags on the sidewalk that were really human beings, unable to look them in the eyes because they didn't know what to do about them. The people in these photographs, though, looked directly at you. Formally posed but relaxed, they sat in the Gothic murk of historic Trinity Church, in the eighteenth-century airiness of St. Paul's Chapel, in the utilitarian fluorescent light of a drop-in center.

Delphine was twenty when this picture was taken. She is thin in her oversized sweater, but she looks beautiful, even elegant, as she looks calmly out at me. The plain table behind her, laden with paper cups, ketchup bottles and the other detritus of institutional life, is out of focus: our eyes are drawn to Delphine's lovely face, with its high cheekbones and intelligent, challenging eyes.

The original of this photograph was given to the mayor of New York. Delphine wasn't sure how she felt about the idea of her portrait hanging in the mayor's office. *Everybody will know I'm homeless,* she said. *But at least people will look at me in my eyes.*

Delphine never had a permanent home. Never in her whole life. She was abused, sexually and just about every other way, from early childhood. She was a drug addict and a prostitute. She would later die of AIDS. But she was a human being, a beautiful young woman whose dignity, though hidden from most, was caught by a man who has photographed the most beautiful models in the world. He has a good eye.

MAY 14

"Write proposal ... loan application by noon! ... develop pictures ... milk, bread, pantyhose ... order checks! ... menu for Friday...."

Some people make lists at the beginning of the day. Lists of things they have to do, errands they have to run, things they need at the store. They cross things off the lists as they finish them. They feel a sense of accomplishment with each stroke of the pencil. The "to do" list gets smaller.

Some people's lists backfire. They have underestimated the time it will take to accomplish each task. By midday, they have fallen behind. Their lists don't make them feel accomplishful. They make them feel guilty.

Setting a goal which cannot be achieved in the time you have to achieve it is like cramming yourself into a dress the size you wish you were: you may be able to do it, but you'll be in agony all day. And you'll look silly, too, a lot sillier than you would look if you were honest with yourself. Be realistic about what you can do, and don't confuse it with what you *wish* you could do. Or—worse—with what you imagine someone else can do.

There *are* irritating people in every generation who accomplish tremendous amounts of work in hardly any time. Some of them are famous, like Mozart. Others aren't, like the office dynamo to whom you can't help comparing yourself. Let it go. The time it takes you to do something well is the time it takes, and that's the amount of time you have to allow.

MAY 15

"There are some of them who have left a name...." —ECCLESIASTICUS 44:9

I do not know if every young girl dreams of being famous. I did, though. I saw myself in front of an audience, singing torch songs with great emotion. I was wearing a dress with sequins on it, and I was beautiful. My hair was dark, not its actual dull brown. I was thin, too, not my actual hefty self. In other daydreams I was not that kind of a singer at all. I was a wonderful lyric soprano. My voice soared effortlessly through the Met. My dress was long and lavish. I was thin in that one, too. And again, I was an orchestra conductor, intellectual—and thin—in a long black dress. My long hair was pulled back into a bun at the nape of my neck. My ears didn't stick out. Under my baton a great orchestra thundered and whispered, each performer stretching every nerve to give me exactly what I wanted. Intimate with each one, intimate with the composer, intimate with the audience, I finished the performance and turned to face them, sweating just enough to glow. The applause was an ocean.

I thought then that my life would be a failure if those wonderful daydreams didn't come true. And then they didn't. How silly they were. But it was so much fun to dream them. Even now, in middle age, I can still see myself in those dreams. I can say with assurance that no one at the Met has anything to fear from me. Kurt Masur's position is secure from any threat I might pose. I do other things, and I am not famous for doing any of them, either. And that is not nearly the unbearable thing I thought it would be when I was nine.

MAY 16

"Cleanliness is next to godliness."

Not true. At least, I don't *think* it is. Being neat is a pragmatic thing. Being godly, whatever that means, is surely a moral and spiritual one. But I invite someone into my office and apologize for the mess. "Welcome to the asylum!" I say brightly, but inwardly I chastise myself. You should have gotten here earlier. Then you would have had time to straighten up. Better still, you should never let it get messy in the first place. If you cleaned up after everything as it happened, you'd never *have* a mess.

Maybe not. But if I spent my time putting things at right angles to other things, I'd also never have a *life*. I don't think anybody ever became neat and orderly as a result of this kind of lecture. You either are or you're not. And another thing: neatness is not a moral issue. It's an aesthetic one, a matter of personal choice.

None of us who have chosen chaos as a lifestyle nag our orderly relatives and colleagues about being rigid and over-controlled; we may talk about it a little among ourselves behind their backs, but we never raise it in public. Not so the other side. They're always after us to become more like them.

I think we make them nervous. They have sold themselves on the idea that it is their orderliness that makes them productive; our productivity, despite our messiness, suggests that it may be something else. Maybe they, like us, are good at the things they do because they have talent and work hard, Maybe it doesn't matter whether or not you count your paper clips at the end of the day.

MAY 17

"My grandmothers were strong..." —MARGARET ABIGAIL WALKER

Today we're going to bake a birthday cake for our friend Greg. "We" is Madeline and Rosie and I, so it's going to take a lot longer than if I just did it by myself. But they've been looking forward to spending the weekend with us and baking this cake since forever, so I am committed to the time and the mess of cooking with grandchildren.

There are some work-related things, though, that I absolutely must do this weekend. I'm up right now, working on one of them. It's four in the morning, and the house is quiet. This was my strategy when my kids were little. They were simply unable to let me alone if we were in the same building and they were awake. So I worked when they were asleep.

The only problem now is that I'm not as young as I was then. I know women my age who are having babies now, and I am full of admiration for them. I don't know how they do it. I am exhausted after the grandchildren visit. I'm not sure I could handle having them all the time.

I am reminded of the fact that an increasing number of children in the United States are being raised by their grandmothers, though. A number of tragedies—drug addiction, AIDS, imprisonment—singly or in combination, have deprived a significant number of children of their mothers. And so women who thought their child-rearing days were over have found that it is not so. How hard a thing that must be, to see your daughter's motherhood shattered and then to have to become a surrogate for her. Life can be so tough. But it's amazing how strong a woman can be when she must.

"If a man has a talent and learns somehow to use the whole of it, he has gloriously succeeded..." —THOMAS WOLFE

I usually buy Girl Scout cookies by the case from whatever girls in my congregation are peddling them. I mean that literally: they sidle shyly up to me at coffee hour with their order forms, and then skip away, wide-eyed, to find their parents and tell them about the windfall. I don't do this because I like the cookies, especially, although the Thin Mints do bring back some good memories. I do it because I like kids. I always buy whatever they're selling. To tell a child I don't need what she's putting herself on the line for seems unacceptably hardhearted to me. They'll find out soon enough about hardheartedness. I do need what they're selling, whatever it is—or rather, I need for them to have the experience of success as a result of their own effort.

We all need for the new generation to believe that what it does will have some effect on its well-being. I shudder to think of what the world will be like if these kids grow up thinking that it won't make any difference whether they try or not. Children and teenagers of the nineties are beginning to suspect that the world is closed to them. The spiral of upward mobility that was a given for decades is gone—never to return, economists tell us. These kids' sense of self and of their own power will be harder-won than ours was. It will be easier for them just to turn on the television and never try. Much easier.

So I buy the cookies and the candy bars and the magazine subscriptions. Because the ones who will change this grim state of affairs are the ones who have tasted their own success and found that it is sweet.

MAY 19

"And God planted a garden..." —GENESIS 2:8

In 1917, someone wanted to reroute the streetcar through Central Park. They didn't do it. In 1918, somebody else wanted to dig battle trenches in its North Meadow as a memorial to American soldiers who had perished in the Great War. They never did that, either. Neither did they fill in the Pond to make a new driveway, as someone proposed in 1923, or erect a giant statue of the Buddha, as was suggested in 1925. In 1964 it was suggested that the park be shortened by four blocks so that another bank of high-rise housing projects could be built and those rolling acres put to some practical use. No dice.

It's not that there have been no changes and additions to the park since it was laid out in 1858. But none of them has succeeded in disrupting this wonderful green creation in the midst of the mercantile capital of the modern world.

When looked at in terms of dollars and cents, Central Park does not compute. We've got a housing problem; let's put up some apartment buildings and get some practical good out of the place. We've got traffic congestion; let's run another avenue straight through the middle. But the lovers walk hand in hand along the cobbled walks and cuddle together on the great rocks. Runners trot along the paths. People sail model boats and ride in big ones. Little league teams play on some of the ballfields and teams of paunchy older guys play on others. Yes, New York means business. But you can't work all the time. Central Park is its rich green jewel, one of the things that even people who hate the city have to love.

MAY 20

"Where sorrow and pain are no more..." —THE BOOK OF COMMON PRAYER

Our friends have just called with the news we have feared to hear for weeks: their twenty-year-old daughter has lost her long battle with cancer. Her dad runs through the arrangements for the funeral in a mechanical voice; he sounds wearier than the whole weary world. We say several times how very sorry we are, aware of the ludicrous inadequacy of our words. But we know that he hears our sorrow in them, and that's all that matters anyway.

I cry when we hang up. I cry because life is a beautiful, beautiful thing, and because young people should have the chance to live it to the hilt and sometimes they don't. I cry because this young woman was so brave in her illness, trying all kinds of different painful and exhausting treatments, only to watch each one fail, and because young people deserve to see their efforts rewarded with success. I cry because there are people who long to die and cannot, and because this young woman wanted with all her heart to live. I cry because her brother took the semester off from school to be with his sister and because he has lost a companion he loved enough to do that.

We owe our children everything, and we give it gladly. We would give our own lives if we could, without a moment's pause. But we don't get to make those kinds of deals. Tired of crying, I lapse into prayer. There are no words in it: words fail me. I do not know much about where that part of this young woman we call her soul is right now. Nobody does. But I send there what blessing I have to give: *You deserved better. No more pain now, never again. Rest, rest in peace.*

MAY 21

"All your strength is weakness..." —SOPHOCLES

As the flight attendant talks about people sitting in certain seats being willing and able to help other passengers deplane if we crash, and says that if anybody sitting in those seats doesn't feel up to doing that we should change seats with somebody who is, I realize that because of my back, I am one of the people who shouldn't be sitting in one of those seats. I wouldn't be able to open the emergency door or help people slide down the rubber chute to safety. Somebody would have to help me.

There goes Wonder Woman. I have always been able to lift heavy things without asking for help. Now I have to call my husband to help me lift the heavy pot in which I make polenta. A lot of things aren't the same as they were. Most things have a higher nuisance factor than they used to. But I still do those I can. And I still make polenta. Here's how:

POLENTA

Boil 6 c. of water. Add 2 c. coarse yellow corn meal, a little at a time, stirring constantly. Don't worry about the lumps; you will cook them out. Cook, stirring often, for forty-five minutes. It will be very thick, and will come away from the sides of the pot. Add 1 c. grated Parmesan cheese. Rinse a small, deep bowl with cold water and turn the polenta into it. Invert bowl on a plate and lift it off to reveal a wonderful mound of the stuff on which Caesar's legions conquered the world. Serve with melted butter and more cheese, or with tomato sauce. Great sliced and fried in olive oil for breakfast, too. Serves 6–8. *Buon appetito.* May you conquer the world.

MAY 22

"Hope deferred makes the heart sick." —PROVERBS 13:12

Something is wrong with our cat. She is doing horrible things to the curtains in the dining room, so horrible that I can't tell you what they are except to say that I'm having to wash them just about every day. She did the same thing to our down comforter—three times. I think you know what I mean.

Now, cats don't do that unless something is wrong. Especially girl cats. Unlike dogs, they are fastidious in their personal habits. So Jenny is obviously undergoing some kind of emotional crisis. We are mystified. We hope that she will return to her normal self when the weather gets warmer. We can't wait.

She can't talk, so she is telegraphing whatever it is that's wrong. People do that too, of course, even people who can talk perfectly well. There are things we cannot seem to speak about, so we act them out instead. A woman terribly bruised by her divorce plunges into promiscuity, finding no other way than this self-destructive one to bolster her sagging sense of self-worth. A teenaged honors student steals from the dime store, finding no other way than this to ask if she is lovable even it she's not perfect. A man yells at his wife and his children, unable to tell anyone that he feels inadequate to the task of excelling at his competitive job; he dominates his family because he fears he won't be able to master anything else.

But we're not cats. We *can* talk. We have to come honestly to grips with the things that are eating us up inside, find out what they are and then do something about them. We can't act them out and expect to get anywhere: that just alienates those around us. And we still don't fix the problem.

MAY 23

"Big girls don't cry."

W hat a lie.

Sometimes you read in a magazine that crying frequently is a sign that something's wrong, that you're under too much stress, or that you're horribly depressed and unable to admit it. But I cry frequently—always have. I guess I *am* under too much stress; everybody I know is under too much stress, so why should I be any different? I don't think I'm especially depressed these days. But when I read something moving, I cry. Or when I talk about something that matters a great deal to me. It doesn't have to be something bad or sad: I cry when I hear something wonderful and inspiring, like a story about one person saving the life of another.

I'm not sure I agree that there's something wrong with this. I like having strong emotions and the freedom to express them. I have no interest in living a lukewarm life. It's one of women's greatest strengths that the gift of tears hasn't been denied us. Remember when Edmund Muskie lost his chance in the presidential primaries because he cried in public? Women have to be careful about where we cry, too, but at least nobody thinks we're unwomanly if we do.

Actually, things are loosening up for men in the crying department. My husband cries, too, the same way I do, when he sees or reads something moving. Maybe it's because we've had bad things happen to us in our lives; I don't know. Everybody has bad things happen, and not everybody cries easily like we do. People like my husband and me can be awfully embarrassing to non-criers. Whatever it is that has made us the emotional people we are, though, I'm glad we found each other.

MAY 24

"I won't be your friend."

Our five-year-old neighbor has come over to play with Rosie and Madeline. They are always so eager to play with her; they barely get in the door for a visit before they ask if they can go and get her to come here, or go over to her house and play there.

Yet when they play, they often fight. They concoct huge projects, mammoth games of hide and seek, loud races down the stairs on their bottoms, puppet shows, plays with our collection of special hats. Invariably two girls want the same pink hat, or somebody races down the stairs out of her turn. Howls of protest, and then the threat: *I won't be your friend.*

That's serious business. They allow themselves to think about what it would be like for a moment, how they would avoid each other's eyes if they both happened to be in the backyards at the same time, how they wouldn't ever play with the hats together, ever again. A grim picture. A negotiated peace usually follows.

We long for friends. There is little we fear as much as we fear being left alone. The inability to make meaningful connections with other human beings is a hallmark of mental illness, a symptom which becomes the cause of more and more serious debility. It literally makes us sick to be alone.

In my line of work I often visit in nursing homes. Most of the women who live there are widows, alone after years of marriage. I have noticed that some women develop deep and intimate friendships with another resident, a nourishing pairing not unlike a marriage. And I have noticed that those women are the ones who thrive, physically and spiritually. At the beginning of life and at the end—and in between—we are not meant to be alone.

MAY 25

"I died for Beauty..." —EMILY DICKINSON

When I was in high school, I washed my hair every day. I would arise at about five in the morning—long before anyone else was up—and stumble to the bathroom, where I would fill the tub and get in. We did not have a shower, and the water pressure out in the country where we lived was never very strong, so I had to submerge my head to wet my hair and then pour water over it repeatedly from a cup to rinse. Then I would towel it partly dry and roll it up on bristly metal rollers into which I stuck pink plastic spikes to hold the rollers tightly against my head. I would put a plastic bonnet over my head and hook up the tube of my hairdryer to it. At last I would get back into bed and go to sleep with the hairdryer on, having found an angle at which I could hold my head so that one of the pink spikes wouldn't drill into my scalp. The rollers were stiff and uncomfortable; they often hurt, no matter how I held my head. Yet I went through this every morning. I wouldn't have dreamed of not doing it.

Now I jump in the shower and wash and condition my hair. I get out and wrap it in a towel for a minute or two, then comb the tangles out. I give it a shake. That's all I do. That's all most women I know do now.

I cannot imagine doing every day what I did in those days. I would resent it heartily. That was an extra hour a day—on *hair*. But everybody I knew did the same thing then, and I don't remember any of us ever complaining about it. I'm glad I remembered about this. It's one thing I don't miss about my youth.

MAY 26

"I love a parade...."

There used to be parades in every town at this time of year in honor of those who died in the defense of our country. Old guys in uniforms they wore as young men marched along Main Street with the high school band and last year's homecoming queen, and every fire engine the town had crawled through town at the end, blowing its siren. People along the route clapped and cheered. Some of them waved little American flags.

Some towns still have a Memorial Day parade, giving in to the odd human desire for a ceremonial walk to mark important times and feelings. Parades are pretty universal. We have them when people get married and when they die. We have them when people graduate, and years later we still choke up when we hear "Pomp and Circumstance." We have them in churches, when people bow as the cross passes before them. We have them in synagogues, too, parades in which people dance with the sacred scrolls of the law.

Special walking happens in enough different places, and for enough different reasons, that it seems safe to say that it's something human beings need to do. People need to have parades. You don't necessarily need to be *in* the parade. But you probably do need to *see* one from time to time. It gives you a place to remember. Unless there's a parade, some kind of special occasion that demands our attention, we'll just go on being busy. And soon we'll forget that we owe a lot to those who have gone before.

MAY 27

"They are all gone into the world of light!" —HENRY VAUGHAN

A picture of my grandmother and her sister hangs in my study. It was taken when they were little girls. My grandmother appears relaxed and interested in what the cameraman is doing, after the manner of one-year-olds. Aunt Jenny just looks uncomfortable, standing stiffly beside her.

Their dresses are long and heavy. They wear wondrous lace collars; my great-grandmother was a wonderful lace-maker, and I still have pieces of her fine work. The little girls stood there for a long time, I'll bet, done up in their heavy dresses encrusted with lace.

I have another picture of them sitting side by side. This picture must have been taken in the late 1950s. By now they are older women; Grandma is about seventy, so Jenny must be seventy-four. They are seated on lawn chairs. They are wearing soft, shortsleeved jersey dresses in muted flower patterns. Their hair, which was so blonde in the first picture that it looks white, is dark, and they wear it in identical hairstyles, pincurled and then brushed out loosely, styles they adopted in the 1940s and never abandoned. Both of them look relaxed; photography is no longer a big deal.

A number of things got easier for women in the years which intervened between the two photographs. Clothing became lighter, less confining. Hairstyles became looser: everybody's hair got fluffier, in fact, because people began to wash their hair more often. A lightness about their appearance and dress speaks of the changes in women's lives. And that was the Fifties. Imagine what they would think of our lives now.

MAY 28

"Love is an attempt at penetrating another human being..." —OCTAVIO PAZ

My friend was on a radio talk show. She's a psychotherapist specializing in women's issues, and the show was about how men and women have different communicating styles. Her partner on the show was a man. They have given talks together before, and they are funny about the differences between them, so that they embody their subject.

People call in. A woman says that she wants her husband to compliment her when he likes something she does. *I hear about it when something is wrong,* she says, *but he just never says anything when I do something well. So I don't know if he's pleased or not.* Her husband gets on the phone. He doesn't understand what the problem is. *If she knows something is good, she doesn't need me to tell her. If I didn't like something, I would tell her. I can't spend all my time chattering away about how good everything is.*

He thinks she's just asking if he's satisfied with the things she does, that what she wants is really information. But what she really wants to hear is that she is valued, and she doesn't think she is if she doesn't hear it. They don't understand each other.

My friend and her partner bicker back and forth on the radio as the woman caller and her husband listen. Everybody laughs a lot as the two therapists model styles of communicating and the couple hangs up in a good mood. These differences are funny when you look at them in a certain way, but they can really hurt. *You can change the way you communicate*, my friend says, *and sometimes you should. Why cause someone you love pain for no reason?*

MAY 29

"I am heavy-laden with trouble through lack of an intimate friend..."
—ANCIENT EGYPTIAN SONG

A young woman whom I haven't spoken with in a number of years calls out of the blue. I'm so surprised to hear from her. We talk for a few minutes about where her life has taken her, and I am sorry to hear that it hasn't been to very many good places. A series of depressions, hospitalizations, suicide attempts. Now she lives alone in a tiny apartment. She's on anti-depressants and disability.

How are my kids, she wants to know, and remembers their names. I fill her in on where they are and what they're doing, painfully aware as I do so that their progress through the years of growing up has been ever so much gentler than hers. I wish with all my heart that things were different.

I remember her as a sweet girl, eager to please, eager to learn. She had already had a tough life when I knew her years ago: a dad who beat her when he drank, which was just about all the time. I am angry that a lovely girl like this has been dealt these terrible cards to play. How unfair it is. She has a birthday coming up, she says. She'll be thirty-seven. She's going to dinner with a friend, another person I knew as a young man, another gentle soul with some severe emotional problems. They spend a lot of time together, she says. I'm glad to hear that. They are both survivors, both gentle people whose lives haven't worked out. I'm impressed at their bravery: reaching out to each other from their lonely, sad places, able to take comfort in friendship.

MAY 30

"...where thieves break through and steal..." —MATTHEW 6:19

Sometime between my arrival home at 3:30 and our departure at 5:00, a passing thief took it into his head to smash our car window and pull the radio out of its metal sheath. I come out of the building to find my husband standing amid scattered piles of greenish cubes of glass. Car windows break in such a neat and well-mannered way these days. They don't shatter; they just crackle into a pretty mosaic of these greenish cubes. And talk about quiet: we were right upstairs, and we didn't hear a thing.

This makes six radios we've lost out of our car. I stifle an accusing *Why on earth didn't you take it inside with you*; Richard already knows he should have taken it inside. Maybe we shouldn't get another one, I think, as I always do when our radio is ripped off. But damn it, we like to listen to music. I don't want to live a life without music because there are thieves in the world. So we'll get the window fixed and get another radio.

A young man walks by while we're sweeping glass cubes out of the car. He says he knows where they take the radios to sell them. He says it's probably over there being sold right now, and we could go over and get one cheap, a lot cheaper than the one we're going to get from the store. I wonder, a little uncomfortably, how he knows these things and why he happened by just now. Thanks but no thanks. We're not about to reward radio thieves by buying back our own property, or someone else's. So we no longer have a radio. We can still have some dignity.

MAY 31

"Train up a child in the way he should go; and when he is old, he will not depart from it." —PROVERBS 22:6

A young man is convicted of several counts of arson. One of the fires he set destroyed an entire apartment complex. He told the prosecuting attorney that he was bored.

The young man is now receiving psychiatric care. In a bizarre footnote, it is revealed that his father is the fire chief. I think of some other young people I have known: one who stole drugs from his physician father, a police chief's son convicted of burglary, a clergyman's daughter involved in prostitution. Something about the position of authority held by these parents seeped into their children's confusion, causing them to violate not just any law, but the law incarnating values basic to their parents' work.

It is not always easy to be the child of a powerful parent. At an early age, all children behold the competence of their parents with awe. But a parent who seems to have power not just over children, but over other adults—or over an enormous destructive force, like fire or illness—is a tough act to follow. Some children despair of ever measuring up, and unconsciously set themselves to destroying the sacred signs of the parent's power.

It is terribly painful for the parent. He feels as if the obvious link between his profession and the child's crime indicts his parenthood beyond any possible defense. And, both he and his child *do* have work to do with a therapist to help the young adult separate himself in a constructive way. But—as in all hard times between parent and child—the solution does not lie in finding who's to blame. The solution is in finding how to help the situation change.

JUNE 1

"The road to Hell is paved with good intentions."

I want to paint the hallway on my vacation. And I want to get some sewing done. I also want to take a little trip or two with my husband so it feels like we've been away. And, of course, I have this writing to finish. I also owe myself some reading.

I won't get all these things done, I'm afraid. Not if past experience is any indicator of future reality. I usually feel a little guilty at the end of a vacation. I have to go back to being busy and frantic and I haven't done all the things I promised myself I would do when I had a little time. I also haven't rested as I should have. Damn, I can't even take a vacation the right way.

Of course, what is the right way? Overhaul the whole house and exhaust myself? Wrong. Do nothing productive at all and have nothing to show for my time—maybe, but I'm just not built that way. Fill my calendar with social engagements so I don't get any rest?

The best vacation—if you're staying home for your vacation and not renting a villa in Tuscany this year—is one that blends all these things. A little unusual work, not the stuff you normally do but something special, so that you can feel remarkable. A lot of unstructured time in which you are free to do nothing at all and nobody is allowed to complain. A judicious sprinkling of unpleasant tasks you've been saving for when you have time: for heaven's sake be careful here, though. Not too many of them. You're on *vacation*.

JUNE 2

"Three years we waited intently for the herald..." —GIORGOS SEFERIADES

Not every wonderful thing is a big hit right away. Beethoven's *Emperor* piano concerto, for instance, now acknowledged as one of the most difficult and most brilliant works ever written for the instrument, was greeted with a yawn when it first came out. So was *Moby Dick*; the reviewers said that Melville didn't know how to write.

Seven days into the Clinton administration, there were already those who talked about the "failed Clinton administration." I guess they expected the budget deficit to disappear sometime during the Inaugural Ball. Not every-body wanted to give Bill a chance.

That sometimes happens with less famous people, too. All you have to do to check this out is go to your high school reunion and not recognize the class geek, who is now a well-dressed, high-powered lawyer. Some things—and some people—take awhile to catch on. Obvious potential is only one part of eventual success, and it's not always present. Some people's gifts are anything but obvious at first. You just never know.

So if something or someone new seems all wrong or really silly, don't give it a bad review right away. You could end up looking pretty foolish. Wait and see how it turns out. New things are usually distrusted at first, for most of us react negatively to change. But all of the traditions we honor were at one time new.

JUNE 3

"You seem a little short on credentials...."

My friend is outraged. She is looking for an academic position after years of childraising, and she is fuming because of a conversation she had with a woman she knows. "You made a choice," the woman said. "Now you have to live with the consequences."

I didn't make a "choice," she says. *I couldn't find a job in my field that would permit me to stay in the same town as my husband and children. That's not a "choice." It's a fact.*

The woman to whom she was speaking had pursued her profession and didn't have children. She now has a long and impressive resume. My friend's anger bewildered her. *I'm not complaining because I don't have children,* she told her, *so why are you so angry?*

A disproportionate number of women whose academic careers go back several decades fall into either of these two camps: the frustrated independent scholar or the childless tenured professor. But having children is a pretty basic human right, and it carries with it some pretty basic responsibilities. It shouldn't be viewed as a career choice. You don't hear men talking about whether they should have a child or a job.

Surely there's a place for stages in a woman's life. Why must there be only one way to manage a career, only one chronology that denotes seriousness? Fathers are more involved in parenting these days. Some of them have even taken parental leave, one hears. But it's a very small percentage of those who are eligible. Looks like the bulk of the responsibility is still on the mom.

So let's not ignore that reality and treat everyone the same. We're not all the same. Thank God.

"Those whom God has joined together, let no one put asunder."
—THE MARRIAGE OFFICE, THE BOOK OF COMMON PRAYER

June is the month for brides. The society pages are thick with pictures of them in June. Grooms, too, these days, as more and more couples opt for a photograph of both for the newspaper. It is still jarring to see male faces in those formerly all-female precincts, but it makes sense. The groom is more than a fashion accessory. He's getting married, too.

Such a hopeful thing, a wedding. Such a fresh beginning. Even if things aren't perfect: lots of these brides and grooms have tried marriage before and failed. Lots have lived together for years. Some of the marriages won't survive. Everyone who goes to weddings knows these things. Even so, the hope for a union that endures and flourishes fills the room at every wedding. Not every guest prays consciously, but everyone does say—to Someone—*"Let it last, and let it be good."*

Some people think remarriage is a second-rate sort of thing. Damaged goods. Or that the people involved take marriage lightly or cynically. Not me. I think the courage to try again after a disappointment is a beautiful thing. More beautiful, even, than the untried bravery of those who have not known this failure. Nobody would say that the death of a marriage is a good thing. It's not. It's bad. But people can survive it and learn from it. And try again. Not innocent anymore, but older and wiser.

JUNE 5

"When angry, count ten before you speak; if very angry, an hundred."
—THOMAS JEFFERSON

Notice that our most brilliant president is not advising us to not get angry. He only suggests we give ourselves a little time to think, so that we can choose our words carefully.

I get angry a lot. More than anyone who knows me would suspect, because I don't always show it. I hardly ever lash out, though. I have to think about it for awhile. This is because I sometimes get angry quickly and then it goes away. If it dissipates that quickly, how important can it be? I know not to pay too much attention to it.

Another thing that I'm not sure about, always, is whether I'm right or not. It's not always easy to tell. I may be genuinely angry; but if I'm in the wrong, I'm probably better off not sharing it. I also get very dramatic when I'm angry, and am likely to get carried away with my own rhetoric if I don't stop and think a little about how I want to express what I'm feeling. Otherwise I might wound with my words, and cause permanent damage to a good relationship over something quite minor. That has happened to me, and I've regretted it each time. If you jump too quickly on something that offends you, it may run away with you. You may start bringing up all kinds of other things while you're at it, and before you know it you're having an argument about something that happened in 1968.

I know we're supposed to get things off our chests. But, before we begin to shout, shouldn't we check first to see if it should have been there in the first place?

JUNE 6

"Should auld acquaintance be forgot, and never brought to mind?"
—AULD LANG SYNE

There are lots of good-byes at this time of year. The people who have been a part of a student's life for four years will be taking their places in the past. They will never sit together as a class again. They will scatter, go their separate ways. And when they meet again, they will not be the same people. They will have changed.

As students, as workers, as neighbors, we don't usually stop to think about how much people mean to us. Not so with the near and dear ones: we always know how important they are. But what about the casual friends? The people in the office or at the store? The janitor? We don't realize, until it is time to leave, how much we have loved the familiarity of seeing the same faces. And so we find it hard to say good-bye to people we weren't very close to at all. And then we feel a bit absurd at how hard it is.

New York City, 1992. A blind man, who has sold pencils on Fifth Avenue for years, is struck by a car that jumped the curb. Hundreds of people read about it in the paper and send him money. They have walked by him two or three times a day for a long time. They may never have stopped to buy a pencil, but he is important to them. They didn't realize how important until he was no longer there. He belongs there. Now that he is gone they miss him. Besides being concerned at the bad thing that has happened to him, they are aware that something has happened to *them*. In a way, they love him.

Yes, love. It's not always a grand passion. Sometimes it is just a benign comfort with the way things are.

JUNE 7

"I am the very model of a modern major general" —GILBERT & SULLIVAN,
THE PIRATES OF PENZANCE

In this famous patter-song, the major general lists his accomplishments at great length. He goes on and on about the things he knows and has done. The more he talks, the more ridiculous and pompous he appears.

This is the time when people graduate from school. They are given diplomas which, in formal language and fancy lettering, certify their completion of the requirements, for graduation. Sometimes the diplomas are written in Latin, in which case the majority of their recipients cannot even read them.

Nobody is much disturbed by this. A diploma's wording doesn't matter much. Although a diploma represents a great deal of work, it does not by itself demonstrate what you are. It just gets you in the door. You still have to show that you know what you're doing.

What you know and what you have done is important stuff. But it is not as important to you as what you *will* do, for that is the part of your history you can do something about. Once you've accomplished something, you've accomplished it. You can be proud of having done so, but you can't live in it forever. The reverse is also true: once you've messed up, you've messed up. But then it's over, and the future is still yours. We don't get to stay on our peaks and we don't have to stay in our valleys. Today is a new day. Yesterday is over.

JUNE 8

"The bird is on the wing..." —OMAR KHAYYÁM

No matter where you live, you can probably hear birds singing in the morning. They thrive in cities as well as in the country, so you don't have to be able to see trees from your window to hear birds. In the city they are a real gift: something small and alive, something whose modest voice can still be heard among the bigger noises of cars and sirens and unloading trucks.

The birds wake up before we do. Ordinarily they will begin to sing before it is light; when you hear them you can tell it's morning without looking at the clock. I hear them through the open window early on a summer morning and I am awake. I get up and look out. Already they have some human partners, people unloading trucks in the dark here in the meat market section of Greenwich Village, walking back and forth in their white coats, slinging enormous slabs of beef from the truck to the loading dock. Yet they are too far away for me to hear the noise they make, and so they look like a silent movie as they work, a silent movie accompanied by birds singing hopeful little songs.

The birds don't know they're in a movie. I think they're singing about mating or something else of interest to birds. The meat market men don't know about it, either. They are thinking about meat, I suppose, or about something else of interest to them. But they are part of the early, early show. Men working, birds singing. We're in the movie, too. I am the woman watching from an upstairs window. You're the one reading in bed, listening to the birds sing.

JUNE 9

"Clarissa lives!" —SAMUEL RICHARDSON, *CLARISSA*

These two words are a coded signal from the villain in this eighteenth-century novel to his co-conspirator: they mean that his long-drawn-out seduction is successful at last. He has just raped the heroine, who surprised him by refusing his advances. Now her life is beginning, he thinks. Now she is a real woman. But Lovelace is wrong. What happens in the book is the reverse: this event seals her doom. Seven or eight hundred pages later—the eighteenth century didn't rush through things—Clarissa dies.

Women who have been raped often report feeling that their old selves have died. Men who have committed rape uniformly lack a genuine sense of having done something irrevocably wrong; typically, they do not perceive the event as having repercussions beyond the few moments of its actual occurrence. Often they maintain that the rape was not unwelcome at all, that it completed a desire on the part of the victim. And the increased publicity that has centered around rape and its causes in recent years has not seemed to reduce its frequency. This crime is as common as it ever was. Maybe more so.

It may be that you are a person to whom this has happened. Perhaps it was years ago, and you never told anyone. It may have been someone you knew, and you have felt ashamed, felt that somehow it must really have been your fault. That is not so. If your participation in what happened was against your will, sin happened, and that sin was not yours. You may be scarred. But you are not stained.

JUNE 10

"Uh, oh ... I think we're just about out of gas...."

Someday we will run out of fuel. It is hard for us to really believe this. We are certain that scientists will come up with something so that we can go on about our merry way and not change our energy habits. We'll always be able to switch on the lights. We'll never have to give up our air conditioners.

Every once in a while something happens that shows us what such a shortage would be like—the oil shortage in the early 1970s, for instance, when we lined up in front of gas stations for hours at a time and big cars almost disappeared. That passed, though. *It was just politics,* we told each other. There's plenty of oil. Big cars are back now.

There may be plenty of fuel, but there's not an infinite amount. We may not run out. Our children may be okay, too. But our grandchildren could be in trouble,

Oh, they'll find a way to deal with it, we think. *Somebody will come up with something.* But I don't want Rosie and Madeline to have to clean up after me. I don't want them to live with the knowledge that their physical world is a hostile place because their grandmother's generation couldn't control its appetites and took everything, knowing as we did so that there would not be enough for them. We don't have children so they can take care of *us.* We have them so we can take care of *them.*

JUNE 11

"The eye is bigger than the belly." —GEORGE HERBERT

As always, my husband is appalled at the size of the serving of rice I have heaped on his plate. *About a quarter of that would be fine,* he protests. It's always the same: he measures things out in teensy quantities, and I make about twice what we need. Leftovers drive him nuts; I like having them around. Saves cooking twice, I tell him.

Actually, he is right. But the right amount looks somehow stingy to me, as if I were ungenerous in my hospitality. I want to be able to say, "Here, take some more" without putting someone else in the position of having to take the last portion. I love the feeling of there being more than enough of everything. That's what I think life should be like: more than enough.

It's not, of course, for so many people. A solicitation arrives in the mail. The enormous eyes of a dying child in the African desert beg me silently for something to quiet the pain of his hunger. The check that I stick in an envelope will arrive too late to help him. The child in this picture was probably dead by the time I received it. I think of my piles of food, and of his want, and my mouth goes dry. I will never know why I am here and he is there. It could so easily have been otherwise.

And so I cook up more food than we need, and send off a check to the hungry. The two actions are related; they are whistling in the dark, one a foolish and ineffectual talisman against the world's hunger and the other something that will actually do some good. Too late. Not enough. But something.

JUNE 12

"All work and no play makes Jack a dull boy."

I recall a radio commercial for car phones. You heard a man singing along with the radio as he drove to work. "I'm so happy," he sang, a bit off-key, as the car radio crackled in the background. Then the announcer came on. *This man is wasting time*, he said. *If you were this man's boss, wouldn't you want him to be making contacts or selling things or doing whatever you pay him to do, instead of wasting time singing? If you got him a car phone, he could put that driving time to use. He could be more productive. This would ultimately mean more money for you. Find out about a car phone today!* Then you heard from the man again. He wasn't singing this time. He was talking from his new car phone, making deals. He sounded crisp and authoritative. All business.

Every time I heard it that commercial used to make me sad. Leave the poor guy alone, I thought. Let him sing. Is it such a crime for a person to begin or end the work day with a song? So he can't carry a tune—there's little enough song in the world; we can ill afford to give up any of it. It's not good for us not to sing.

Sure you have to work overtime sometimes. Sometimes you have to take work home. Often you have to put in long hours to achieve a professional goal. No problem; it goes with the territory. But there is such a thing as quality of life, and you need that, too. Work should not be allowed to intrude everywhere. We need some time for ourselves.

JUNE 13

"Nobody is indispensable."

I was hit by a car while on my way to drop off a manuscript at the publisher. I was walking along on the sidewalk, looking in shop windows, when I felt a merciless series of bumps on my back and legs. I was thrown into the facade of the building I was passing. Reasoning that someone eccentric enough to drive up onto the sidewalk might also be odd enough to back up and run over me again, I crawled awkwardly out of range of his wheels, realizing as I did so that my right leg was not working.

I'm a busy woman, I thought to myself as a sympathetic crowd gathered, I don't have time for this. Someone put her jacket over me so I wouldn't go into shock. I began telling people that the envelope I was carrying was extremely important and would they please be sure it was safe. They said my life was more so. Yes, I said, but give me the envelope. I then asked for my purse and pillowed my head with it so it wouldn't get stolen, a savvy accident victim of the Nineties. I told the emergency people that I thought I was all right and maybe wouldn't need to go to the hospital; they murmured reassuring things and immobilized me for transport.

My calendar was suddenly a lot clearer. Things I was supposed to go to were attended by others. Meetings I should have chaired went on under the direction of others or were postponed. Some things worked out pretty well in my absence. Some didn't. But nobody died, and so I re-learned one of life's big ones: nobody is indispensable.

JUNE 14

"I pledge allegiance to the flag..."

This is Flag Day in the United States.

Flying the flag has meant many different things in our country in just the short time I've been alive. It was simple when I was little: everyone displayed the flag as a symbol of patriotism. Then, during the 1960s, flag-flying grew suddenly more complex. The flag was used during the Vietnam War, both by those who supported the war and by those who opposed it. "These Colors Don't Run" read one of the bumperstickers you could get for your car if you thought we should stay in Southeast Asia. If you wanted out of Vietnam, you could get a peace sign colored like Old Glory, suggesting that withdrawal was the action more suited to the tenets of freedom America espoused. Other people flew the flag from enormous poles erected in their front yards.

Those were hard times. There's some nostalgia for the Sixties these days, but we forget what a bitter thing it was to be so at odds with each other about what love of country meant. I sure don't want to go back to that kind of name-calling. There is room in my universe for people who disagree with me, even about important things. In fact, how important can a thing be which *does* not prompt strong feelings? Disagreement among people about things that matter is not a sign that something is wrong. It's a sign that something is right.

JUNE 15

"You set the solitary into families." —THE BOOK OF COMMON PRAYER

One of our three cats appointed himself my home health aide when I was laid up after my accident. He installed himself on the bed where I was supposed to be most of the time, and would escort me on my brief trips to the bathroom. While I was in there, he would knock over my cane so I couldn't get it, and then he'd flee from the noise. That was the extent of his assistance.

Except that it was nice to feel his round cat body curled up next to mine. I think of the way litters of kittens sleep, all tumbled together in one mass of fur and eyes and tiny tails. They like the feeling of being next to one another.

108

Children love it, too; if you're not careful, they'll train you to cuddle them to sleep so well that they'll be unable to drop off without you, and pretty soon you'll have World War III getting them to sleep by themselves at night. Yes, I speak from experience.

But even so, I would not have traded those cuddly years for all the money in the world. Baby care manuals used to warn darkly against letting your children climb into bed with you. I can't imagine what on earth they were thinking of—sex, I suppose, as if the only reason for human physical contact were seduction. That's a weird attitude. No wonder people today have trouble with intimacy.

The cat gets up, stretches and jumps off the bed. I remember those other little bodies that used to lie next to me, and move over onto the warm place where he was.

JUNE 16

"Somebody's got to listen." —JONATHAN KOZOL,
RACHEL AND HER CHILDREN

You run into sad stories no matter where you go. All of us know someone who is living through a tragedy right now. If it is a close friend or family member, you cannot help but be involved in it. If it is a more distant acquaintance, you may see her from time to time and wonder to yourself how she manages to go on day after day. But you may never speak to her of it. *I hardly know her*, you say. *I'm not going to intrude. Besides, what good could I do?*

Probably a lot. Going through a tough time in semi-public, with everyone knowing about it and nobody saying anything, is a terrible strain. Whatever the trouble is, it belongs to the sufferer to sort it out and resolve it as best she can. But surely that doesn't mean that other people can't help by supportive listening. You don't have to offer advice. In fact, you should try *not* to give advice if it is not explicitly sought: your advice will not be welcome or of much use. Just listen and express your concern. Say you're sorry all this is going on and that you wish it weren't. That's enough. It's a lot.

JUNE 17

"Six days shalt thou work and on the seventh thou shalt rest."
—THE TEN COMMANDMENTS

Sunday afternoon. Anna and I are taking Rosie and Madeline food shopping. The market is filled with other people who are trying to get it all done before Sunday evening, so they can get some rest for the week which starts tomorrow. Lots have small children with them, as we do. Anna and I have commandeered two carts, and each of us wheels a little girl, Remembering some practical wisdom from my own days in the trenches, I had fed the girls before we set out on our shopping trip, so that everything we saw wouldn't look appetizing to them. My memory is that this used to work better than it seems to be working today; Anna and I are turning down numerous requests for salty, sugary snacks as we walk.

Everybody else is pretty much in the same boat. Some are worse off: their darlings are whining and crying in an attempt to use terrorism to get the things they want, and the moms and dads push the carts grimly through the aisles, wishing they were anywhere else but here.

In the dark ages when I was a kid, no stores were open on Sunday afternoons. If you didn't get it on Saturday, you did without it. Whatever implications that nationwide practice had for the doctrine of separation of church and state, it did give us a day that was slower than other days, on which there wasn't much to do because not much was open for business. That wouldn't work today as an official practice. Businesses aren't going to close down. But *we* can, and we should, even if it's only for a few hours in the evening.

JUNE 18

"What are they after our souls, travelling on the decks of decayed ships...?"
—GIORGOS SEFERIADES

A ship model exhibit opens at the Seamen's Church Institute. There's a model of the *Queen Mary*—twenty-two feet of her. Lots of other vessels, too: the *Excalibur*, the *Alciente*. Some of the old guys are here, wandering around among the models. *I was on the "Excalibur,"* one of them says, and so were several of the others. They peer into the portholes at tiny replicas of the cabins they once inhabited, half-expecting to see miniatures of themselves asleep in the tiny bunks or writing home at the little desks, shrunken down to a centimeter's height by the passing of decades but still there, still manning the ship.

Would those of us who work in large office buildings come to an exhibit of them in miniature thirty years later? I doubt it. There's something about a ship that stays with the people who have made it sail. These old men define themselves as seafarers in a way that is still alive to them decades after they stopped shipping out. Their closest relationships are with each other. They love remembering their life on the sea. They say that nobody else quite understands how it is.

I guess not. Teamwork matters in any job, but at sea it's a matter of life and death. A ship can break apart like an egg if it's in the wrong place at the wrong time. A rogue wave can come from nowhere and knock a person into a bulkhead with a force of tons—just like that. People don't face risks like that for decades and remain as they were before. The old men look at the ship models, and they know they are lucky to have survived.

JUNE 19

"The fear of death is more to be dreaded than death itself." —PUBLIUS SYRUS

My friend has had a persistent cough for months now. It gets better and then it comes back. *I've got to see a doctor,* he says grimly, and I can tell that he is afraid. His companion of many years died of AIDS four years ago. Is this cough the beginning of an AIDS-related illness? Every abnormal physical symptom brings this thought. It is always in the back of his mind. He has never been tested for the virus.

What? That's crazy.

But not all that much crazier than going for years without a pap smear, as lots of women do. Or without a mammogram. People in high risk groups for HIV infection are not the only people who sometimes bury their heads in the sand. The desire not to know bad news can be pretty powerful. My friend cannot bring himself to face it all again. His partner's illness was long and hard. He cannot allow himself to know about it if he, too, is stricken.

But the sooner you know, the sooner you can start treatment that will help you live longer and better. I know healthy people who have been HIV-positive for ten years and longer. Long-term survival like that is directly related to early detection and good self-care. Sure, it changes your life. Staying healthy becomes a second career. But a changed life can still be a good one. Most people want to stay in this world as long as they can, and are ready to do what they must in order to do that. But you can't if you won't let yourself know for sure what's going on.

JUNE 20

Slow Down

A colleague is wearing a cotton pullover from Sweden, a rich blue fabric with a narrow white stripe. Turn around, I tell him, so I can see how it's made. He obliges, and I examine the sleeves and the back yoke and the collar. I could copy it easily. It's just the sort of thing my husband loves to wear.

But when would I have the time? Something has happened to us: we are no longer in control of our schedules. When I want to do something, I have to ask permission of my datebook, as if it were the warden. I have less personal freedom than the average teenager. I love to sew, yet I hardly ever do it. It is always near the top of the list of things I want to do when I get the time, whenever that is. I know a lot of women who feel this way. We carry those little

111

books, maps of our lives, everywhere. I would rather lose my money than my datebook any day. A friend from Italy used to ask me to lunch a lot; wait a minute, I'd say, let me get my book, and he would laugh. He carried no book. Couldn't understand why I had to. I couldn't understand how he survived without one.

Of course, we are extremely productive. Doing more and more in less and less time. What we don't have, though, is time to dawdle over coffee with a friend. Or to make something that must be put together painstakingly and slowly. Those are things some people need to do for their spiritual and emotional well-being. We do them because they are fun. We have a right to some fun. I'm going to put a block of sewing time in my datebook—I'll call it a "design meeting" in case somebody sees it—and I'm going to make that pullover.

JUNE 21

"No more monkeys jumping on the bed!"

With supervision, Rosie and Madeline are jumping on the bed and shouting this at the top of their lungs. I am afraid they will fall off, so I make Anna stand in there with them as a spotter. Up and down they jump: two, three, four jumps and then they draw their legs up under them and hit the mattress sitting down. They sit there and look at each other, cackling insanely. Then they get up and do it again.

I remember loving to jump on the bed when I was little. It seemed to me that I jumped very high, that I almost flew. Sometimes there were circus performances with trampoline artists on Ed Sullivan in those days. Jumping on the bed, I imagined myself as one of them, doing incredible feats in a brief outfit of gorgeous blue sequins. I didn't actually do any incredible feats. I never got beyond the suddenly-sitting-down-and-laughing stunt.

My mother hated it when I jumped on the bed. I think she thought I might break it. But it may be that she was afraid I would hurt myself, as I am afraid for Rosie and Madeline. I can hardly bear to think about those peals of laughter turning to wails, hardly bear to think about what might happen if somebody fell off, or landed the wrong way.

I am more nervous about kids' injuries as a grandmother than I was as a mom. I remember that my mother was, too. She got very angry at me once, I remember, for letting Corinna ride her two-wheeler at the age of four. *She's too young to do that*, she said, but there Corinna was, riding it perfectly. We don't know our grandchildren's bodies as well as their parents do. But we cannot help but fear that *they* may not know how easy it is for something terrible to happen very quickly.

JUNE 22

"Pity would be no more, If we did not make somebody poor." —WILLIAM BLAKE

On our living room wall is a spectacular piece of embroidery which we bought from a Hmong needlewoman who had immigrated to Minnesota. The Hmong, who lived in the mountains of Laos, came to America by the thousands after we pulled out of Vietnam. During that endless conflict, they were frequently a source of support to American troops in Laos; they were to pay heavily for that role when the Communists overran their neighbors. That is why so many Hmong have come here as refugees.

The embroidery is large and brilliantly colored. It depicts a sort of Hmong Garden of Eden, animals of all description living peaceably together in the trees, birds drinking from the silver stream that flows out of the distant mountains, a friendly red sun beaming over all. It is executed with a cheerful disregard for matters of scale—a couple of the butterflies are as big as the elephant. Historical accuracy is not central, either; there's a dinosaur, for instance, grazing along with the modern fauna.

It is a beautiful piece of work. It probably took a very fast embroiderer between forty and sixty hours to make. We paid about forty dollars for it, so let's see: that means that the woman who made it—who probably sent it here from Laos for her countrymen to sell to the Americans—got between seventy-five cents and a dollar an hour. That's if she keeps all the money, which she probably does not. *It's a lot of money to her*, somebody might say. Maybe. But that's only true because she lives in a land made poor by other people's wars and colonial habits. She's at least as gifted in her work as I am in mine. And I have so much. And she has so little.

JUNE 23

"Thou art not for the fashion of these times." —*AS YOU LIKE IT*, ACT II SCENE 3

Bellbottoms are back. So are miniskirts; that's old news. So is long, straight hair parted in the middle and cameos on black ribbon chokers and platform shoes. So are Twiggy-esque waifs. So are Edwardian-looking greatcoats and romantic long-sleeved dresses.

Young woman look wonderful in these clothes. Older women can look pretty silly in them, so I think I'll sit this one out. Somebody has recommended the following rule: *if you wore them last time, don't wear them this time.* Say no more.

It is amazing how styles come back. I remember the return of the sack, which had been *sacque* in the nineteenth century, when it was a shapeless coat-like affair worn over a dress. And then it was the chemise of the 1920s. Men hated it when it appeared again in the late Fifties—they'd been spoiled by the wasp waists and full skirts that followed the Second World War. But then the miniskirt came along and everyone felt a lot better. It was the first thing in a long time that was really new.

It's nice to walk down the street and see young people looking like I looked years and years ago. It's like seeing my friends of those days back again. I even feel like my then self, when I see them, as if I had gone back in time. But then I catch sight of myself in a shop window and am almost surprised to see the pleasant-looking lady with glasses who looks back. She looks a little like my mom.

So this is how I turned out.

JUNE 24

"You can't please all of the people all of the time..." —ABRAHAM LINCOLN

More military base closings were announced this morning. The past week has seen the usual scuttle of congresspeople trying to save the bases in their districts and then, when they failed, dissociating themselves from the closings. The political opponents of these lawmakers are already making hay with the closings; *If you'd elected me last time around,* they say to the electorate, *I would have saved the base.*

It's pretty easy to say what you would have done if you're not in office. You can appeal exclusively to people's immediate selfinterest. *I'm the candidate who will see to you and you alone,* croon the hopefuls in the next election.

But American public life is not *about* me and me alone. It's about *us.* It has never been true that each person pursuing his or her own interests will magically make everything just wonderful for everyone. Being a leader of any kind sometimes means doing something unpopular because it must be done. The troubles of political figures are the ones that make the headlines, but it's true for all of us: You can't please everyone, not in any walk of life. That's not leading; it's following.

This list of closings is actually fairly modest, the Secretary of Defense begins to say, but he is interrupted: *Unless you're on it,* a congresswoman says, and he acknowledges the truth of what she says. Sacrifice doesn't feel modest when it's yours. It hurts. But that doesn't make it unfair. The reality of our common life is not that nobody should sacrifice. That's a lie. The reality is that *everyone* must.

"To thine own self be true..." —HAMLET, ACT I SCENE 3

There are some things you absolutely must do. There are some things you really should do. There are some things it would be nice to have done. And there are some things which aren't important to you at all, but which someone else thinks you must do. There's no way you're going to do all these things. So you have to prioritize them.

When you begin prioritizing, it feels as if everything on your plate is a must-do. But it's not; ask yourself what will happen if you don't do it, and the answer will tell you where it belongs. Besides, the fact that something is a must-do doesn't mean you're the one who must do it. Ask yourself if it has to be you.

It also helps to remember that not everything needs to be done perfectly. Some things deserve an all-out effort. Some don't deserve much effort at all. It is very important that you yourself make this determination and that you base it on your own reality, not on what you imagine someone else's to be. For example, you may be a terrible and resentful baker but think that it's important to your daughter that the cupcakes she brings into school on her birthday be homemade. It probably isn't. Buy them if you'd rather not bake them. Good enough for you is good enough, period.

Finally, don't do the things somebody else thinks are important unless *you* think so, too. If something is so important to your husband that he makes a fuss about it, it's probably important enough for him to do it *himself*. This can be a real shocker at first, but stick to your guns and the noise level around the house eventually goes way down.

JUNE 26

"Your teeth are okay, but your gums will have to come out..."

The dental assistant looks at me reproachfully over her mask. *You're going to have to be more serious about flossing,* she says, and goes to work on my gums, digging around the roots of my teeth with a couple of different sharp tools. She draws blood. She compliments me on my high pain tolerance. *A lot of people wouldn't sit through this,* she says. I can't believe I'm paying to be here. I resolve not to be so brave next time.

Actually, I couldn't be less serious about flossing. I just don't do it. So I have to get my gums tortured twice a year instead. My suspicion is that the fascination with gum disease which has arisen in dentistry in recent decades is related as much to the decline in per capita tooth decay—and the corresponding decline in revenues from filling cavities—as it is to progress in preventive dentistry. It's not that I don't think there's such a thing as gum disease, or that your gums don't change for the worse as you get older. Or even that I might slow down this process by flossing religiously. It's just that I'm not sure it matters much.

You are so wrong, says my husband, and shows me a pamphlet about people's teeth being burrowed from within because they didn't floss. So you lose a couple of teeth eventually, I say scornfully, is that the end of the world? And how do we know this isn't a complete invention? What a terrible thing to say. I go to the dentist and get my gums sliced to ribbons again anyway. Cowed by her stainless steel implements and her mask, I don't tell her I suspect the whole gum thing is a sham. I tell her I'll try to remember to floss.

JUNE 27

"Proper words in proper places" —JONATHAN SWIFT

My mother-in-law was a champion speller when she was a girl. She followed the old method of dividing a word in order to spell it aloud: *Mississippi; m–i–s–s, miss, i–s–s, iss, i–p–p–i, ippi, Mississippi.* Throughout my husband's boyhood she impressed upon him the importance of correctly spelled words. He is now an English professor who takes off for misspellings in his students' papers, as a number of his colleagues do not.

These days his mother can't hold much in the way of a conversation. She has had Alzheimer's disease for many years, and hasn't the attention span to do much more than answer a question with a yes or a no. Often she cannot even do that. She does not recognize most people. Sometimes she doesn't even recognize him.

She can still spell, though. *Try to be a little more flexible,* one of her nurses told her when she was being difficult about something. *Flexible: f–l–e–x, flex, i–b–l–e, ible, flexible,* she shot back with a look of triumph. A memory of a long-ago spelling bee in which *flexible* was the winning word? Who knows? She cannot tell us; she has already forgotten. But that skill, drummed into her head when she was a little girl, remains there after most of her other memories have flown away.

People need to be good at something. We need to know that we do something well. We need to be what we can be, whatever that is, and despite our limitations. My mother-in-law is making excellent use of her education, doing the very best she can. Education isn't just job training. It is part of the glorious task of realizing our potential, something that is good simply for its own sake.

116

JUNE 28

It is better for people to think our bathroom is a work in progress, I tell my family, than for them to think the wallpaper in there was something we choose. So I rip the offending wallpaper down one day. It was a brilliant yellow vinyl flower print from the 1970s. The flowers were the size of dinner plates. So now the walls are no color at all, just the grayish hue of Sheetrock. It stays like that, I tell them, until I can get around to doing something about it.

And it does. Our bathroom stays Sheetrock gray for five months, maybe longer. Then I finally paint the walls a caramel color and sponge white glaze onto them to make a sort of marble effect. I pry the hideous chrome medicine chest out of its hole in the wall; a man comes in and puts new Sheetrock over the space. I paint and glaze that, too, and hang an antique mirror over the place where the medicine chest was, so no seams show. *What are we going to do without a medicine chest,* my family asks. Never mind that, I say, and make room for cosmetics and toothpaste in the linen closet right next to the sink. Every bit as easy, I tell them. And it is.

I wheel in an old marble-top dresser from my childhood and hang another antique mirror over it. I stretch a sheer white curtain across the window, gathering it on café rods at top and bottom. Richard hangs a plant in front of the window, and puts Shaker-style pegs high up on the walls for towels. I hide all the odd-colored towels we've accumulated over the years and demand that people use only beige and white ones from now on. As a finishing touch, we hang Richard's grandmother's wedding picture in there. She is young and pretty, caught in a candid shot that's rare in nineteenth-century photography; she is gathering her full skirt in her hand as she takes a step toward the camera.

We think the bathroom looks fabulous. We had to wait forever for it, but we're busy people. Besides, speed isn't everything. And at least we didn't spend six months looking at those malignant flowers. Not everything worth doing has to be done right away.

JUNE 29

The day after the last presidential election, all of the candidates who tried their best to destroy each other during the campaign pledged wholehearted support to the winner. The one who had told an audience that his dog had a better grasp of foreign policy than did his opponent said a week later that the

Democrat had run a terrific campaign. The president-elect complimented his former foe on a lifetime of public service.

Outside a courtroom, I am amazed to see two attorneys who cut each other to ribbons yesterday slap each other on the back like old friends and go out to lunch. *It's just business,* my attorney says when I comment on it. *You can't take this stuff personally.* I sure could, I thought to myself. Lawyers and politicians have to be extraordinarily thick-skinned, able to survive vicious attacks on their motives, their intelligence, their families, you name it, and then joke with their assailants the next week.

A certain type of person is not bothered by personal attacks at all. That person should seek out the jobs where such occurrences are inevitable, like litigation or politics. Others of us are better off not choosing to put ourselves in harm's way.

Or—you can learn to be tougher. You can educate your emotions by facing criticism and personal attacks and surviving. The first time it makes you want to die. The second time keeps you up half the night. And the third one is not so bad. Awful as it is, people do get used to it, and they grow in self-confidence when they do. Nobody can avoid personal attacks completely anyway, no matter how gentle a profession she may have chosen. But you do have some control over how you will handle them, and you do improve with practice.

JUNE 30

"Who steals my purse, steals trash." —SHAKESPEARE, *OTHELLO*

On a crowded subway car, the man crammed in next to me suddenly decides to leave. He pushes his way through all the packed bodies and out the door. As he goes, I feel my shoulder bag move. *Uh, oh.* I try to reach down and explore its contours with my hand. I think my wallet is missing, but I can't be sure; the car is too crowded to lift the bag and examine it. I'm right, though: when I get out at 14th Street, the wallet is gone.

Here is the list of my missing wallets: one today out of the subway car, two out of the church (!), one out of a crowded bus, one out of the train station. That's just in New York. There was also the bag stolen from my hotel room in Venice while I slept right next to it, and then there was the bag stolen out of my shopping cart in the supermarket. That's a fair amount of theft for one person to sustain. It has become so routine I'm not even upset by it. I haven't had a driver's license since Venice, so this guy didn't get that. I haven't carried credit cards since the first theft from the church, so he didn't get any of them, either. He got a little cash, a wallet I liked, and one of my husband's antique cuff links. That's about it. I feel worst about the cuff link.

So I'm not in a frenzy about canceling credit cards. And I can borrow some money from my daughter to buy a train ticket home. No real problem here. Hee-yah! Take that, pickpockets! I've beaten you at your own game. I have nothing left for you to steal.

JULY 1

"Thank God It's Friday!"

A young man comes to see me. He responded to being on the wrong end of a "downsizing" by going into business for himself as a word processor. He does résumés and brochures, and he's getting a fair number of clients. He is also an organist, so he has a job at a church on Sundays. He also tunes the organ at another church. Then he's got a children's choir—the one at my church, in fact—so he does that once a week. *All in all*, he says, *I make more money than I did at the job I lost.*

But I feel so spread out. I'm here, then I'm there. I did this because I wanted to be in control of my own schedule, yet somehow I don't feel I am in control. I feel that I have to accept every two-bit job that comes along because I don't have a regular paycheck. That's what I miss about working for someone else: you have your job and you do it and then you go home, and every two weeks you get a check. But when you're the boss, it never ends.

I tell him I think we're supposed to regard that uncertainty as part of the thrill of entrepreneurship, and he laughs ruefully. But what I say is true: uncertainty is built into running your own show. It may be unsettling, but at least it's yours. So *make* it yours, I tell him. Get tough with yourself and with others about the boundaries you need. One of the principal satisfactions of freelance work should be a feeling of autonomy. But you *need* an "off" switch. Otherwise, you're not really working for yourself: you're working for everybody *but* yourself.

JULY 2

"...a wise and frugal government ... shall not take from the mouth of labor the bread that it has earned." —THOMAS JEFFERSON

Coal mining is the most dangerous occupation in the world. Several times a year we join a vigil beside a mine on the evening news, see the forlorn cluster of wives and children and ministers, the grim-faced rescue teams, the trench-coated reporters. It seems to me that these vigils usually end in sorrow: the rescue teams are forced to leave the mine by pockets of the same methane gas that caused the disaster, or they come upon the miners, dead where they fell in the explosion.

People call us ignorant hillbillies, says a young woman from West Virginia. She's being interviewed after her husband has actually survived a mining accident. *I wish they'd come here and go down in the mines and see what it's like.* Her voice grows angry as she warms to her subject. *It's like our lives aren't worth protecting because we're from "Appalachia," like we aren't human beings, too. Well, if they came here and saw what it's like, they'd listen when we ask for simple safety protection. After all, it's the law. My husband's supposed to be able to refuse to work if there's a violation. But if he doesn't go down, he'll lose his job. They'll make up some lie—that's what they do.*

So you have the right to refuse, but you"ll pay if you exercise that right. A number of labor "rights" work that way. And in a coal mine, it's a matter of life and death. That's not true everywhere. That woman in West Virginia knows she's lucky her husband's alive. But she still has a right to be angry.

JULY 3

"Of warm lights and all-night vigil..." —SOPHOCLES

Madeline stirs in the night and starts to cry a little. Before I can swing my legs out of bed, my husband is up and across the hall. I hear his warm, rumbly voice saying something soothing to her, and in a few minutes he comes back to bed. Nice reflexes, I tell him, you'd make a good mother. *Man-basher!* he says. *That's not a mother reflex. It's a parent reflex. Dads have it, too.*

I had been congratulating myself on my own nighttime mother reflexes during this overnight visit of the grandchildren. Mothers have a more acute sense of hearing than normal people; noises no one else can hear will have us up in no time flat. I had this reflex when mine were little. And now, fifteen years later, I have it still. But now here is Richard, a male, doing the same thing. I guess he's right: dads have it, too.

Everyone knows that uninterrupted sleep is important. Not everyone knows, though, that there is a dispensation from that natural rule for parents. People who don't have children would consider a night during the course of which they were awakened two or three times to be a pretty rotten night's sleep. People who do have kids have that kind of night every night; they learn quickly to go right back to sleep as if it never happened. Their sleep isn't ruined by it; it's just the way things are with kids.

If you don't have kids, I'm not trying to scare you off. Maybe you couldn't handle a night like that now. But you will then, and it won't even seem like anything much. It comes with the baby, like stretch marks. And many other wonderful things I'm not going to tell you about just yet.

JULY 4

"I came to the United States at age four through Ellis Island. I had to stay in the hospital alone. My mother went on ahead." —MARY ALICE KLEIN, BEAVER, PA.

You can visit Ellis Island now and see the dining rooms, the Great Hall; you can look at pictures of the immigrants. The people who entered the country through this checkpoint were exhausted, sick, poor and frightened. They were also tremendously brave.

It is hard to travel with children. We all think that, although for us that is likely to mean a drive along large, well-lit highways in an air-conditioned car with plenty of restaurants and gas stations along the way. I can hardly imagine how hard it must have been to come here from across the sea, leaving behind parents and aunts and uncles forever, trying to keep the children calm when the parents themselves must have been terrified. A hard trip. A strange new place. Unfamiliar.

One picture shows a rooftop playground for children who were detained—denied entry because of some medical or legal problem in the family. Five of them sit in a magnificent cart, decked out with American flags and pulled by two other boys. "Uncle Sam" is emblazoned across the side of the cart in fancy script. Another child sits on a splendid rocking horse, holding an American flag. Another rides a tricycle. All of them are engaged in some kind of play, yet none of them is smiling. They're not having fun. They're scared and homesick. I imagine their parents watching them in that garden of childish delights, seeing those grim little faces. Wondering if they did the right thing in coming. But here we all are. Happy birthday, America.

JULY 5

"Last rose, as in dance, the stately trees, and spread their branches..."
—JOHN MILTON, *PARADISE LOST*

I remember lying on my back on the grass in the summertime, looking up at the sky through the branches of trees. It seems to me now that I spent hours as a child doing that. I can close my eyes and see it still: the blue sky peeking through the green leaves, the sunlight coming and going as the branches swayed in the breeze. I also remember looking at clouds and pretending they were people and animals. And making twig dams in a stream, and leaf boats.

I helped my mother some, but I sure had a lot of free time. Life was different then. Nobody thought twice about letting a little girl play in the woods alone. We were unescorted in our play, and it was safe for us to be so, I am sure that I wouldn't have spent so much time looking at leaves and clouds and dreaming up things if I'd been as monitored as kids have to be now. But these days we are afraid to leave them alone like that. We think something may happen to them. And it might.

We have to find a way to give them that dreaming time. Kids need to dream. We have to find a way to give it to ourselves, too. We haven't outgrown our need to dream. The sky and the leaves and my time on this earth seemed limitless to me as I lay there and looked up into the trees. I felt as if I were forever. As confined as time and space are now, we all could use a little of that limitless feeling.

JULY 6

"The wild God of the world is sometimes merciful to those that ask mercy..."
—ROBINSON JEFFERS, "HURT HAWKS"

I have vague recollections of being taught to swim, but more specific ones of teaching my own children. Step one, of course, is to put one's face in the water and blow bubbles, something that seems very daring the first time. Down go the little faces and up they sputter. A shout goes up: "I did it!" And then learning to float, and gradually feeling the great peace and grace of moving through water. There's always something new to master: jumping off the side into waiting arms; then learning to dive from a crouch; then doing a standing dive; and then a running leap.

There are some who cannot conquer their fear. To them the triumph of the ones who can cuts like a knife. They watch the divers and the jumpers, watch the others go fearlessly under and pop up laughing. *If only I could do that*, they think, imagining themselves strong and graceful, their bodies arcing over the water with power and purpose. And they try again to summon the courage to put their faces in. And again it eludes them.

People need time to master the things of which they are afraid. Children should be given that time, not shamed into humiliating paralysis by being compared with others who are not afraid. Time and encouragement, lots of both. *That's good*, we should say to them, *really good. Try it again.* And we should say it to ourselves, too, when we face something which scares us to death. *You can do it—just take it slow, one step at a time.*

JULY 7

"Little GTO, you're really lookin' fine..." —JAN & DEAN

Young people today have a hard time believing that a major portion of the 1960s was spent listening to songs about cars. Maybe their parents would just as soon forget, too, but the truth is that a fair amount of the decade had passed before most people knew what "psychedelic" meant, and many of us spent that time listening to blond adolescent boys sing about sports cars and their engines and their gearshifts. The great wave of postwar babies had their drivers' licenses and were ready to have a good time. Ready to go to California. Ready to surf, or at least to look like they knew how. And the boys sang about their cars. And the girls listened. I don't remember ever thinking it strange that some of my favorite songs were about automobiles.

Feeling the summer heat now reminds me of those songs and the carefree life they celebrated. So does the smell of suntan lotion. Of course we now know that the American love affair with cars has not been an unmixed blessing. The same can be said about deep, dark suntans. And most of us have had rather enough of watching admiringly while men did daring things. All of us left the place in which our leisure pursuits defined who we were. Today we think we're lucky if we even *have* leisure pursuits.

Yeah, those songs were dumb. And so we grew out of them. But when one comes on the radio as I drive to work, I remember the way it all felt. The way we were then. And I can't help but smile.

JULY 8

"In all, let nature never be forgot." —ALEXANDER POPE

For some people, working in a garden is the best means of stress reduction there is. They like to get down and dirty out there, to tie up tomatoes and prune bushes and mix unmentionable things with the soil. They like to sweat.

There are others for whom it is enough simply to *think* about working in the garden. They don't actually have to *do* it to feel at one with the earth. Walking by a garden is enough for them. Which is why office workers like to go out at lunchtime and sit in a park, if there is one nearby. When you're cooped up in a hi-tech environment all day, it's good to see some green. *Outside.* Office plants just don't cut it; they are not free.

But a plant growing in the earth, even one set out in the most rigid of orderly rows—that plant is *free.* It stretches its toes into the soil and feels terrific. It unfolds its leaves to meet the sun and doesn't worry about skin cancer. It drinks water deeply and gratefully. And that's it. Even if it has only a season to live, it is enough. No more is required of it than to purify the air and look beautiful.

More is required of us. No wonder we are not as beautiful and serene as the plants; they don't have to run around like we do. But they are here to help us: *slow down,* they say. *Sit and look at us for a minute. You and we are both part of something bigger than ourselves, something that was here long before we were and will be here long after.*

"Thanne longen folke to goon on pilgrimages..." —GEOFFREY CHAUCER,
THE CANTERBURY TALES

This is the time of year when you sometimes find yourself covering for someone else who is on vacation. Later on, someone's going to have to cover for you. It's hard to do that: you've got your own job and part of someone else's.

Maybe you work alone—maybe there's no one to cover for you if you're not there. Lots of people fall into this category, stay-at home mothers being the most numerous, with their continuous twenty-four-hour-on-call routine. If you're basically *it* in your work, it can be tempting just to not take off at all. A vacation can feel impossible. *I can't get away. Nobody but me can do what I do.*

That's probably true. Nobody does what you do. But somebody can do something that's good enough to pass muster for a short time, long enough for you to get some R&R. Everyone needs it, even if it can only be a day here and there. Otherwise, a bitter attitude can set in, even toward the work that you love, and you will be robbed of the satisfaction you deserve to have in a job well done.

Watch it, though—make sure your holiday gives you a chance to get some rest. No point working so hard at having fun that you get back home more exhausted than you were when you left. It's supposed to be *fun*. You're supposed to feel rejuvenated afterward. Whatever it takes to make you feel that way—*that's* what you should do.

JULY 10

"With what sense does the tame pigeon measure out the expanse?"
—WILLIAM BLAKE

I sit at my window and look out. A flock of maybe a hundred pigeons comes careening through the air, around the corner of a building, and hovers over one of its favorite spots: the sidewalk in front of a store's loading dock, where a dependable supply of crumbs can always be found. They flutter down, all of them at once, beating the air with their wings, their white undersides flashing, making the air and the sidewalk shimmer. Then they are up again, as if the leader said, "Okay, everyone, let's go!" and they all shoot down the street and around the other corner in an airborne slalom that amazes me every time I see it. Through the canyons of the buildings they swoop, making the turns, shooting straight up and gliding down, fluttering their wings, catching the sun.

I am sure they are playing. I am sure they are enjoying their own skill, their teamwork, their sheer numbers. It seems to me that they couldn't perform this spectacular air show for me unless they were also doing it for themselves. They don't *need* that rhythm, that precision, that excellence just to get from one place to another. They do it because they like it. They do it because it's fun.

They are so good at what they do. Really good. I could watch them all day if I didn't have to get to work. But I'll remember their excellence all day, the way they made something spectacular out of picking up bread crumbs off the sidewalk.

JULY 11

"Doubts are more cruel than the worst of truths." —MOLIÈRE

It seems to my friend that her boyfriend's feelings for her are cooling. Although they have talked of marriage more than once, she's noticed that they haven't done so for a long time. *He seems uncomfortable when I try to have a conversation about the future. We went to a friend's wedding and he spent almost the whole time talking with his friends from college—he would barely look at me all evening. But when I ask him what's wrong, he says everything's fine.*

She is suffering over this. She knows she's not being told the truth, and it's a nightmare. What her boyfriend does is speaking so much more loudly than what he says. This makes her behave unnaturally toward him. *Which is probably going to drive him even further away,* she says. *I can't help thinking every time we're together that it may be the last time.*

Her doubts are well-founded; she's not stupid. The pain of a love affair coming to an end is made worse by the uncertainty. She is driven into a humiliating state of passivity: what is he going to do, and when is he going to do it? She is paralyzed by her doubts. She cannot just say *Never mind what he's going to do, what am I going to do?* and take matters into her own hands. What if she drives him away?

The answer is that she won't. He'll drive himself if he's leaving, which is certainly what it sounds like to me. All she can do is be clear with herself about what is acceptable behavior. If this is acceptable, so be it. If not, she should say so. Maybe he'll change. Maybe he won't—and that's an answer, too. Not the one for which she might have hoped, but at least she'll know.

JULY 12

"Ask not what your country can do for you; ask what you can do for your country." —JOHN FITZGERALD KENNEDY

There is a shortage of volunteer firefighters in many small towns, I read in a magazine. Older guys say that young people today just don't have any interest in it. They have a hard time understanding why: being firemen has been such an important part of their lives. The guys at the station are their best friends.

They are a team. They have saved one another's lives on occasion, and they've saved the lives of countless fellow citizens. Why wouldn't a young person want to serve others and test his courage, they want to know.

Well, you can get yourself killed fighting fires. But thousands of small towns throughout America have been protected by volunteer firefighters for years and years. What kind of person risks his life to protect his neighbors? And, more important, what has happened to that kind of person? Are they gone? Have we just become too selfish to produce that kind of person any more?

Interestingly, I do know some volunteer rescue workers who are women, something the old guys at the station probably aren't thinking of when they talk about "young people today." A petite young woman talks to me about being able to lift a two-hundred-pound man and carry him out of a building on her back. *I can do what you have to do*, she says, with calm pride. *No problem.*

JULY 13

"That toil of growing up..." —WILLIAM BULTLER YEATS

There's a new hotel going up across from the World Trade Center.* I pass the construction site all the time. No matter when I walk by, there is always a little knot of men standing and watching the goings on. Bulldozers bury their shovels in the dirt and then lift them high in the air; they reverse their direction and carry the load to a dumptruck. The guys on the sidewalk watch in silence as the bulldozer repeats the loop over and over: dig, reverse, dump, dig, reverse, dump.

There aren't any women watching; I don't really count myself among the watchers—I'm not watching the bulldozer, I'm watching the guys. I wonder why they watch and we don't. The women stroll through the park in pairs or trios, talking and laughing. The men watch in silence. And when a man and woman stroll together, they don't watch the construction work, like two men might: they talk and laugh, like two women.

These men of Wall Street have spent the morning swimming with the sharks in the most competitive environment in the world. At noon they, come out into the sunshine and lift their eyes to behold gigantic versions of the trucks and bulldozers they played with as boys. They used to be the ones digging into the dirt and loading it into a dumptruck back when life was a whole lot saner. Now they shout into telephones and pound computer keyboards and run like hell to stay ahead of one another. The women swim with the sharks all day, too, and at lunchtime they come outside and stroll

---

*I thought a minute before deciding to include this just as it is. But I like remembering those days. I still can't believe it's gone.

around, just as they did in the playground years ago. They want to be playing outside, these grown-up boys and girls in pinstripes and Burberrys.

JULY 14

"Now give me a big smile-great! Hold it!"

We have an enormous picture of Marilyn Monroe in our dining room. *Why*, you ask. Because Anna loves Marilyn: she has all kinds of Marilyn memorabilia in her room and on her walls, has seen all of Marilyn's movies. And then my husband, of all people, thought when he saw this particular picture how nice its colors would look with the color of the dining room wall. *Besides, Marilyn and I are about the same age*, he says. *Not that we knew each other that well, but still it would be nice to have her picture on the wall.* So I end up with a picture of Marilyn in my dining room.

In it she is standing in a bedroom; the walls are covered with flowered wallpaper, and you can just make out the bed behind her. She is wearing a sequined sheath with spaghetti straps; one strap has slipped off her shoulder. In one hand she holds a large bottle of Chanel No. 5; with the other she applies a touch of the perfume between her breasts. Her eyes are closed and she is smiling slightly, her lips parted just a bit to show her teeth.

Poor thing. I know what it is that makes people love her, although I can't really put it into words. Something childlike. Something vulnerable. Something about being just a little inappropriate and not realizing it. Her life was a mess: pills, booze, marriages she somehow couldn't stay in for long, depression. And yet she looked innocent and happy in most of her pictures. Whatever was happening in her life, she knew she had to smile for the camera.

JULY 15

"Fear no more the heat o' the sun..." —CYMBELINE, ACT IV SCENE 2

I want to lie in the sun the way I did when I was a teenager: gleaming with suntan oil, baking in the heat until I can't stand it anymore and have to jump in the water to cool off. We thought it was good for us. Not anymore. There's no such thing as a healthy tan, a skin doctor has told my husband, and so Richard covers himself with high-octane sunscreen when he works in the yard.

When my kids were little, doctors counseled mothers to sunbathe their children. Vitamin D came from the sun. So you put your baby on her tummy out in the sun with nothing on, and then you turned her over after two minutes, like a pancake. It's worst of all when you're young, they say now; even one bad childhood burn puts a person in a whole new high-risk category when she grows up. And women who lie out in the sun are going to have faces like catchers' mitts when they reach middle age.

So I don't lie in the sun. I sit in the shade and read books. I scold Anna when she comes home sunburned from the beach. Corinna doesn't sunbathe her kids for two minutes on each side, like I did. I compliment her on her choice of industrial-strength sunscreen for them.

But when I give them their bath, I see that they have little white ghosts of bathing suits on their naked bodies, just like their mother used to. I always loved that. I liked the way I looked with a suntan, too, and I liked the way the sun used to bleach blonde stripes in my hair. it still feels wonderful to turn my face into the sun, and I still do it for a surreptitious moment here and there. The sun was a good friend in the old days. At least, we thought he was. I miss him.

JULY 16

"How beautiful you are, my love." —SONG OF SOLOMON

I read that nine out of ten women wear shoes at least two sizes narrower than their feet. I knew a woman who cut out all of the "Size 16" labels in her clothes, so that nobody at the cleaners would see them. And I know many women who buy clothing a size too small and stuff themselves into those too-small dresses like sausages.

At dinner, I happened to mention some work I was doing on Dorothy L. Sayers, the famous English writer. One of the men present said that he had met her. He made a few cursory remarks about her translation of Dante's *Inferno*, and then went on, *She was quite unattractive, really, she was hugely fat, you know.* He continued at some length about Sayers's appearance. He wanted to confine the significance of that brilliant and productive woman to her physical appearance. C. S. Lewis, also no beauty contest winner, had been this man's tutor. Why didn't he fill us in on whether or not Lewis was good-looking and the proper shape, I wonder?

The desire of women for smallness is a holdover from another day, when a woman needed to be smaller, shorter, younger, and dumber than whatever man she was with. The male ego, we were assured, could not withstand equality. We have climbed out from under some of this: most women no longer feel they should play dumb in order to make men feel smart. So we shouldn't try to shrink ourselves in any of those other ways, either. Our feet are the size they are, and we should be comfortably shod. Our bodies are the size they are, too, and deserve clothes that fit and flatter them. Women come in all sizes. So do men. So does beauty.

JULY 17

"We do not know, yet must choose." —PAUL TILLICH

I visit a thirty-five-year-old woman with breast cancer. She had a mastectomy with reconstruction a few days ago. The operation took seven hours. The doctor says it was very successful, and the tests on her lymph nodes have come back negative. *Looks like they got it all*, she says. Now she has to decide what further treatment, if any, she should have. She is quickly learning that medicine can be a most inexact science. Chemotherapy or radiation? A combination of the two? Autologous bone marrow transplant? None of the above? She's going to get a second opinion, and maybe a third. Her doctor admits that the approach to treatment depends on the physician's philosophy. There are no universally-accepted rules about what to do. *I feel healed*, she says. *I'm really tempted not to do anything at all.* But then she would feel so angry at herself if her cancer recurred.

The disquieting truth is that the decision is hers. All the experts can offer are educated opinions, and those opinions are not all the same. In the end, she is on her own. Modern medicine heals all sorts of things that were once incurable. The things surgeons are able to do are nothing short of miraculous. This is a blessing, but not an unmixed one. All these new possibilities make things harder to decide, not easier. *This treatment problem is just like the rest of life*, she says. *More things among which to choose. More consequences to face.*

JULY 18

Call Your Mother

An English friend has just returned from a visit home. *It was fabulous*, she says, *my mother spoiled me rotten the whole time.* Her job is an extremely demanding one: long hours, lots of stress. She is young, single, and far from home. No wonder she loved being spoiled for a while.

She is surprised and a little embarrassed at how badly she misses her parents since her return. *I even cry sometimes*, she says, *isn't that silly?* But I remember crying every time I left my parents. And I still cry when I leave my father. He is old and frail. We look into each other's eyes when we part. Neither of us speaks—it is not our way—but we are both thinking that this could be the last time we see each other in this world. We think that every time we say good-bye. One of these days we'll be right.

My friend's parents are not old and frail; they are still in vigorous middle age. She's not crying about their deaths. In a way, she cries about her own: the death of the child she was when she lived at home with them, the girl who lived on that English farm and looked out that bedroom window every morning, the girl who came down the stairs to breakfast, smelling the same delicious smells every morning. *It is all still there.* Everything is just as she left it when she emigrated to America. It is she who is missing. She closes her eyes and sees her home like a picture, and tears fill her throat. *I've called so many times since I came back,* she says. *I shudder to think of the bill.*

Big deal, I think. Call while you still can. Things won't always be the same. Call. I used to talk to my mother every day when she was alive. I'd give anything to talk to her now.

JULY 19

"Nothing succeeds like success."

A friend will arrive soon for coffee and counsel. She is out of work, and my job is to help keep her spirits and confidence up while she looks for another job. She's never been unemployed before and, although the reasons for her predicament are purely economic—"downsizing" is the current term for the process that cost her her job—she feels as if she's been fired.

I know how good she is at what she does. She's really good. Really smart. Dedicated. The kind of person who's going to be hired again, soon. All these things are clear to me. But I want them to be clear to *her.* She'll sleep better. She'll feel better. And she'll interview better.

So how can I help? By telling her how great she is? I do that. She looks at me with a mixture of gratitude and annoyance. *If I'm so terrific,* she says, *what am I doing out of work?* But we begin to talk strategy: whom to contact, where to apply and where not to. What to stress in the cover letter. I can tell that this practical problem-solving feels good to her. Of course it does: she's *doing something.* It's *doing something* that out-of-work people miss most, the feeling of putting effort into a task and seeing a result. Just about everybody has this basic need. Most of us don't feel quite like ourselves without it. The sooner my friend has it again, the better.

JULY 20

"Life is short."

M y daughter called late last night to let me know that she'd be staying at a friend's beach house rather than coming home. I appreciated the call. I appreciate everything about her these days, the last few weeks of the summer after her senior year in high school. I like her in her fast-food restaurant uniform. I like hearing her incomprehensible music slamming away behind her bedroom door. A fashion magazine left in the bathroom doesn't make me angry. It makes me glad she's here.

The day she was born seems like a few weeks ago. Day after day and year after year of picking up after her collapse together into a very small package of memory. I remember how she and her sister used to fight like cats over who would sit in the front seat of the car. I used to get so exasperated at this pointless argument. Now the two young women slide into the car with no apparent interest in who sits where.

They so much *are* the way I wanted them to be! I used to wonder sometimes if we would all survive their upbringing. Now we have, and they are beautiful and interesting and kind. Could stand to be a little neater, perhaps, but maybe that's coming, too, like everything else.

Time seems to stretch out when you're standing at the beginning of a hunk of it. Twenty years looks like forever. But when it's over you realize it was nothing. And the people you held close: when it's all over, you realize you didn't hold them for very long.

JULY 21

"Nice customs curtsy to great kings." —HENRY V, ACT V SCENE 2

You can't go to the supermarket without seeing something at the checkout about Prince Charles and Princess Diana.* *What's wrong with the royal family*, people want to know. *Why don't they behave themselves?* I've heard people say that it's a sign of the times: in these degenerate, anything-goes days, not even the Queen of England can keep her family in line.

That's not really it, you know. The problem is not that the royals are behaving more disgracefully today than they have in the past. It's just that we all know about it now. George IV was every bit as neglectful of his queen as Charles was of Diana. It just wasn't in the papers. Edward VII was a second-class dandy and a first-class womanizer; he had a long affair with luscious Lillie Langtry, no doubt working off the sexual guilt instilled in him by his mom, Queen Victoria. The list of royal mistresses, if such a list were to be compiled, would be lot longer than the list of English monarchs. It's just that the newspapers print things today that they would never have touched in the past. This most recent crop of royals is not so awful. They've just lost the mystique that used to make things like this off-limits to reporters. They're even ringing up the media themselves, apparently. Royalty only works if the system of communications which links it with the world is spotty. That is, in the right spots.

So let's not be too hard on them. The royals are not a different species. They never have been. They're behaving the way some of our more embarrassing friends and neighbors are behaving. And the way their ancestors did.

---

*Poor Diana. I have elected to keep this just as it was.

"...old and merry..." —HENRY IV, ACT II SCENE 4

My stepmother may need to have her gallbladder removed. What used to be major abdominal surgery in which the patient was all but cut in half has now become an outpatient procedure. People used to take months to recover completely; now they're back up to speed in about a week. This is great for an older person. Everything is slower and more difficult in old age, including healing from a huge incision. Now she doesn't have to have one. She'll just have a scar about an inch long, maybe two.

She has been a nurse for almost sixty years. The practice of medicine has changed so much since she began. Some things that used to be forbidden are now recommended. *We used to have people on complete bed rest for weeks after heart surgery,* she says. *But now they get them moving right away. I'm all for that. Less chance for pneumonia: that was a real problem in the old days.*

So she looks forward to her operation with her usual brisk common sense. I admire her flexible approach to life. One might expect an older person to be suspicious of so radical a departure from the way she was taught, but she does not cling to the old ways if she thinks the new ones may be better.

Old people aren't always rigid. Conservative, maybe, but not rigid. It's young people who think they know everything. Old people have lived long enough to know that things change.

JULY 23

"...the names of those ought to be written in gold, who died so cruel a death."
—BERNAL DIAZ DEL CASTILLO

An archaeologist has uncovered a group of human remains in the Italian city of Herculaneum. They were piled on top of one another at the mouth of a tunnel to the sea: they had been running for their lives from the river of lava behind them, hoping to reach the water before the lava reached them. That was as far as they got.

One of the skeletons was that of a young girl, the skeleton of a baby still wrapped in her arms. Around the baby's wrists and neck were gold bracelets and a gold necklace. The girl wore no jewelry. Signs of wear on the bones of her lower spine suggested that she had carried heavy burdens for a long time, even before her bones were fully grown. The difference in their attire tells us this was not her baby: she was a servant girl.

Poor thing. I imagine her terror as she ran as fast as she could through the narrow streets, carrying her precious bundle, separated in the confusion from the baby's parents. A hard life and an early death.

But she did the right thing, trying to get to the water, and she almost made it. She might have reached the water if she hadn't been carrying the baby, if she had cast it aside and sprinted. Who knows? But she didn't. This young child-care worker of ancient times died trying to save the little one committed to her charge. I think of her as I walk to work and see the toddlers in the park with their nannies.

If there's a job more important than the one they're doing, I don't know what it is.

JULY 24

"One grand sweet song..." —CHARLES KINGSLEY

On the radio they are playing a Jerome Kern composition recorded in 1931. Fred Astaire and his sister Adele sang it when they were still a team. His reedy, sprightly voice is immediately recognizable; her tremulous soprano helps me to understand why he branched out from that youthful partnership to something more sophisticated. But oh, the sweetness of these old songs, the innocence of their lyrics about love and being swept off one's feet and dancing the night away: has it really only been the lifespan of a person since we were like that? Or were we *never* really like that? Was that sweetness always only in the movies?

I remember veterans of the First World War marching in parades on the Fourth of July, old guys in their funny uniforms. None of them are left now. My mother remembered veterans of the Civil War marching in parades when she was a little girl. I listen to these sweet songs, songs about love and romance, songs about life and love and trust as we have always wished they were, as soldiers of distant wars died believing they were. That was real music. Then I am assaulted by one of our songs, something about sex and power, the way we measure love now. I wish things were now as they were then.

Of course, those sweet old days were also the days of Jim Crow laws. Institutions from colleges to country clubs were openly anti-Semitic. All kinds of unfairnesses were institutionalized in those sweet old days, unfairnesses that our gruff era is still trying to heal.

Those days were not as thoroughly sweet as I want them to have been. I guess what I'm longing for is the world of those songs. It may have been an imaginary world then, too.

"Farewell! Thou art too dear for my possessing..." —SHAKESPEARE, SONNET 87

I visit a church that I have visited many times before. The rector of the church has just left, after being there for seven years. Person after person comes up to me to tell me how hard it was to say good-bye. One lady showed up with a rich suntan: *I knew I couldn't stand to be at the good-bye party,* she said, so *I just chose this week for my vacation and went to Aruba.* This guy worked hard to be a faithful companion to his people. He was a wonderful priest. They will miss him tremendously.

At the coffee hour after the service, someone said something about love being too hard, something about not wanting to care about the next rector, so that it wouldn't hurt so much when he or she moved on. That's the price of connecting with one another: we miss each other when we part. The only way to avoid that pain is not to love at all.

The relationship of a priest with a congregation, if it is a good fit, always hurts when it ends. But even work relationships that aren't nearly so intense matter to us, much more than we think. We spend long hours with our colleagues. We share the excitement of doing something really well together. Or we share the annoyance that only people who work for the same psychopath can ever truly understand. We may share a great deal of our private lives with the people at work, or we may share hardly any at all. But we depend on one another. And we miss each other when it's time for one of us to move on. We care more than we thought we would.

"I seek a father, who most need a son." —JOHN MALCOLM BRINNIN

I am listening to an interview with a father and his son. The father was a member of a gang when he was a teenager in Los Angeles in the late Sixties. The son has joined one, too, and at age seventeen has already begun to have many of the same problems his dad remembers. So the dad, who is now a poet and newspaper publisher, wrote a memoir of his gang days. He wants his son to understand what he did in those days—including the things of which he is ashamed. He knows what the appeal of the gang is: it functions as a family in which loyalty is very strong. He is painfully aware of the pain his divorce from the boy's mother caused, painfully aware that his son suffered when he moved to another city. *The gang is there for me,* says the boy to the interviewer, and his young voice reminds me how it feels to need friends when you are young.

The father does not forbid his son to be with his gang. He knows that it would be to no avail. *All I can do is be there for him and tell him the truth.* I can hear the love and fear in the father's voice. He knows firsthand how bad it can get. They talk a lot about the future: what the boy wants in life, and what he needs to do to get it. The father sees some changes in his son. *He's working. He's back in school.*

It sounds to me like the son is also getting the attention from his father that he craves. That has a lot to do with the hold the gang has on him, and it will be important in giving him the strength to go his own way. They edge along toward his adulthood, an inch at a time, as if they were negotiating a tiny ledge over a deep abyss. And I guess that's exactly what they *are* doing.

JULY 27

"But who is to guard the guards themselves?" —JUVENAL

My daughter's friend is moving home to live with her parents. She is twenty-nine. *It's not the money,* Corinna tells me. *It's just that she doesn't want to be alone.* My daughter shakes her head. I don't say anything.

I have never lived alone in my entire life. I went at a very young age from being somebody's daughter to being somebody else's wife. Then I was somebody's mother. So it has never been just me. I don't know what it's like. On those occasions when everybody has been somewhere else overnight—and you could count those occasions throughout my entire life on the fingers of one hand—I am embarrassed to confess that I have been afraid.

As if having children in the house made it safer. Which makes no sense at all.

What am I afraid of? I seem to hear creaks in the house I don't recognize, but it's not really an intruder I fear. I think it is loneliness. I've gotten used to being needed. I know it's hard to say in just what sense one is needed by people who are in their beds asleep, but one is. And I feel lonely when there's nobody here who needs me.

Don't get me wrong: I often resent being needed. Heartily. I have fought for time to myself all my life, and I have savored hours of solitude as if they were chocolate. I have imagined the well-ordered house I would have if there were nobody in it but me, even though all the offices I've ever had, where there has *always* been nobody but me, testify that it probably would not be well-ordered at all. But the fact is that I can't imagine myself permanently in that empty house. I would have to remake myself. A whole new person.

Which is what I'll be having to do someday, of course, unless I die before my husband. I'll be old, I hope, but I'm afraid I won't be any further along in self-sufficiency than my daughter's homesick young friend.

JULY 28

"Sing, heavenly Muse..." —JOHN MILTON

A woman, well into her middle years, has begun to write. Her mother was a writer as well. She won some prizes for her poetry. The woman remembers how the neighbors looked askance at her mother's writing, how they gossiped about the way she let her girls run around outside—sometimes with nothing on!—while she sat inside the house and wrote poems.

Her mother stopped writing, though, while her girls were still young, and never went back to it with any seriousness. An uncle says he thinks maybe she just got whatever it was out her system and didn't have to write anymore. My friend doesn't think so. She thinks her mother grew tired of being labeled irresponsible and feckless by people who didn't even read poems, let alone write them.

For years my friend froze whenever she tried to write. She'd sit in front of blank sheets of paper and no words would come. She thinks that this was because of her resentment of her mother's writing. But she began to remember that she hadn't always resented the writing. Sometimes she liked it. She loved it that some of the poems were about her. She even—sometimes—liked it that her mother was unique. She began to remember that her mother's writing wasn't always a bad thing. Sometimes it was a wonderful thing. It was a mixed blessing.

As she began to remember these things, her writer's block began to disappear. She lived in New York City, a place where they don't talk about you if you're unusual because it's normal to be unusual there. She is free to write. She wishes her mother had had the chance to be as free.

JULY 29

"We hold these truths to be self-evident, that all men and women are created equal." —ELIZABETH CADY STANTON

Four women in their mid-forties are having lunch. One of them has two toddlers. One is unmarried and has no children. One is a grandmother, and the other has two teenagers from a previous marriage and a two-year-old from her current marriage. *I can't believe you're a grandmother and I'm just starting out,* says the one with the toddlers. *That's nothing,* says the one with the fourteen-year gap between her first two and her third, *Look at me.*

The one who has no children observes the others as if from behind a veil. There are moments when she'd love to be a mother, too, but she has to admit that she usually feels okay about not being one. One of the others tells her she should have a baby alone, like Murphy Brown. *Oh, please,* she says. Another says she should marry the office creep, whose only redeeming feature is that he's single, and she pretends to scream and choke, as if she had swallowed poison.

Seriously, though, says one, *aren't you lonely? Well, yeah,* she says, *sometimes I am. But I like my life.*

You don't have to be single to be lonely. There are great gulfs of loneliness in lots of marriages, too, made more bitter by the facade of companionship the married couple presents to the world. The single woman of the quartet has thought a great deal about her life and feels at peace with her single status. It's not what she expected, but it's certainly not bad. She enjoys the richness of solitude, and the freedom of it. She is a person in her own right.

JULY 30

"...greet me with that sun, thine eye..." —SHAKESPEARE, SONNET 49

I hurry along the empty sidewalk, afraid I'll miss the downtown train. A man with a briefcase hurries toward me, and I smile and say "Good morning" as we briefly meet. He gives a startled murmur and we pass each other.

Having grown up in the country, I find it unnatural not to speak to a stranger if we happen to find ourselves face to face and more or less alone. So I always do, and the person I meet is usually somewhat at a loss for a reply. Even so, most people manage to summon a smile. In a small way, an exchange of smiles between strangers makes the world a better place. Modern civilization can be savage in its refusal to recognize the worth of the individual, and yet we all crave that very recognition. So much in our lives makes us feel unwelcome in the world. A smile and a greeting ennobles us.

You can see this in the rooms across the country where people who live with alcoholics or other addicts gather to encourage one another's healing. People literally change in appearance as they get better; women get prettier, lose the worried brows and grim, straight mouths they came in with. Peals of laughter and bursts of applause greet their stories of things they used to cry about all alone. Laughing together literally saves their lives. The people whose substance abuse drove them into the group may never stop using. But whether they do or not, they come to know that they are persons who matter in their own right. It ennobles them. You can see it happen. It's a beautiful thing to watch.

JULY 31

"Get me the police."

In 1992, twenty-five thousand Americans were robbed or assaulted by people posing as police officers. I read this in a magazine, and that's all it said, so I can't tell you if the felons were wearing police uniforms they had stolen or if they were impersonating plainclothes cops. Certainly the latter would be easier.

I am told that many of the victims of such crimes are elderly people who fall prey to a confidence game that goes like this: a person accosts the victim in a bank, identifying himself as a policeman. He asks the victim to help him apprehend a crooked bank teller by making a sizable withdrawal. Asking to count the money after the withdrawal, he takes it and runs. Apparently this is a common enough occurrence that some banks post signs warning customers not to give money to anyone claiming to be a police officer.

You hear a lot of stories about crooked cops. A pervasive cynicism has infected us, nationwide: there are many, many people who believe that most people who have risen to positions of authority have done so by crooked means. It's hard for many people to believe there are any good people left running anything, anywhere. But not all of us are cynics. Enough people trust the office of the policeman that twenty-five thousand of us fell for a scam like this transparent one. We want to believe the things people in authority tell us. We want to trust; our society is built on our ability to do so. What a mean thing, to play on that trust. And what a powerful thing that badge is.

AUGUST 1

"Let us reason together." —LYNDON BAINES JOHNSON

We are thinking about trading in our car for a new one. That would be something of an emotional wrench, as we anthropomorphize our cars, give them names and genders. This car's name is George, and it's a boy. My van was a woman by the name of Estelle. When I had her junked it was like putting a favorite pet to sleep.

It will be emotional for another reason. My husband and I have never bought a car together before, and there could be trouble. I think cars should be convenient. Extremely convenient. They should have air-conditioning and power steering and their workings should be self-evident to an experienced driver such as yours truly. You shouldn't need to took up how to fasten the seat belt. Richard thinks air-conditioned cars are bourgeois. He likes things pretty much the way they were in 1947. No air. No frills. I'm surprised he even has a radio in George. And he loves nothing more than diving into a good operator's manual. So it's Baby Boomer meets Lad of the Depression. Who will win?

We both like a standard transmission, but there will be controversy over that, I can tell you right now. If I'd been smart, I would have pretended to want an automatic, so I could negotiate it away for air-conditioning. The mind doesn't always work fast enough.

Your resale value is much higher for cars with air-conditioning, I point out. Nobody wants one without it. *I do*, he says, and the race is on.

AUGUST 2

"It is better to wear out than to rust out." —RICHARD CUMBERLAND

You should take it easy, my friend's daughter keeps telling her. Betty is nearly eighty-five. She lives alone and takes care of her own little house. She drives her old car the few places she goes: to the store, to her church. She hires a neighbor boy to mow the lawn, but does the rest of the gardening herself. *This is nothing*, she tells me. *My garden was five times this big at the old place.*

Why don't you let me get someone to come in and clean, says her daughter. *You shouldn't be doing that any more.* She really means it, and she and her mom have real arguments about it. *You should rest more. You've worked hard all your life. Why don't you call me when you want something at the store? I can pick it up on my way home from work.*

I don't know what she thinks is wrong with me that I can't take care of myself. *She forgets that I raised nine children. I do just fine.* She waves her hand around the tiny living room. She is right. Her house is spotless and cozy. She makes the boy who does her lawn take cookies home to his mother.

Betty thinks her daughter doubts her abilities. Her daughter doesn't realize that this is how she's coming across. *It's not that at all*, she says. *I've never known anybody who was a better housekeeper. I just want her to enjoy life and not worry about the house and all that. She's earned a rest.*

But a rest is not what Betty wants as she nears the end of her life, *I get plenty of rest*, she fumes. *It was when you kids were little that I needed a rest!* Betty knows that the time will come when she won't be able to do what she does now. She's not going to give up her ability to care for her home until it does.

AUGUST 3

"Be not made a beggar by banqueting upon borrowing." —ECCLESIASTICUS 18:33

My husband wants to pay off our credit card bills. *See how much interest you're paying*, he says. *That's not deductible anymore, you know. You're just throwing money away.*

He is right, of course. But I don't want to show him the bills. I incurred most of them. While few of the purchases were luxuries for my own use, I *have* racked up large bills buying things for my children and grandchildren. I know I have bought things he would not have bought, and I feel embarrassed, like an irresponsible teenager. Up until now, I had enough money coming in that I could just pay the minimum and never say anything about the balances that were accumulating. And I could tell myself that people who make money have the right to spend it as they see fit. But now most of the money coming in is his, so he's got to see these totals. I hate the thought of showing him, and I hate myself for letting things get to this point.

I am harder on myself than he turns out to be on me. He looks through the purchases and listens to me tell him of my plans for not making so many of them anymore. That will work if I stick to my rules, and I tell him how I intend to do *that*. I also tell him I intend to pay him back. He does not act like a stern father about any of this, and I appreciate it. Afterward, I feel like a person who has just attended an AA meeting. Imagining myself confessing was terrible. Actually confessing wasn't nearly as bad.

AUGUST 4

"All the world's a stage...." —AS YOU LIKE IT, ACT II SCENE 7

Sometimes I wonder if I'm going anywhere, a young woman tells me as we drink coffee together. *I'm working all the time just to pay the bills. I have forty thousand dollars in school loans to pay back.* **Forty thousand dollars.** *I take acting classes when I can, but I spend so much time just trying to stay alive that I really can't attend auditions the way I should. Did you know that I have four jobs? Some days I look at this and wonder if I'm ever going to make it.*

This is a very talented young woman. If anybody deserved to make it as an actress, she does. But she lives in New York, where the restaurants are full of talented young people like her, working as waiters. She knows that a large portion of success in show business is luck, simply being at the right place at the right time.

Sometimes I fantasize about what I would do if I were rich. If I were, I would make a deal with her: *here's enough to support you for four years. Go to your classes and your auditions and concentrate on your career. Four years ought to be enough to see if you can make it. And then, if you haven't made it big re-orient your theater work and make it an avocation. Make it a hobby, and make yourself another career that will support you.*

I wish I had the money to do that, but I don't. All I can do is buy her a cup of coffee and be her friend. Which helps, I think. Being frustrated and discouraged is terrible. But feeling that way with a friend sure beats feeling that way alone.

AUGUST 5

"Now I lay me down to sleep..."

Three A.M. Why am I awake? I turned down coffee after dinner. Lord knows I was tired enough when I went to bed. And I *need* to be asleep, too: tomorrow's going to be another killer. Carefully, so as not to disturb my sleeping husband, I turn over on my back. I try not to dread starting the day with a sleep deficit: I could keep myself awake for hours worrying about not getting enough rest, and there's something wrong with that picture.

After a few minutes of fuming, I remember that praying is a good thing to do when I can't sleep, and I begin. I have extensive lists of people to pray for, and then there is myself. And then there is the further prayer of quiet contemplation. I relax. I wake up a few hours later, rested and ready for the day.

What do you pray for? a friend asks. I have found that it's not easy to explain prayer to someone who doesn't do it. I believe they think it's somewhat like shopping by phone: you put in your order and then, if you're lucky, you get most of what you want. Or that it's sort of like relaxation therapy.

But it isn't like that. I don't know what life is like for people who don't do it, but I know praying is something I need to do. I have no more certainties about God's nature than anyone else has—people don't have certainties about that. We have beliefs. So not having God figured out is no reason not to pray. Neither is not knowing what to say. I am often at a loss about what to say when I pray. When that happens, I just say so—I say something on the order of, "Hello, I don't know how to begin." Prayer is not all that different from other endeavors in that way. It's not important to start well. What's important is that you start at all.

AUGUST 6

"We are becoming the servants ... of the machine we have created to serve us."
—JOHN KENNETH GALBRAITH

A computer store. A young man in a white shirt and bright tie wants to help me. He is about twenty-three. *What are you interested in?* he wants to know. I can barely answer: there are too many different brands, too many exotic features. I just want something I can write on, I mumble sheepishly.

I tell him that I don't know what a spreadsheet is and don't want to know. He goes swiftly down the line of machines, scanning the specs on each one. He tells me to try one or two and see how their keyboards feel. They feel fine, I say, feeling a little foolish.

The fastest, most powerful computers cost the most, of course. But you don't really need that kind of speed for what you do, Justus says. *There's no need to pay good money for things you don't really need.*

Good advice. Electronic equipment changes so quickly it's hard to keep up with it. The rapidity and amount of change intimidates the buyer—at least, it intimidates this one.

We are being changed by what our machines can accomplish. We can no longer wait for a letter: we want a fax right away. We are also more verbose: revision is so easy on these machines, words so easy to come by, that we put out a lot more of them. College professors report that student papers are wordier than they used to be.

But they are not better. Maybe there is something about gnawing on the end of a yellow pencil and looking at a blank sheet of paper that we need to do. Maybe it helps us consider our words carefully, choose slowly.

AUGUST 7

"Sterile prayer pierces heaven" —THERESA OF AVILA

A young woman comes to see me. She wants to talk about prayer. *I don't know what I believe in,* she warns me. *Just so you know, sometimes I think there's a God and sometimes I don't.* I tell her that seems fair enough, that nobody really "knows" about these things, at least not in the way people know that Harrisburg is the capital of Pennsylvania. Spiritual things are really about desire, not about information.

She wants to talk about what she should pray for. And how she should do it, given the way her beliefs are shifting lately. *Isn't it hypocritical for me to pray to God if I'm not sure God exists?* she asks. Doesn't that depend on what you say? I ask. *I have so many feelings inside me that are not expressible in any way I know about,* she says, *and so many people I care about are in trouble.*

We talk about what her prayer might look like. What she might say if she happens to be having a day on which she's not sure whether or not there's a God. I tell her to be honest with herself about that; her life will teach her the answer to that question.

Everybody has a spiritual life. I remember a little girl whose mother was an atheist; she very carefully explained to me that they didn't believe in God, but in Mother Nature, which was clearly a proper noun for this child. We are all animated at the deepest levels of our being by a part of ourselves which we cannot understand and which does not follow the protocols of human logic; the name by which this domain is called is less important than our acknowledgment that it exists. We can't ignore it. It has somewhere to lead us. It is part of being a person to explore it.

"Remember me when this you see."

I have a book about the Names Project, the great quilt friends and families of people who have died of AIDS have made. The quilt is so enormous now that it cannot be fully opened in any one place; there is no public place big enough to display all the names at the same time. So parts of the quilt travel around the country for people to see this homemade testament to love and loss.

Looking through the book always makes me cry. I think of the months of suffering which preceded each of these deaths. I think of the burden of watching that suffering, and of the hard work it is to nurse a terminally ill person as he prepares to leave this life. Toward the end, the people who love the patient spend most of their waking hours involved in his care. And then, suddenly, he is gone. There is sorrow, and there is even genuine relief that it is over, but there is also the definite and disconcerting feeling of being at loose ends. Most of the other things in life were pushed into the background while he was ill. *Now what do I do,* they ask themselves.

One of the things that more than 50,000 of them have done is to make a single panel of this enormous quilt. Some of the panels are simple: just the name of the person being remembered lettered onto a piece of cloth. Others are elaborate works of art, using special fabrics and exquisite designs. Many offer sad and simple little messages of love and longing, but some of them are funny, choosing to remember the deceased with the humor he spread liberally around when he was alive. Some of the panels remember babies and toddlers, and have images of teddy bears and building blocks sewn onto the fabric: the sweet artifacts of childhoods never enjoyed.

This is one more thing we can do for him, the people who have loved the dead say to themselves. *We can make something that remembers him to the world, something that is him.* They sit around tables with fabric and needles and thread and make a panel for the quilt. Some of them have made dozens of them. *It helps,* they say, *to do something concrete with my sorrow. I put a lot of hours into taking care of him. I'm used to spending time with him. Making this panel was sort of like that. I look at what I have made, and, in a way, I am looking at him.*

AUGUST 9

"She looks well to the ways of her household and does not eat the bread of idleness." —PROVERBS 31:27

So that's where this whole thing started. She's a busy little bee, that woman in Proverbs. Running her own business, sounds like, and raising all those grateful children. And where's the man of the house? "Her husband takes his seat with elders of the land." Wouldn't you know? She's working her tail off and he's out with the boys every night.

I include this only to prove that there are working mothers in the Bible. There seems to be a movement across America to turn back the clock to the time when women didn't work. Now, just when was that? When they drove three thousand miles across the continent with their families in wagons? When they pitched hay in the fields with their husbands? When they worked seven-day weeks of twelve-hour days in the sweatshops of New York City and cooked dinner after they got home at night? When they worked ten days on and two days off in aircraft factories during World War II?

The decade of the Fifties was not the norm in our history. It was unusual in our history for women to absent themselves from the workforce in the numbers they did then. It was a privilege to be able to stay home with the children, but it was never the universal practice: not even in the Fifties. And it has never been enjoyed, before or since, by as many women as it was in the years after the Second World War. Then as never before, women concentrated on childrearing as a profession.

Those women can testify that they worked hard, and most feel good about having done it that way. It was not without its pitfalls, though. The generation of children who were the object of all that focused parenting grew into what is arguably the most self-absorbed generation this country has seen to date. It may not be the best thing in the world for a child to think that the world revolves around him. Maybe being forced to accept responsibility at an early age is not such a tragedy. Maybe the whole family is responsible for its well-being, not just the mom.

AUGUST 10

"Thursday come, and the week is gone." —GEORGE HERBERT

Apparently, there is such a thing in the auto industry as a "Friday car." These cars, put together on Fridays, are said to be lemons because the workers are thinking about the weekend and not about their work.

I wonder if that's really true. I do know, from my own work, that lots of people in crisis seem to wait until Friday afternoon around four to come forward, and that it can be hard finding appropriate help for them at that time of the week. Everybody's cut out a little early to get the jump on the weekend.

A friend of mine does all her cleaning and laundry on Thursday night. Then at work on Friday she thinks of her clean apartment and has the feeling that the weekend has already begun. I remember seeing my yuppie niece saunter out the door for work one Friday morning wearing shorts with her blazer instead of a skirt. *Friday is Dress Down Day*, she explained. *Everybody chills out before the weekend.*

If this is the way we are, then a four-day week really makes some sense: knock yourself out for ten or eleven hours a day for four days and then enjoy a three-day pass. For some of us, though, it could spell trouble: I'm trying to imagine an eleven-hour stint at daycare for a two-year-old, and I can't quite see it.

And we'd all have to agree: no cheating, no "Wednesday come and the week is gone" syndrome. No cynical sayings about "Thursday cars." We've got to get *some* work done.

AUGUST 11

"I have laid aside business, and gone a-fishing." —IZAAK WALTON

An excellent idea.

A friend has returned from a fly-fishing expedition with her son. Fly-fishing. *It was fabulous*, she says. *I'm going back in a few weeks to do it again.*

All manner of things became clear to her while she was fishing. She realized that she didn't want to stay in her job forever—she likes it, but she doesn't love it, and so she's going to change jobs in a couple of years. She also realized that she doesn't want to grow old all alone on the East Coast: *I can't do much about "Old" or "alone" but I am a Westerner. That's my home, and I'm going back there.* While fishing, she thought about how stressful her life is, and decided that from now on she was going to take mini-vacations—three or four a year for several days at a time. *That's just a better way for me to do it*, she says. *I need a break more frequently than once a year.*

The combination of clean air, sparkling water and the patient self-control that fishing requires is conducive to taking stock of oneself. Maybe it has something to do with the brevity of the fish's life: one snap at the wrong thing, and it's all over. Could happen to any of us at any time. Spend a few hours in this enterprise, and you're bound to get a little thoughtful about your own journey. *Where am I going? Where do I want to end up?* Better get started getting there—you don't have forever.

AUGUST 12

"There was an old woman who lived in a shoe; she had so many children she didn't know what to do."

Let me come and get the kids for an hour or two.

My daughter says no. She's been trying to clean her house, but the little one dumped a box of dry cereal on the bedroom rug and the older one cut up a newspaper and refused to pick up the pieces. *Nothing I've tried works. I talk to them and explain why something is wrong, and they listen and then they go and do it again. I've had it.*

She doesn't want me to trouble myself. I have her sister call her back and say we're coming anyway. Women have to stick together at times like this.

Anna and I pick up Rosie and Madeline. I yell at them in front of their mother, telling them how bad it is to be so messy when she works so hard. My aim is to make them feel awful, and I do. Anna digs me in the side; she thinks I'm going a bit too far. Tough, I say, and we sail out the door, each of us holding a cowed little girl by the hand.

We go shopping for school clothes. Grandma, who has cooled down a little by now, buys each child two expensive outfits. This is not consistent with the tongue-lashing I gave them previously. Tough. Grandmothers don't have to be consistent.

Then we go to lunch. Afterward, we rent a Shirley Temple movie and watch it while the little girls lie down on a sleeping bag. Then I take them home. Their house is spotless and their mother is glad to see them.

My mom would have done the same for me.

AUGUST 13

"Got a minute?"

The phone rings. It is a man who calls me frequently to say very little at great length. I groan inwardly at the interruption, grab a pad and pencil and sit down. I have found that I can write letters or balance my checkbook or touch up my nails with no greater investment than an occasional murmur or chuckle to keep the soliloquy going at the other end of the line. For my caller doesn't really want me to talk to *him*. He just wants to talk to me.

What a life he must lead, I think as I listen to him talk on and on. His discourse is so unremitting that our talks cannot accurately be called conversations. They are more like lectures. After I've given him twenty minutes or so, I break in and say I've got to go. *A couple other things have happened,* he says, and would plunge ahead for another hour if I let him. I repeat that I've got to go, and say good-bye. Then I hang up. He is never miffed. I suspect that others are not nearly as nice to him as I am. My husband, for instance. He'd like to meet this guy, he says, so he could punch him in the mouth. I imagine many people respond to him in much the same way. Poor guy.

Don't encourage him, my friend Joe says. Joe is right about one thing: this guy will never run out of things to say. Many of them are even interesting, although afterward it's hard to remember what has been said. But just because he's a pain in the neck doesn't mean he doesn't need somebody who will listen to him. It's a service I can offer at no cost to myself, and within limits that I control. When it's over, it's over. And my nails look terrific.

"You can't go home again." —THOMAS WOLFE

Today Anna and I will go out to New Hope to browse around in the little shops and have lunch somewhere. New Hope is an eighteenth-century town with uneven streets and dozens of antiques stores.

We're going on this little outing because she'll be leaving for college at the end of the month. My last child. From now on I'll go into the bathroom and it will be just as I left it the last time I was in there. No makeup in the sink. No towel on the floor. Her room will stay clean; nobody will be in it. It will take us a long time to fill up the dishwasher without Anna's contribution of a dozen glasses a day. Not that she's going that far. She'll be less than an hour from home, and she'll only be about four blocks from our apartment in the city.

But the Anna who lived here will never live here again. She won't be the same person when she comes home. We won't have the day-in day-out life together we have now, not ever again. Eighteen years of waking up in the same house every day and taking each other for granted are almost over.

Anna doesn't know it, but I dread her leaving. When her sister left, I still had Anna. I was still Mom to somebody who lived here, and that defined my days and my spare time—this even though I have worked outside the home throughout Anna's entire life.

But from now on, I will not be a part of her day-to-day present. And still less a part of her future. Well, I wanted them to be independent, didn't I? You bet I did. And I'm so glad they are.

But, just today, I wouldn't mind doing it all over again.

"Hail, Mary, full of grace…"

Painted on the wall of a tiny church in the Italian village of Monterchi is one of the very few representations in the world of the Virgin Mary in which she is obviously pregnant. Her blue dress is partially unbuttoned to accommodate her extra girth, and her white shift peeks through the opening along her stomach. She rests one hand on her swollen belly; the other is planted firmly on her hip, and she looks challengingly and piercingly—and not at all sweetly—out at us.

I study Mary's face. She is young. Something about the set of her mouth and the lift of her chin seems defiant. So does that hand on her hip. A young girl pregnant out of wedlock. The whole village buzzes with gossip about her. *Go ahead and talk*, she seems to say. *I don't need your approval*. But there is a hurt behind the challenge in those piercing eyes. So she is human, after all.

Centuries of the devout have focused on the physical particulars of the tradition of the Virgin Birth. Was she or wasn't she? How did it happen? Of more use to us, I think, is the personal cost of Mary's aloneness. None of us becomes pregnant without having sex. But many of us *have* found ourselves alone and in disgrace because of an unwanted pregnancy. History has sweetened this anguish in its treatment of Mary, as if it were easy to be in that predicament. It's not. It's hard, and it takes guts.

AUGUST 16

"Talk gently; act frankly." —WILLIAM HENRY CHANNING

A rapid clicking sound begins on one branch of a tree outside my window. It is made by an insect, one of the midsummer bugs of the Northeast. Other insects join the first, and the sound spreads from tree to tree like a wave, mounting to a crescendo of a thousand clicking insects and then suddenly melting away.

What on earth are they doing? Maybe they're checking in with each other, keeping track of all the members of the family, like kids at a swimming pool yelling "Marco!" "Polo!" to one another. Or maybe they all want to fall in love and get married, after the manner of insects, and this wave of clicking noises is a kind of corporate personal ad in which the bugs advertise their availability and attractive qualities to one another.

Whatever it is, there is no question that it's intended to communicate something. It starts with one tiny animal, but swells in seconds to include thousands who click back to one another. Even insects need to talk to each other.

They do it instinctively. We aren't so lucky. Although we have many more ways of reaching out to one another than insects, human beings often just choose not to do so. People live whole lifetimes side by side and never say much about what they really think and feel. Then they wonder why the people they love don't know.

Life together is too short to be lived in silence and isolation. Everybody needs to talk to somebody.

AUGUST 17

"I can do it myself."

I got up early this morning to get some writing done. I got myself all set up in the living room with a nice cup of tea, my record player, and a yellow pad. I wrote one page. Then I put my pen down and looked around the room. I've been meaning to rearrange the furniture in here. Talked about it with my husband yesterday. We should put the two couches in front of the fireplace. They used to be there, in fact. I don't know why we ever moved them.

I can do this *now*, I thought. It was about six in the morning. I can move the couches little by little and roll the rug up under them little by little. Then I can move the padding into its new place and drag the rolled-up rug over there. It would work. I began. Kneeling down and using my shoulder to lift the first couch, I rolled the rug up and nudged it under the legs. It worked.

After the first couch, I lay down for a moment. Some pain shot through my back. It wasn't the worst thing I ever felt, but it wasn't the best, either. This is probably a stupid thing for me to be doing, I thought uneasily. But there was no turning back now. As it turned out the second couch wasn't so bad. I was eager to get it done before my husband got up. And I did. He's on his way down now.

I hope I'm not sore from moving the furniture. He'll be annoyed if I am, and justly so. He won't be able to understand why I couldn't wait for him to help me. I don't quite understand it myself, actually, but I do know that sometimes a person just wants to do things herself.

AUGUST 18

"The city that never sleeps."

The New York street on which we used to live led directly to a hospital. Ambulances used to scream up it at all hours. There was a popular restaurant across the street from us which was open until about four in the morning; every night we'd hear people shouting goodnight to each other and laughing. Sometimes we'd hear them arguing loudly out on the sidewalk. A motorcycle club used the same restaurant as its base, and every week or two the gang would roar up. I guess those things don't have mufflers. And then somebody's car alarm went off every few minutes. New Yorkers pay no attention to car alarms, so it would howl for fifteen minutes or so, until it ran out of juice.

People who visited us invariably asked how we could sleep through all that racket. *We barely hear it*, we would answer, and it was the truth. After the first night, it became white noise, the soundtrack of the night, and it faded out of our consciousness. One learns to live with noise. In a way, it ceases to exist.

When we come out of the city, the quiet is amazing. It is four in the morning in my house in the suburbs as I write this. On 12th Street, the bikers would just now be mustering for the ride out of town, gunning their engines over and over again. I would turn over in bed, mutter something to my sleeping husband and go back to sleep. But here the road in front of our home is still. An occasional car goes by, its tires making a hissing noise on the surface wet from last night's rain, and that's it.

I didn't mind the noise on 12th Street. I even liked it: being able to ignore it made me feel tough, like a New Yorker is supposed to be. But the quiet of the nights here satisfies my soul. I feel my own presence more. And minutes pass more gently.

AUGUST 19

"Do not go gentle into that good night." —DYLAN THOMAS

I visit a lady who is dying of cancer. She and everybody else know it, and she is not afraid to die. She is eager to get on with it, in fact, for she has been ill a long time. She is tired of her wasted body, tired of her increasing weakness, tired of her pain and her nausea. Yet she continues to get dressed when expecting visitors. She still curls her hair and puts on makeup. She was very annoyed at me once when I dropped in unannounced and caught her in her nightgown; she went on to brush aside my suggestion that she just stay that way. Yet she is up half the night, washing out her underwear after repeated and humiliating bouts of incontinence. Then she is exhausted and sick the next day. *Don't you think you need someone with you all the time now*, I ask her. *You really shouldn't be doing laundry.* But she wants to be alone. She doesn't want people in her house all the time. She hates for people to see her this way. Even nurses.

It's going to be hard for her to give up her strong need to control her own life. She's a fighter: it won't be easy to stop fighting. She's worked hard her whole life. She's working hard at dying now, only she doesn't know how. All she can do is cling desperately to the routines of living: looking pretty, sitting up to entertain, washing her own clothes. None of these things make much sense now. Yet she cannot stop doing them.

I'm able to see that she needs to give up now. But I know that I would be the same way if I were in her shoes. We don't know how to die. We only know how to live.

AUGUST 20

"Rachel, weeping for her children..." —MATTHEW 21:18

My daughter is coming into the city. We're going to meet for tea at a favorite place. Then she's going to take my credit card and shop for school clothes. Next week she's off to college.

What a life. She goes back and forth on the train and up and down on the subway like she owns the place. She's got a fine eye for style and a realistic sense of price and value. She hangs clothes on her perfect body as if they were works of art. On her, they are.

In some places, there are girls her age whose parents have sold them as prostitutes. Some girls her age live in refugee camps, filthy and hungry, easy prey for violent men in the night. Some girls her age look half that, their bellies swollen with hunger, their eyes sunken deep in their skulls, their legs impossibly thin little sticks. Some girls her age are dead. Anna strides along the sidewalk blessedly unaware of how carefree her life is. It will not always be so. But what a pleasure it is for me to see her like this, for I know just how otherwise things could be. Anna at seventeen has just the kind of life all seventeen-year-olds should have. If only all of them did.

Yeah, I've worked hard to give her that life. But there are lots of parents who work harder than I do, only to have their efforts mocked by something cruel and bigger than they are. I am lucky. Don't I know it.

AUGUST 21

"The magazine for the woman who wasn't born yesterday."

I'm glad there are some models with gray hair now and then. They remind us that it's okay to get older. That's a relief. Grown women have no reason on earth to feel inferior to fifteen-year-olds with collagen pouts.

But can we take it further? Could we see some models who are not only not young, but not glamorous either? I'm not sure I am really freed by looking at someone ten years my senior who looks better than I did ten years ago. I already know that bony women look fabulous in clothes. How about a few who resemble some of the rest of us? I know a lot of incredible women with big thighs. Is the only appropriate thing to say to them that if they work tremendously hard they can have a young, hard body again, even if they are old? Maybe there's something *else* they'd like to be doing with that kind of time investment besides spending it in the gym. Is young and hard the only beautiful kind of body there is? What's so terrible about soft and comfortable?

One of the joys of getting older is freedom. Freedom from some of the important demands others have made on us for so many years. Freedom not to conform if you don't want to—possible at any age, but much more thinkable later in life. I'd also like to be free not to care about how I look if I don't want to—even though I know the world's going to judge me by my appearance anyway. Let 'em. I don't want to be a woman who needs validation. I want to be a woman who validates herself.

AUGUST 22

"Healing is a matter of time..." —HIPPOCRATES

Have you tried acupuncture, my friend wants to know when she hears that I still have a lot of pain months after my accident. She is not the first person to ask me that. I have also had friends inquire about my vitamin consumption, whether or not I've seen a chiropractor, and whether I know about an obscure form of spiritual healing that involves massage with exotic oils. I answer a little apologetically, saying that I want to go as far as I can with my sports medicine doctor and his exercises before branching out. Besides, I feel I ought to try one thing at a time. If I start both acupuncture and vitamins in one month and feel better, how will I know which one worked?

When you hurt yourself, everybody has a treatment to recommend. It's hard to listen to them after a while: you commit to a course of treatment and you want it to work. You don't want to pull out and try something else a week or two later. But what if you're turning down the magic bullet in favor of a dud? There's no way to know.

I couldn't walk, says my friend, *and in an hour after having acupuncture I had no pain at all. Haven't had any since.* Wow. I think of my doctor and my exercises, of my slow progress, of his reassurances, and wonder if I'm barking up the wrong tree. I take her acupuncturist's number.

I never knew there were so many people with sore backs in the world. Or maybe backaches are basically a twentieth-century phenomenon: maybe we just notice our aches and pains more in this century, now that we have fewer of them overall.

AUGUST 23

"Ride on over all obstacles, and win the race!" —CHARLES DICKENS,
DAVID COPPERFIELD

Today I read an article about two sisters who are celebrating their birthdays. One is 100 years old; the other is 102. They have lived extraordinary lives. One was a teacher and the other a dentist; they were professional women of color in a society stacked against them, and they achieved in spite of it. I can only imagine the daily obstacles these two women overcame. One of them said that her hundred years didn't seem that long a time as she looked back on it.

Other old people I talk to say the same thing. I even feel it: Watergate was twenty years ago? Get outta here! So let's experience each day fully, and enjoy the moment fully. Life is too short to rob ourselves of the joys we can have by dwelling on the ones we can't.

There are people who go to work every day in wheelchairs. There are blind people who hold down fulltime jobs. There are quadriplegics who teach. So, I tell myself, I'm also going to accept whatever happens and enjoy whatever ability I have. And focus on my gifts, not on my problems. And, however many more years I have left, it's going to seem like a short time when it's over. No time to waste whining about the parts of my life that are difficult. I'm lucky just to be alive.

"The water of life..." —BERNARD DE VOTO

A thunderclap shakes the house, and the lights flicker. It is five-thirty on a summer afternoon, but it is dark outside. The rain is pouring straight down, and I can hear it gushing out of the downspout.

We have been wanting this rain for weeks. The heat has fallen on each morning in a wearisome blanket and stayed all day, every day, for what seems like forever. People can't keep up with their windowboxes: the plants droop, gasping, over the sides, and they seem parched again almost as soon as they are watered. The cats sit on flat places in the shade and do not move. Anna can't understand why we don't have air-conditioning, and even I am tired of hearing my bright comments about how comfortable a few fans can make a house.

But now the storm is awesome, great sheets of water hurled to earth, and I sit by my window watching it. I remember an open window upstairs, and climb slowly up to check on it. The rain is not coming in, but the cold air is, deliciously cold and fresh. Feeling it cool my face, I want more. I go back downstairs and outside into the yard. Immediately I am drenched, and I don't care. This is only water, my primordial friend. Our former home, if the theory of evolution is true. Certainly our home for the first nine months of our existence. I have felt drained of energy by the heat, motionless as the cats. Now I am myself again. I look like a fool standing out in the yard in the pouring rain, and I don't care.

AUGUST 25

"What is life? It is the flash of a firefly in the night." —CROWFOOT INDIAN PEOPLE

It is nearly dark, but we are still sitting outside in the garden. Rosie and Madeline are waiting for the first lightning bug to show, and pretty soon one does, turning on his lamp for a tantalizing moment and then turning it off again. The little girls scramble in the direction of the last flash and try to compute the bug's trajectory in order to plot his location. Then he turns on his lamp again—nope, he is still just out of reach.

We used to collect these insects in glass jars with holes punched in the lids. We'd give them a leaf or two to munch on. We told each other that scientists would pay us money for lightning bugs: five dollars for a thousand bugs. Who these scientists were, or where they were, or what they wanted with the bugs, we didn't know. And in the morning the night's catch was usually dead.

There were other things we did to bugs. Sometimes a kid would pull the light off one and stick it on his or her finger, saying that it was a ring. The light stays on, by the way, when it is disconnected from the insect's body. Another thing we did was tie a string to a June bug's leg and then let him go. He'd fly around and around in a wide circle, buzzing furiously.

We weren't mean kids. We would never have hurt a cat or a dog. But these cruelties to insects didn't seem to us to count, somehow. It was as if the bugs had no feelings. I can't imagine trying to escape from a string knotted around one leg felt good. It *was* mean. I don't tell Rosie and Madeline about how we used to put lightning bugs in jars. I make them let the bugs go. I don't tell them about the June bugs, either. Or about the rings.

AUGUST 26

"Happy birthday to you."

My mother would be seventy-seven today if she were still alive. I woke early and lay in bed for a few minutes before remembering the date. I feel sad, thinking about what she has missed. When she died at sixty-four, I didn't realize that sixty-four was middle age. It seemed old to me—I was twenty-nine, lightyears away. But now that I'm middle-aged myself, it seems much too young to die.

She didn't see her great-grandchildren. She didn't get to enjoy the fruits of retirement. My father took her on a lovely trip to Canada the summer before she died; cruelly, the whole happy memory of that last trip was erased from her mind in a stroke she suffered the following winter. *I don't remember a thing about it,* she said. *It sure sounds like we had a good time, though.*

She worked hard her whole life long. Raised three kids. Nursed his mother and then her mother through their final illnesses and deaths. Helped in his business and later worked full time until her heart began to give out. And that began to happen when she was in her early fifties. By the time retirement came around, she was too weak to do much in the way of enjoying it.

But she was a person who was able to get a lot of pleasure out of not very much. Extraordinarily willing to make do with what she had. Always had been. If she felt cheated, she didn't show it.

I think she was good at living in the moment. If something is good right now, it's good right now. Something else not being so good doesn't change that. Hold that thought: it's the key to a life that's as joyful as your life can be, whatever good or ill befalls.

AUGUST 27

"Honor your father and your mother." —EXODUS 20:12

My grandmother did not know how to drive a car. One morning at breakfast my grandfather said to the assembled family, "Today is the day Mother learns to drive the car." And after breakfast, they all trooped out and got in the car, the two little girls in back and my grandmother in the driver's seat. She started out pretty well until they reached a pond. For reasons which have never been clear to me in the forty years I've been hearing this story, she drove into the pond. Everyone piled out and waded ashore. Men came and helped my grandfather raise the car.

Some time later the same announcement was made at breakfast. They all went out and got in the car, same as before. She turned on the ignition, stepped on the gas, and drove through the back wall of the garage and out the other side. After that, my grandfather just drove her wherever she needed to go.

Funny—although my grandmother lived with us, I don't remember *her* ever telling it. Just my mom, when Grandma was not around. The mental pictures which made us howl with laughter—a black Model T up to its running board in the pond, a Model T–shaped hole in the back wall of the garage, like in the cartoons—would have embarrassed her to no end. She was a remarkably competent woman—cooked and baked and canned things, sewed beautifully. It was unusual for there to be something she couldn't do. Thinking about it now, and remembering how I hate not being able to do something I should be able to do, I'm a little sorry I laughed at the story of My Grandmother and the Car. I'm glad she didn't know we told it. I can think of a few stories I hope my kids don't tell their kids about me.

AUGUST 28

"I am not done with my changes." —STANLEY KUNITZ

Rosie has just this moment lost a tooth. It has waggled disgracefully back and forth for three or four days, and only just now did it give up the ghost.

Do you remember the anguish of that waiting, how you pushed the tooth around with your tongue and fantasized about tying it to a door and having somebody slam the door shut? I was always afraid to show a loose tooth to adults, fearing that they would reach in my mouth and pull it out. And that it would hurt.

Of course, it *doesn't* hurt when a loose tooth is pulled. Just as everybody tried to tell you, only you wouldn't believe them. So many rites of passage are accompanied by fears about physical pain, as if discomfort were a penalty for growth. When I was a girl I thought menstruating must be painful—the bleeding itself, I mean, not the cramps. As if it were an injury. My friends and I told one another the same thing about sex. *It hurts a whole lot*, we'd whisper with the assurance only complete ignorance bestows, *but you do it anyway because you want a baby*. And with the forest of myths about childbirth, and the chorus of women with horror stories about that cataclysmic moment, it's a wonder anybody ever goes through with it. But then after it is over the pain is put in its proper place.

We think our life is going to come to an end when we look ahead at a transition from one stage to another. And, in a way, it really does: one life ends and another begins. Toddler to child, child to young woman, daughter to mother and into old age. But change is not the enemy—at least, it doesn't have to be. Maybe change closes some doors, but it opens others.

AUGUST 29

"...a life of simplicity, independence, magnaminity, and trust."
—HENRY DAVID THOREAU

The Hutterites, who still live in colonies scattered through the midwest and Canada, speak German in their daily interactions and in their homes. They cling to a simple lifestyle, one which contains little in addition to the nineteenth-century accoutrements they went out there with. They live on communal farms in which everyone shares in the work and in the fruit of it. They don't have radios or televisions, so the children read a lot. If they want to hear music, they sing.

They do permit a certified teacher from the outside to teach the children in the subjects they refer to as "English," by which they mean anything outside the sect's beliefs and religious teachings: geography, math, science, music. They don't believe in competitive sports, so there's no football or baseball. Hutterites stop school at fifteen to go to work on the farm in occupations that are strictly divided as to gender, the boys in the fields and the girls in the kitchens and sewing rooms, where everyone's clothes are made and everyone's food prepared. They earn the money they need by selling the things they make and grow to the outside would. They marry one another.

A life like this is so different from the one I lead that it could be on another planet. I envy the pure interconnectedness of belief and practice. I couldn't live within its limits, though. I wouldn't want *not to know*, and in order for a community like this to remain as it is everyone must agree not to know some things. I can't have a life like that, even though I envy it. But I do like knowing that it exists.

AUGUST 30

"I cannot praise a fugitive and cloistered virtue..." —JOHN MILTON

At the top of the ornate tower which surmounts the Borough of Manhattan Municipal Building is a gilded statue. You can't make out its details very clearly from my building six blocks away, but I know that it is intended to depict "Civic Virtue": a serene goddess with flowing robes and outstretched hands conferring a benign nondenominational blessing on what has got to be one of the crankiest cities in the world.

"Civic Virtue" was actually commissioned for Brooklyn. When she was unveiled over there, though, the borough fathers angrily rejected her. Here is why: "Civic Virtue" is not wearing a shirt. She's not wearing anything, in fact, from the waist up.

But up on top of the municipal building nobody can tell *what* she's wearing. And nobody cares: this is New York, and it's her life. "Civic Virtue" has found a home where so many other people who chafed at the constraints of their places of origin have found one: Manhattan, home of Wall Street and the Street of Dreams; home of the tawdry allurements of Times Square and the acadian loveliness of Central Park. In its teeming anonymity many have tasted the first freedom of their lives. And, like "Civic Virtue," they have never left.

My aunt Harriet came here in the late 1940s. She told her mother in Minnesota that she was staving at a chaperoned residence for young ladies, but she was really renting a place in the Village with a friend. Her mother wouldn't have liked that, but once a young person arrives here, she feels a need for some real freedom. Lots of young women have the same experience "Civic Virtue" had on her high tower: *Oh, boy. Free at last.*

AUGUST 31

"Raised by a perfect mother..." —WALT WHITMAN

When my elder daughter was little, she liked to stop for a swing before going on to the rest of the day. We lived in a poor neighborhood; there were no swings nearby. But there was a park with swings on the way to the college I attended, and we would leave early in the morning so we would have time for a swing before work. I can see her still, her skinny little legs pointing straight up to the sky, her long hair flying out behind her. There was a pond with geese there, too, and sometimes we would bring bread for the geese to eat. These visits to the park lasted only ten or fifteen minutes. Then we would get back in the car and go to the babysitter's house.

Corinna never wanted to leave the park. She never wanted me to leave her at the babysitter's. *I love you so much I can't say it,* she would sometimes say to me. Three years old. *You are my favorite girl in the whole world,* I would say to her, and bury my face in her hair to smell her wonderful little-girl smell. I never wanted to leave her, either. But I knew that I was going to need an education if I was ever going to get her a swing set of her own. Or any of the other things she was going to want as she grew.

She is all grown up now, with little girls of her own. She has become everything I hoped she would be, and more, and it hasn't always been an easy road for her. Not that it is for anyone. Did we stop for a swing often enough? I hope so. All I can say for sure is that we did it as often as I could manage.

SEPTEMBER 1

"...that they may with some judgement contemplate upon moral good and evil."
—JOHN MILTON

It is almost time for school to begin. Even if you've been out of school for years, it is easy to remember what the first day was like: new pencils and clean sheets of paper. The smell of the hallways, with their fresh coat of wax. The smell of chalk. The sound of bells ringing.

These school sights and smells and sounds speak to us of fresh resolve and new beginnings, so much so that we call any chance to start over a "clean slate." Vacation time is over. Something new begins. Something new to learn. We are going to become more than we are now.

The first years of a person's life are spent accumulating and learning to use a tremendous amount of information. More all the time: there are things our children learn that the world didn't even *have* when we were their age, like computers. Somewhere along the line, though, a person has to acquire a set of principles by which it can all be sorted out. What kind of woman am I going to be? How will the world be better because I was in it for awhile?

When you're young the sky's the limit: you're going to be a famous actress, a star, a genius. But even if that doesn't happen, education has to have a moral dimension to be truly meaningful. It isn't just the accumulation of facts. We don't want only to be smarter. We want to be better people.

SEPTEMBER 2

"Nothing endures but change." —HERACLITUS

It is late in the day on which I have taken my youngest child to college and left her there. We didn't get much chance for a good-bye—the elevator was waiting. I was just as glad: less chance for us to mist up. We both cry so easily.

But now I'm home, listening to the radio. There is a snap of autumn in the air already. Fall is here early. For years that has meant absorbing the events of my children's first days of school. Now those days are being lived somewhere else, and it will be the roommates, not Mom, who gets the first reports. I have a *grandchild* who will start school in a few days. She'll tell her mother all about it, not me. I guess nobody needs to talk to me about what happened in school anymore. I guess nobody ever will again.

I've wanted to be undisturbed for years, but I've always known that it would be difficult when it finally happened. This is like that first day of your first child's kindergarten, when you walk out the door alone, leaving your child behind. What am I going to do with this sudden freedom? And like my own first day of school, which I remember only dimly: that same exciting feeling of separateness from my family. Exciting, but not entirely comfortable. Here my life is up to me. What am I going to do?

Put us somewhere new and we are new people. We are not fixed; we change. Experience molds us. That's both good news and bad news. I don't want to stay the same; I want to grow. But I will miss the way things were. The way I was. The way the kids were. The way we were.

SEPTEMBER 3

"Come, labor on! Who dares stand idle?" —JANE LAURIE BOTHWICK

The period of time just before a woman gives birth is called "labor." Earlier in the history of the English language it was called "travail." Both mean "work," of course. Most of us will agree that this is an appropriate choice of words. Giving birth is hard work. You're exhausted afterward. It's work for the baby, too, and after a few howls of greeting most of them are glad to be wrapped up in a blanket and allowed to sleep.

So the first moments of human society are marked by work. It's hard to become a person. It takes teamwork; the mother and baby both work hard. And the rest afterward is only a temporary one. The work of growth and learning begins. And throughout life, even into very old age, work never stops.

It's not good for people not to work. Not everyone has to earn money, but everyone who is able does need to work, to contribute something to the world that justifies the space they take up and the air they breathe. It isn't enough simply to *be*. We also have to *do*.

The first Monday of every September is Labor Day. When the labor movement was strong, it was a day for parades and speeches honoring the worker. Now it's primarily a day for storewide sales. That's a change: a holiday which used to be about work is now about shopping.

Don't let Labor Day be just about consumerism. Or about the closing of the swimming pool. Honor yourself and those you love for the work you do. It's part of what makes you a human being.

SEPTEMBER 4

"Skirts, plaid (3); Blouses, white (5); Sweater, brown (1)..."

Some schools require that all the students wear a uniform. Less competition. More equality between students in different economic circumstances. A sense of community and common discipline.

Jobs have uniforms, too. People who do the same work tend to dress alike. You get used to being judged by your appearance in the workplace. Women used to worry a great deal about the business uniform, about how they could dress to communicate their competence. We went through a phase of wearing suits that looked like those men wore except they had skirts instead of trousers. Just now it's snappy little outfits in very bright colors, so that people will know you're not only briskly competent but also deeply and happily feminine and wouldn't hurt a fly. It can be exhausting and expensive trying to keep up. Some of us have bailed out altogether.

Those old school uniforms were intended to case social differences; nobody would have an advantage over someone else who was poor because all would look alike. Adult uniforms are not about that; they signal that you know the game and are willing to play. They signal that to men as well as women.

I find the uniform a little irritating, and I don't wear it very well. I know people who look better when they're dressed to wash the car than I look when I'm dressed to go to work. I suppose I'm signaling an unwillingness to play the game. But I still envy colleagues who look comfortable in the uniform. I'll bet even their leisure clothes are chic. Mine look like hell. I can't wait to get home and change into them.

SEPTEMBER 5

"I'm sorry honey—we just can't afford it."

This is an expensive time of year for people who have children. It costs an arm and a leg to get them ready for school. Clothes, books, tuition, uniforms, sports equipment, musical instruments, haircuts, physical exams—add them up and pretty soon you're talking about real money.

This is a time so full of hope for their futures, a time full of your love for them as they begin another leg of the journey. You want them to have everything they need. And when your financial resources aren't up to the demand, a feeling of failure and of dread can settle on you like a dark cloud. *Maybe my child won't succeed because I can't give him this or that.*

That's probably not true. Some of the world's most successful and inspiring people emerged from childhoods of terrible deprivation, Of course you want to give them everything, but *nobody* gets everything. The best you can do will have to be good enough, and it probably is. Anyway, the most important thing you can give them is you. Your sense that this time in their lives is important. Your sense that they are incredible human beings. Your sense that they are competent and good. Your sense that being with them is fun. Your sense that the family needs the contributions they make to its common life. Kids work hard and well when they think it matters that they do. They are not so different from us in that regard.

SEPTEMBER 6

"One writes of scars healed, a loose parallel to the pathology of the skin, but there is no such thing in the life of an individual." —F. SCOTT FITZGERALD

Frances is going back to school. She is in her mid-forties. She has survived the unimaginable tragedy of losing two of her children. She is not sure how she lived through that. *I still just go from day to day,* she says, *and I guess I always will.*

So both she and her surviving daughter are college students. Frances is studying religion. She loves the classes, loves to talk to the professors. She interrupted her education to have children, and the years of being busy with them were good years, years that defined her in a way that was more than enough at the time. But now that her motherhood has been so badly wounded, she rejoins an earlier self: the young student, who knew nothing of what Frances was to learn so painfully.

I'm in awe of her ability to do this. She says she wants her life to matter, and that it's hard sometimes to feel that it does, after what has happened. *So I just take what I can get. I love school. I'm immersed in it, and it feels good. I like the certainty of study and intellectual discussion. I know it's removed from "real life" a bit, but I know how hard real life can be. I need to be removed from it sometimes.* She is happy among her books, going to her lectures. Her work makes her feel better. It's good that there is something that gives her some happiness. God knows she deserves it.

SEPTEMBER 7

"Stop! In the name of love!" —THE SUPREMES

Walking south on Seventh Avenue, I am standing at the comer of 24th Street waiting for the light to change. Standing next to me is an old man with a cane. He steps into the street, and his wife, who is on the other side of me screams "Stop!" in the harsh whiskey tenor some older women have. *The traffic's bad enough without your crossing against the lights,* she says as she crosses in front of me and grabs his arm angrily. He steps back up on the sidewalk and says nothing.

I walk on, now out of earshot. She made him feel foolish in front of all those people, I could tell. But she loves him, and he scared her. She thought he was going to be hit by a car. I know all about that: I am like that with the people I love. Anna is furious when I cry out in fear as she steps into the street. I can't help it, I say. I thought you were going to be killed. *Like I don't know how to cross the street,* she says. I made Rosie cry once by yelling at her when she was dancing on the coffee table and I thought she was going to fall off. I was scared, I explained to her when I saw her tears. I'm sorry. She sniffled and did not understand, withholding forgiveness for a while. I had made her feel foolish.

But I was standing on the sidewalk once and a car came right up over the curb and knocked me into the nearest building. People do have accidents. Stuff happens, as it says on those bumper stickers. We know this, and we try to protect those who could break our hearts very easily by suddenly not being around any more.

Get a grip, Mom, Anna tells me. I make my family angry with my fears about their safety. I will try to control myself. But it's not easy.

SEPTEMBER 8

"Nothing can be said to be certain except death and taxes."
—BENJAMIN FRANKLIN

I am listening to a radio program about breast cancer. I learn that having had my babies at a young age puts me into a low risk group. But then having female relatives who have had breast cancer may cancel that out. Except that my mother wasn't one of them, so maybe I'm all right after all.

Then would you advise women to have their babies early? the interviewer asked one of the doctors on the program. *Only if they want to structure their whole lives around avoiding breast cancer,* he said. He went on to talk about his daughters, who are pursuing single lives happily into their thirties so far. *Let's not retreat into fewer choices,* he said. *Let's develop the technology that will let us live with the increased choices we have. If you're at risk because you wait to have children, let's work on reducing that risk in some other way.*

He's right: you can't build your life around fear. Every magazine I pick up has a new scare story about a household appliance that might kill us.

We can't live in this society and encounter no risks to our health; there are too many of them. So we just have to do the best we can and keep walking. Get a mammogram now if you've never had one, and keep getting them every year or two after you're thirty-five. Examine your breasts after your period each month—don't be squeamish about it, and make your doctor show you how if you don't know. Detected early enough, many cancers can accurately be described as curable now, and one of these days cancer will be preventable.

Do what you can to be safe. But then you've just got to let it go and get on with your life. Because there's more to life than trying not to die.

SEPTEMBER 9

"Slow and steady wins the race." —AESOP

Y ou just do a little bit each day and it won't get ahead of you. Then, when your paper is due, you'll have it done and you won't have to stay up all night the evening before. That's what I tell my daughter about staying in control of her college work. *But Mom,* she says, *you don't do that.* Never mind that, I say.

She's right, though. I don't practice what I preach. She knows that I have never in my life been the kind of person who does a little bit each day and thus is easily done on time. I'm one of the ones who stays up all night the evening before. And she knows, too, that I've done all right for myself being that way. There's nothing wrong with the slow-and-steady model; it's just not the only way to get things done.

Still, that's not what I tell her. I find myself giving her advice I've spent a lifetime ignoring.

This is because I have a voice inside me telling me that my way is wrong. Never mind that I get good results and am happy. I should be disciplined, slow and steady, not given to the bursts of activity that have characterized my entire working life.

Yet we are what we are. And she is what she is. I did all right, and she can, too, so long as she works hard, one way or the other. Obviously you can't write a book in an evening; there has to be some reality in your bursts of energy. But if it's bursts of energy and deadlines that get you moving, for heaven's sake don't try to be another way. Find a way to use your energies the way they naturally flow. Trust them. Be the way you are and be it well, and you will do the things you need to do.

SEPTEMBER 10

"My thoughts are not your thoughts." —ISAIAH 55:8

I *missed the train,* Anna says glumly as she trudges into the house. *The professor freaks out if you're late,* she tells me. So she's going to skip her first class and go in later. I stifle the anxious things I want to say, like are you sure you can afford to miss class, and how many times have you missed this class this term, and why didn't you get up earlier. Anna is a young adult. It is no longer my job to schedule Anna. It is her job.

But the tendency to organize other people's lives takes a while to die in a mother. You don't do it for twenty-five years and then just stop cold.

Anna feels managed by me when I ask questions like that. But it feels necessary to me, and I can honestly say that *I* don't mind when people try to help *me* get to all the places I need to go during a typical, hectic day. I appreciate it. I forget things a lot, and I need all the help I can get.

But some people do mind. My family, for instance. They interpret my help as a smothering lack of confidence. That's not what I intend, but that's what happens. Since that is true, I have only one course of action open to me: cut it out. Stop saying the things that make them think I don't trust them to run their own lives. My intentions are good, but intentions are not the important thing here. Transmission is what matters when we talk to each other. So if I want them to understand me, I have to stop saying the things I say and say other things instead. You don't get different results from doing the same thing over and over again. You get different results from doing something different.

SEPTEMBER 11

*"Time heals all wounds."**

A young woman who has just started college comes to see me, distressed and puzzled by her strange new moods. *I think I may be crazy*, she says. *All I can think about is dying. I'm afraid that my mother or father will die. Or that I will die. I'm afraid to be alone because I can't stop thinking about it. I like my new roommates, but I can't stand not being around people who love me. I keep thinking I want to go home and live, and commute to school. But my parents would be disappointed in me if I did that.*

She's not crazy. Many young people are surprised by the violence of their homesickness when they leave home for the first time. That's why college students get into trouble with alcohol or drugs. You don't have to think about things when you're stoned. You don't have to feel. And they are afraid of the power of their feelings.

Why does she think about dying when her life is about to begin? Because that new beginning is scary. All new beginnings are. What does it mean to have a new role in the world, to be responsible for myself, to be an adult? She longs for a return to childhood, she tells me, to when she thought her parents could take care of everything. Her sudden responsibility for herself frightens her.

She shouldn't give up and go home to live. She should wait it out for a few months, go to a counselor, and see if it gets better. In all likelihood, those few months will be more than enough time to get used to life on her own and come to terms with it. She'll stop worrying about death and start enjoying college life.

Or maybe, at the end of a few months, she will still want to go home and live. Then she probably should. She shouldn't feel like a failure about this, and the people who love her should help make sure she doesn't. She can try again

---

*I have not changed this essay to reflect what happened on that other September 11. Perhaps the title will suffice.

in a year or two, and, in the meantime, go to school and live at home. Or maybe take some time out and work for a while. See what that's like.

We should make more room for unconventional behavior than we usually do. People don't have to go to college right after high school. They can wait a while. They don't have to finish in four years, either. They can explore other things and come back. Some people don't have to go to college at all. Everything has its season, and everyone's seasons are a little bit different. This is not bad news. It's good.

SEPTEMBER 12

"We hold these truths to be self-evident, that all men are created equal..."
—DECLARATION OF INDEPENDENCE

For a mere $720, plus shipping and handling, you can buy a replica of the lap desk on which Thomas Jefferson wrote the Declaration of Independence. It's a wooden box, with a table top that unfolds and fits on top so you can write on it. You can store your papers and inkwell and quill pen in the box, and carry the whole thing around by its brass handle.

This piece of portable furniture was the eighteenth century's version of the laptop computer, like the one I am using right now to type today's rumination. I've gotten pretty good at it, and I no longer erase whole documents without meaning to. I've joined the ranks of commuters who use their laptops on the train. I used to admire the productivity their machines made possible. They could start work at six in the morning with those little honeys: talk about dedicated. I hoped their employers appreciated the fact that they worked on the train like that.

That was before I realized that they were not working at all. They were playing solitaire on their computers. An addictive game that replicates the one you play with real cards, the Windows solitaire game is a popular one on the trains. So is one called "Minesweeper." And why not? We work hard. We schlep to the train every morning while it is still dark and we don't get home until late at night. We deserve a little fun.

I wonder what else Thomas Jefferson kept in his traveling desk.

SEPTEMBER 13

"I'm just a girl who can't say 'no.'" —RODGERS AND HAMMERSTEIN, *OKLAHOMA*

Today is a bad back day. Last night was a bad back night, too. I twitched around with the hot water bottle for hours, trying to find a comfortable position in which to sleep. It's my own fault, I said grimly to myself in the dark. Yesterday I talked the physical therapist into turning the speed on the treadmill up as high as I could stand it, just to see how high that was. It was pretty high. Then we lowered the speed a little, and I walked for about ten minutes at a respectable clip. *Does it hurt?* Judy kept asking. *Nah*, I said, *it feels good*. And it did, too, until a few hours later.

That's the problem. You don't always know you're hurting yourself until you already have, and by then it's too late to do anything about it. That's why I need Judy: God only knows what I'd attempt if left to my own devices. She won't let me talk her into anything again any time soon.

Actually, a lot in life is like that. Take the layering on of commitments, for instance. Women don't start *out* with a back-breaking load of things they've said they would do: they just keep saying yes to this or that small obligation, one at a time, and eventually they all pile up. Pretty soon you have no life that you can call your own, and finally you get fed up and pitch some of the things you really can't afford to do.

What is really close to your heart? Which, among the things you've said you would do, are so much *you* that you can't imagine not doing them? Keep those things. Jettison the rest if you have to, until you're safely below your pain threshold. Then stay there. Tell people "no." You might hurt yourself.

SEPTEMBER 14

"Do you not know, my son, with what little understanding the world is ruled?"
—POPE JULIUS III

Like most American children of my era, I went to school every day under the stern inspection of George Washington and Abraham Lincoln. The same two portraits hung in every classroom. Washington's face spoke austerely of excellence, strength, and virtue. *Be good, little girl, better than you are now*. Lincoln's weary eyes looked down on me with somewhat more understanding. He looked to me as if he already knew he was going to be assassinated when he sat for that portrait. The cruelty of schoolchildren came as no great surprise to this sad-eyed man.

These political leaders of the past were like gods to us, full of mythic virtue and superhuman strength. Washington threw a silver dollar across the Rappahannock. Lincoln walked ten miles—or was it twenty?—to return a penny he had overcharged a customer. But now the leaders are my age, people who grew up in the same world I grew up in. They are *not* larger than life; sometimes they seem disconcertingly smaller. How dumb does he think we *are*, I wonder as I listen to one of them say something transparently selfserving on the radio.

Ours is not an august age. But theirs was probably less so than we imagine it to have been. Political satire was a popular sport in the eighteenth and nineteenth centuries. Still, there is such a thing as excellence. The human family remembers it when it happens. We didn't have a picture of Millard Fillmore on the wall where I was a girl in school.

SEPTEMBER 15

"Appearances are often deceiving." —AESOP

I am leafing through a magazine in the doctor's waiting room. I stop at an article about Ted Bundy, the convicted serial killer. There's a picture of him standing at the kitchen sink with a beautiful blonde woman. She's washing, he's drying, They were friends. She says he was wonderful company, charming and fun. She would not have taken him for a sadistic killer, not in a million years. He was a great guy.

So I guess you never know. Such a gulf between appearance and reality as existed in Ted Bundy is rare, though. Most of us are what we seem to be. Still, I am often surprised by people's other lives. An old man who has always seemed a little foolish to me turns out to have been a war hero, a man of uncommon valor who repeatedly risked his life for his fellows. A quiet old woman who looks like everyone's stereotype of a grandmother turns out to have been a singer in the Harlem renaissance. A man I've known for years turns out to have been a ballet dancer when he was young. I never knew that.

There's more to all of us than the face we choose to present to the world. We don't ordinarily feature the less-than-lovely parts of ourselves on the front page: we let people find out about these a little later on. But we also hide some beautiful things under our everyday exteriors. Why? Maybe sometimes the contrast between the pedestrian present and a more exciting past is a painful one. But hey—not everybody's famous. We're all getting older. So who cares? We should at least seem as interesting as we really are.

SEPTEMBER 16

"I yam what I yam and that's all that I yam." —POPEYE THE SAILOR MAN

In the Caribbean, the lizard occupies the same place as the squirrel does in North America; it too dominates the Ubiquitous Small Animal category. Lizards are everywhere, inside the house and outside, sitting motionless on rocks for hours on end and then suddenly darting off somewhere else. Sometimes one will show off to another, puffing up his throat to reveal a pocket of brilliant color hidden in the folds of skin at his neck, or doing a series of solemn push-ups while staring expressionlessly into the middle distance. I believe this is the behavior of a lizard in love, just like the mad dash of the squirrels in cooler climates is a kind of foreplay.

These little lizards are not scary at all. And they are *not* slimy. That is a nasty rumor, and it's not true. Their feet walking casually along my arm or over my knee are as soft and dry as a whisper. I'm not sure they know that something as big as I am is alive. If they did, they probably wouldn't use my extremities as roads and bridges so casually. A Jamaican lady I know says that a lizard walking over your hand means you're pregnant. My own life has not borne this out, but that doesn't mean it's totally without foundation.

My point is that lizards conform to their sinister stereotype just about as well as most other groups conform to theirs, which is to say not at all. We are what we are, and deserve the chance to show others what that is without people making up their minds about us in advance.

SEPTEMBER 17

"It's beginning to look a lot like Christmas."

One year my friend was determined not to be caught at the last minute in her holiday preparations. She began in September. *With so much time to get ready*, she thought, *I can do something really nice for the neighbors.* And she did: made loaves of cranberry bread, wrapped them up in foil, and put them in the freezer. All she had to do on Christmas Eve was take them out, put a red bow on each one and send the children around the neighborhood with them. Everything went according to plan. All the neighbors were delighted with their homemade Christmas treats. All except for the one puzzled family that received a foil-wrapped brick of left-over *rice*, tied up with a lovely red bow.

Another friend decided she'd use the time she spent taking her kids to the pool in July to get a leg up on the family Christmas cards, Every day she'd set up her lounge chair, smooth on her suntan lotion, and take out her box of cards, She wrote personal notes on each one. By the first of August, she was finished. Everything was stamped and ready to go.

But when the second week of December rolled around, the notes she remembered having written in July were a little out of date, and something less than spontaneous. A family decision to move to another state, which had been made in October, was not reflected in any of them. Now she was going to have to send out "We've moved" cards.

We all know it's not good to be late. But there is such a thing as being too early.

SEPTEMBER 18

"I've gotta be me..." —FRANK SINATRA

A middle-aged woman visits me for a talk. She has been extraordinarily successful in her career. But she recently changed jobs to become the head of a brand-new initiative in a non-profit corporation, and she's having a hard time now. The man who hired her to do this job left the organization shortly after her arrival. She feels the loss of his advocacy keenly. The board can't quite make up its mind whether or not it *wants* the new initiative, and she often feels that she is selling something that doesn't have a market.

She feels like a failure. She is accustomed to producing good results that people applaud, and the ambivalence that greets her hard work these days is discouraging.

I don't know why I'm there, she says, if I'm trying to do a job nobody really wants done. I'm not a failure, and I'm not going to keep on feeling like one. We're either going to come to terms with whatever it is this thing should look like and just do it, or we're going to decide we don't want to do it and I'll leave. No hard feelings—but I'm not going to let this go on!

It sounds to me she's on the right track. People need clear definition in their professional lives: I am a teacher, so I teach. A carpenter builds things. A singer sings. The woman who came to see me knows who she is. She needs to do the things which flow from that. Maybe those things are not the things her agency needs, but that's a problem of fit. Bad fit is not the same as failure. Maybe she'll have to change jobs; true, nobody wants to do that. But she needs the certainty that she is productive as much as she needs her paycheck, and she'll do what she must to have it.

SEPTEMBER 19

"Never underestimate the power of a woman." —LADIES' HOME JOURNAL

My daughter is buying a condominium. The paperwork that she must assemble is inches thick. Everything has to be substantiated, somewhat beyond the limits of reason, it seems to me. Not only is the money *in* the bank, but how did it get there? What portion came from the savings bonds she accumulated so slowly and painfully? How much was a gift from me? They need canceled checks and sworn affidavits. Good grief.

Her credit record for the last several years has been exemplary for a single mother of two on a very modest salary. But why was there a late payment in 1989 on a charge account which has now been paid up for two years, the bank wants to know. How dare they even ask, I think with maternal indignation. I have watched my daughter scraping by, shopping for children's clothes at thrift stores and garage sales, buying day-old bread at bakery outlets—at an age when many young women spend their money on CDs and Caribbean cruises. These bank people don't know what a struggle it's been. She's done damned well, thank you. Give her the loan.

This piece of the American dream that she hopes to buy is an apartment about the size of the one she now rents. By any American standards, it could only be described as modest. But she is thrilled at the idea that she might own it. She's been saving for years. *I never thought I'd own my own home*, she says. I never thought she would, either, at least not this soon. Not with all she's got on her shoulders. Guess I underestimated her.

SEPTEMBER 20

"See you after work. Have a good one!"

A woman has just gotten on the train with her little boy. It's crowded this morning, so they join a couple of men in graysuits in a three-seater bench. The little boy is sitting on his mother's lap, looking out the window and commenting on what he sees.

You just don't see many kids on the 7:24 commuter train. People seem surprised but not displeased. The boy's treble voice adds a pleasing note to the rumble of the men's voices, the mellow altos of the women, and the chugging of the train.

I suppose she's dropping him off at daycare on her way to work. What a long day for a little boy. But his long day is bracketed at either end by a train ride on which he has his mother all to himself. That's not such a bad deal.

In centuries past, children saw a great deal of what their parents did to earn the family's living. Even little ones helped out as soon as they could, so the whole family was involved in the work which sustained it. Let's not romanticize that: life was hard back then, and the work especially so. But at least everyone in the family understood what everyone else was doing. Things are different now. Grown-ups go somewhere else to work, and home is the place where the family spends its leisure time. Small children do not see their parents' lives outside the home as very real, because they never see them happening.

But this little guy does. He and his mom commute, he to his place and she to hers. So he shares a little of her world, the world of work he will one day enter.

"Old age is the most unexpected of all the things that happen." —LEON TROTSKY

My mother-in-law needs some new shoes. The nurse says to get 8½ medium. I don't think her feet are that big. They also tell us to buy clothing two or three sizes larger than the ones she used to wear when she was well. I guess they want things to be loose.

My mother-in-law used to be very proud of her good looks and style. When we closed up her apartment and put her in a nursing home, we found more than a dozen copies of a picture of her, well into her seventies, wearing her 1924 wedding gown in a fashion show. We laughed at her vanity—all those copies! But it was remarkable that she could wear that dress with such flair after more than fifty years. So I don't think she would like the Velcro sneakers we've been asked to buy very much. Or the baggy dresses. Or the pull-on knit trousers.

They take good care of her at the nursing home. She is always clean, and her hair always looks neat. Dinner is beautifully served in an elegant dining room. The food is good. The more able residents have a quiet and pleasant social life. There is nothing she needs and does not have, nothing for us to do for her but try to tempt her to eat some shrimp cocktail or taste her vegetables. But often now she does not know her son. She will look at him despairingly and tell him she wants her mother. Her mother has been dead for forty years.

It is terrible not to be able to do anything that will make her life happy again. I buy the shoes and the clothes, and he takes them to her. He sits beside her and rubs her back. A back rub used to work wonders but now she doesn't even seem to enjoy it. Often she doesn't even appear to notice what he is doing.

Here is a need we can't fill: she needs to lay down a life that is no longer a happy one, to leave this world with her body as she has already left it with her mind. And we can't help her do that: it has to happen on its own. So she is kept comfortable. But comfortable is not the same thing as happy.

SEPTEMBER 22

"In front of excellence the immortal gods have put sweat...." —HESIOD

James Galway is playing his flute on the radio while I am sitting here eating breakfast. His virtuosity is breathtaking. Such control. Such speed. Such phrasing. And yet such lightheartedness. Despite Galway's awesome technical skill, his flute-playing sounds like fun.

He practices for hours every day, I'm sure, and has for years. I've never met him, but James Galway has got to be extraordinarily single-minded about playing the flute. Almost all performers are; you may find a few who just wander onstage and do it, but most of them work heroically to become and remain excellent.

I am often aware that I am not single-minded like that. I've always had a hundred different things going at once, each one clamoring for my time and energy. I turn from one thing to another and do each as well as time and strength permit. Sometimes it's pretty damn good. Sometimes it's not so hot. *You should do fewer things*, someone with a calmer life tells me, and I suppose I should. But I've been like this for decades, so I am unlikely to change. Besides, if I am honest, I must admit that I don't want to change very much. I like doing many things. The demands of such a life may drive me crazy at times, but not crazy enough to stop. It appears that this is just the way I am. And, for the most part, I like it.

Still, I am glad there are people like Galway who pursue their art with the single-minded intensity I lack. Me and a lot of other people.

SEPTEMBER 23

"It's your life."

A woman whose husband and two sons were all racing car drivers mourns the loss of her second son; he was killed in a helicopter crash on his way to a race. The other son was killed last year in a wreck of one of his race cars. Her husband is alive, but he has been seriously injured in a crash, and continues to feel the effects of it.

Automobile racing is dangerous. Everyone who does it knows that. It puts a special strain on the mothers and wives of drivers. Everyone wants the people they love to do that which is closest to their hearts. But to send them out every day into such a dangerous occupation, especially after having sustained one devastating loss—the self-control that mother has had to develop is beyond my imagination. I think I'd lock them in their rooms.

I say that. But I probably wouldn't really do it. People have the right to do the things that challenge them to the utmost. If it is the conquest of speed, then that's what it is. Don't get me wrong: I think auto racing is foolish. I would never recommend it as a career for anybody who wanted to live to be old. But I'm not involved in it. It's not my right to tell other grown-up people what to do. Even the people I love. I can tell them what I think is wrong with a course of action they contemplate. I can tell them how it scares me just thinking about it. But I can't tell them what to do. People have to make up their own minds.

A woman disapproves of her daughter's boyfriend. Vehemently. I listen to her explain why, and I've got to say she has a point: he sounds like trouble. But the younger woman is in love, utterly devoted to her swain, blind to his faults in a way that drives her mother nuts and scares her to death. *I'm not going to have anything to do with her as long as she's with him*, she threatens grimly. I tell her I think this is a mistake. I tell her that it will probably cause her daughter to dig her heels in, and delay even further the time when she comes to see the problem in her relationship with her boyfriend for herself. As hard as it is to see someone you love walking down a path toward certain heartache, you don't have the right to forbid them that walk. And it won't do any good if you try. They have to find out for themselves. And all you can do is love them and pray for them and be there. They have a destiny and so do you, and ultimately, they are not the same destiny. You are separate people. That's a hard one, but it's the truth.

SEPTEMBER 24

"People who live in glass houses shouldn't throw stones."

A young friend of mine is an actress. She works at several different part-time jobs: one is in an agency that writes advertising jingles. Another is as a waitress. The third job makes her more money in an evening than she makes all week at the other two: she's a Slammer Girl.

Here is what a Slammer Girl does: she wears a skimpy outfit with a gun holster around her hips. In the holster, she carries two squirt bottles, one of tequila and one of lime juice. Across her chest, bandolier-style, she wears an ammo belt, with shot glasses in the little pockets where the bullets would be. She sets a shot glass on the customer's table and shoots tequila and lime juice into it. Then she pours the fiery mixture down the customer's throat, grabs his head and shakes it back and forth a few times, uttering a high-pitched "Yi-yi-yi-yi-yi!" as she does so. Mary usually gets two hundred dollars in an evening. Sometimes she gets more.

The men who come into the restaurant say disgusting things to her. *I don't even listen to them*, she says; *it doesn't bother me in the least*. One night, though, a young woman came in. She looked Mary up and down unsteadily, and sneered, *I'm glad I don't have your job*. Mary was hurt. She was surprised at how much that woman's contempt stung her. *I thought women were supposed to stick together better than that*, she says. *I know it's a degrading job. But I'm a human being. Besides*, she goes on, *that woman was really drunk. That's degrading too, you know. And I didn't sneer at her.*

"He who possesses, let him learn to lose." —SCHILLER

It's been six months since I was here last. I see that Michael, the owner of the restaurant, has gotten very thin. His companion died of AIDS several years ago. There is a special look, a special way the skin of the face begins to stretch over the cheekbone, a special way the eyes sink deeper into their sockets, that I have come to associate with this disease. Michael has The Look.

He's done well for himself. Everyone in the Village comes to his place for coffee and pastry. He has a home in the country and just got a new BMW— *I'm embarrassed about owning it every time I take it out,* he says, *but I don't know: I just wanted it.* I ask him how life's been. *Oh, it's been hard without Robert. We were together for twenty-three years. But I'm okay.*

Michael loves his restaurant. All his friends come in to gossip. It's like the general store in a small town. Today he's running around behind the counter as usual, smiling and talking to everyone. Nobody mentions his thinness; so many people in this neighborhood are HIV-positive. Some are already ill. Many of his customers have The Look, too. Most of them are doing just what Michael is doing: living and being as happy as they can for as long as they can. They keep on. Their lives keep them alive.

Tomorrow is promised to none of us. Michael can be fairly certain that his life will be curtailed, but I have no assurance that mine will be a long one. Since nobody knows how long she has, we'd better all focus on milking *today* for all it's worth. Taste every drop. Enjoy it deeply. There will never be another today.

SEPTEMBER 26

"The white-robed army of martyrs...." —TE DEUM LADAMUS

Most of us know something about martyrdom. Some of us cultivate it. There is something very satisfying in the grim knowledge that others are not really pulling their weight and you're the only one who really works around here. *Look at them, laughing at their desks when they should be working. Or at him, reading the paper while I'm doing the laundry. Oh, do continue, by all means. Don't stop on my account. Go ahead and have a ball. I'll just keep on working, like I always do.*

Had enough? We all know habitual martyrs, and more than a few of us have *been* one from time to time. It's hard to say why it feels so good to feel so bad, but it can. Still, nobody would call it attractive. What martyrdom is, of course, is an indirect way of asking for help. The hope is that the slothful ones will see the error of their ways. They'll apologize, and ask you what they can do to help.

But I've noticed something: even when someone *does* apologize and offer to help, the offer is frequently refused. Sometimes the martyr is reluctant to give up her high moral ground, She'd rather be angry about being abused than have it stop. Her sense of being ill-used, of being the only hardworking person in a sea of shirkers, has become an important part of her. Too important to give up without a fight.

That's not pretty. And it's a good way to become permanently unhappy and bitter. If you need help, then *ask*, for heaven's sake.

SEPTEMBER 27

"Anything I can do to help?"

Tony worked on ships, in the engine room and on deck, for many years. He is retired now, and comes to the seafarers' club just about every day to sit around with the other old guys and have coffee. He always offers to help: cleans off tables, scrubs the pots, mops the floor. He'll do anything. I have never seen him get angry, or even mildly peevish. What a gift that kind of person is.

He learned to be that way from his years on ship board. Sometimes there are terrible problems on ships, instances of real cruelty. But much more often, a ship is a remarkable laboratory for successful teamwork. The members of the crew are usually strangers to one another. Often they are from different cultures and speak different languages. The educational and social levels of officers and crew can be miles apart. Yet they can take an immense vessel containing a fortune in high-tech navigating equipment and an expensive cargo across the ocean together. And they can get it there on time, with the cargo intact. They accomplish this much more often than they do not. They are able to do this because they know they have to work together in a very interdependent way. It is not enough for a guy to do his job; he has to be sure the next guy can do his, too. Otherwise, everybody could lose big. So they take care of one another. We are not nearly as careful of one another as they are.

But the facts of life are really the same for us: we are none of us sufficient unto ourselves. We do not work or live alone. We need each other.

SEPTEMBER 28

"I grow old ever learning many things." —SOLON

All of the students in my class are working through their lunch breaks. None of us has enough time to get all the reading done. We commiserate briefly with one another and then bend over our books.

We are in a doctoral program that crams all the classes into one day a week. Everybody in it works full-time, and everyone in it is working too hard. Halfway through the academic year, we wonder if we're going to make it through June. At least once a week I wonder if I haven't made a mistake in trying to do this at this stage in my life. A couple of people in our tiny class have already fallen by the wayside.

But the classes are good. The discussion never fails to be stimulating. And we are good, too, my colleagues and I. We bring a rich variety of adult experience to our work. We are all more seasoned than we were the last time we were in school. We are also better managers of time than we were when we were young, as people with careers and families must learn to be. It costs us some of our precious time—a lot of it, in fact—to be here. So we are not about to trash it.

But I'll tell you one thing that is different from when I was a young student: I can't stay up all night and study anymore. Not that I did it a lot back then, but I could if I had to. No more. The words begin to swim around on the page at about nine-thirty. By ten o'clock, I'm gone. I wish it were different, but it just isn't. Willpower just does not do it. Ah, well, such is life and such the passing of time. We must accept ourselves as we are.

SEPTEMBER 29

"This is the very education of our imaginative life..." —HENRY JAMES

My friends, who are teachers, are putting two children through college. Their kids were brilliant all through high school and got some scholarships, but the Ivy League schools they got into cost just a little bit less per year than their mother's annual salary. Each, that is. So their dad took another job—at a liquor store at night—in addition to his weekend work as a choir master. Both of the young women work. And their mom takes more music students and plays the organ at more weddings. As many as she can get.

The kids say they don't understand why we decided to be poor, she said to me. *I almost strangled them right there. We didn't decide to be poor. We just decided to be teachers. It's society that decided that we would be poor. I guess our kids think we should have gone into the bond business or something.*

The girls benefited from their parents' dedication to teaching, and they know it. They wouldn't be the talented young women they are today if their parents hadn't helped them to love learning. But they also know that their house is smaller than those of many of their friends. They know that some of their friends' parents don't have to work as hard as theirs do to pay for college, and that some of their friends don't have to work at all.

But all through the college years they have rejoiced in being able to pull it off, hard as it is. As well they might.

"...those receive me, who quietly treat me as one familiar and well-beloved in that home." —JAMES AGEE

I turn my key in the lock and begin to push the front door open. I meet with some resistance; something has been placed in front of the door. *Wait a minute,* I hear, and my husband comes running to move a picture which is blocking it. I notice that the wroughtiron coat rack has been moved aside.

This means he is having a slide show. He uses that wall as a projection screen. Richard gives lectures about garden design in the eighteenth century, and illustrates them with engravings and paintings from the period. He's a two-projector man when he gets going, scrolling through two sets of pictures at the same time, so his scholarly audiences can compare two different styles of little temples in two different English gardens.

I edge past the coat rack, casting a brief shadow on Lord and Lady Cobham, who are enjoying their new garden in a 1739 engraving that fills the bright rectangle on the wall. Richard has a blank wall in his office: I'm not really sure just why the slide show needs to be in the front hall instead of up there, but I just got home and decide not to ask. I guess he just likes to be where people come and go.

The slide show set-up reminds me of when my kids were little. Sometimes I'd come home and find that they had made a tent in the living room: covered chairs and couches with sheets to make an elaborate labyrinth. They had other places they could have done that, too, but they liked to play tent in the living room where we all were. So we never made *House Beautiful.*

OCTOBER 1

"Christmas won't be Christmas without any presents." —LOUISA MAY ALCOTT

Today I received the first mail-order Christmas catalogue of the season. Surely this is a record: October 1st? Get real.

We used to live near a high-powered fashion photography studio. Famous people came and went every day, and all through the night the street would be illuminated by sudden flashes of bright white light. One time a gorgeous young model took off all her clothes up on the roof of the studio. It was an amazing thing. Just ask my husband.

Often clothing was photographed long in advance of the season in which it was intended to be worn. Bony models in shorts and summer dresses shivered in the January cold out on the cobblestones in front of our building, or sweated in fur coats on the roof under a hot July sun. The modeling business is not always an easy one.

It was jarring to see them—not just the one without any clothes on, but all of the people so hard at work creating an imaginary world to sell us. Mink coats in July. Bikinis in January. Most of us are not ready for the seasons until they are here, or at least until they are very near. I don't want to buy Christmas presents in October. I'm not ready yet. I don't get ready until after Thanksgiving and I don't intend to start now.

Sometimes I receive several editions of the same catalogue, each with a slightly different cover. The first one has just a tiny bit of evergreen in some of the pictures—nothing really Christmasy. Just a hint. Or a reminder. Successive catalogs lay it on thicker and thicker, and they spawn relatives, so that our mailbox is crammed with the things every day for weeks and weeks. We have compulsory recycling in our state—I've got to carry all that stuff to the center, you know. Three or four dozen catalogues are heavy. There's got to be a better way. Maybe I should send out a form letter:

Dear Store:

I'm not buying anything until after Thanksgiving, period. Don't send me a catalogue until then, or I won't buy anything from you, ever.

Your friend,

Barbara Crafton

OCTOBER 2

"Light griefs are loquacious, but the great are dumb." —SENECA

Some people complain about everything: the coffee, the workload, their colleagues, the subways, the line at the bank. The people who are with them every day get used to their nonstop litany of personal affronts, and understand that no action is required or even desired to stem it: the people are just complainers.

But it's the real tragedies in people's lives that are hard to talk about. Hard to ask about, too. People who have them don't want to trivialize them by adding them to the complainers' laundry lists proclaimed every day. So they tuck them away into a private place and don't speak of them. *How're you doing,* other people ask. And they answer that they are fine.

Often other people don't even know about their troubles. I have known people who went through long and painful divorces, long struggles with an adolescent's drug problem, long sieges of a parent's terminal illness without ever speaking of it to the people at work or to the neighbors. It's too painful. They fear being misunderstood or lectured. They feel an odd embarrassment, as if the tragedy were somehow their fault. So they are silent.

These burdens are awfully heavy to bear alone. It helps to talk. Maybe you should think twice about confiding in the office complainer, but there's probably someone else who will be a sympathetic listener. There are also support groups for just about every problem in the world: divorce, bereavement, AIDS, you name it. Find a way to talk about the thing that's tying you in knots inside. It doesn't make the problem go away, but it's good to know you're not alone.

OCTOBER 3

"This is the way we iron our clothes, so early Tuesday morning."
—OLD NURSERY RHYME

I love to iron. I love the way things look after they've been ironed, the way the steam smells when it's rising up from the clothes, the soft hissing sound the iron makes when you lift it. My first paying job was ironing: handkerchiefs and pillowcases and other flat things. I did them for my grandmother at a penny each. She really did arrange the housework like the song said: washing on Mondays, ironing on Tuesdays and so forth. I used to sing the song with her when I was little, with appropriate choreography for the different days: scrubbing the imaginary clothes up and down on an imaginary washboard, sweeping the imaginary iron back and forth.

I don't have time to do all the ironing on Tuesdays, like she did. I usually have to do a shirt at a time, as needed, with an occasional orgy of tablecloths and napkins. *You're nuts*, says a friend. *I wouldn't touch an iron with a ten-foot pole. My kid didn't know what one was until her kindergarten teacher showed the class a picture.*

Well, we all have our little quirks. She shouldn't iron if she hates it, and with the fabrics we have today she doesn't have to. But smoothing out the wrinkles in a garment appeals to the peacemaker in me. I like taking something wrinkled and confused and making it look fabulous and new. And putting clothes into the washer dirty and pulling them out clean: so many things in my life are not nearly so fixable.

OCTOBER 4

"Things that ne'er were, nor are, nor e'er will be." —SIR JOHN SUCKLING

I guess I won't be having any more babies.

This might seem so obvious to the casual observer as not to be worth even talking about. Here I am in my mid-forties, with my husband in his mid-*sixties*, for heaven's sake. My children grown. A step-daughter only a few years younger than I am. I'm twice a grandmother and busy with thirty different professional things every day, all day.

And yet, when a doctor tells me my back injury would cause complications if there were to be a pregnancy, I feel sad. My husband and I would have been good with a baby. I imagine him—he seems to be a boy this time—eating dinner with us in the evening. He could have lain in between us in bed at

179

night. He could have looked a little like each of us. I imagine taking him to school, taking him to the beach, taking him to buy shoes. It would have been so nice.

I am exhausted after a visit from my grandchildren. I tell someone at least twice a week how glad I am to have had my children when I was young. Our house is full of delicate things. My work requires late nights. My husband would turn eighty the year the boy turned fifteen—and that's if he were born today, which he won't be. At the time he'd be trying to find his place in the world, he might also be dealing with a frail parent. Or two of them. Not fair.

And yet. And yet.

OCTOBER 5

"With the consciousness of having done a good day's work..."
—BENJAMIN FRANKLIN

I am working at home today. I'm arranging my life so this can happen more and more, and I'm getting there. Good things about it include: being able to do a load of laundry while working. Not jumping on a train at dawn. Dressing down. Way down.

But there are pitfalls. One is the family: decades of mom's availability when she's at home have taught them that if they can see me, I'm theirs for the afternoon. And those decades have taught me the same thing: if I can see *them*, there must be something I'm supposed to be doing for them. It's hard not to be available for domestic interruptions, which can claim the better part of a day before I realize what's happened to it.

More and more men and women are opting for work at home, saving commuting time and dollars, having more time with their families, reducing their stress levels. Maybe you can be one of them. But maybe you can't, in which case it's good to remember about the grass being greener, especially if your idea is that you'll try to work at home and still be part of a corporation of some size and complexity. You're inevitably a little out of the loop if you work at home. So many work decisions are made informally. If you're not around, that just won't happen for you. Only you can decide how much that matters,

Still, those who have made this switch seem to be pretty unanimous about their satisfaction with it. It's not for everyone. But it could be for you.

"With too much weakness for the Stoic's pride, he hangs between; in doubt to act or rest." —ALEXANDER POPE

I can either plug this computer into the wall or let it work from its battery. The manufacturer claims that it will go 2½ hours on one charge; my experience is that the reality is considerably south of that—an hour, maybe. When the battery begins to get low, the machine beeps softly to signal its impending loss of power. This is my signal to begin the closing procedure.

The machine has a protocol for stopping. First I tell it to "save" all I've done since the last time we were together. I can even tell it to "save workplace" if I want to: it's the equivalent of leaving all my papers out on the desk so that I can come right back to them next time without rummaging around for them. Then I tell it to "close." It asks me politely if I am sure. I say yes. Then I "exit."

The machine is smarter than I am, and not just because it can count 10,000 words in four seconds. It knows when it is tired, and it knows that it cannot go on without sufficient energy. I, by contrast, never admit that I'm too tired to attempt something; I just keep going, dragging myself through one task after another as my strength and productivity ebb. And the machine knows that it needs to keep track of its things, to close covers and put things away so that the place remains neat for next time. I myself leave papers lying around.

Together we are a good team: me with my great ideas and my logical friend with the means to carry them out. Having no ego, he is honest about his limitations. Having a great deal, I am less so. I could stand to be a little more like him, I guess.

Perhaps we will begin to resemble each other as we grow older.

OCTOBER 7

"It gives a lovely light." —EDNA ST. VINCENT MILLAY

The ugliest of buildings looks beautiful at night. Even the New Jersey Turnpike around Elizabeth, a tangle of oil refineries and chemical tanks by day, is a fairy-tale kingdom in the dark. It still smells like hell—literally: there's lots of sulfur—but it looks spectacular.

I'm also better-looking at night. So is my husband. By candlelight both of us look romantic: the lines in our faces which make us look exhausted and old by day make us seem interesting in candlelight. The kitchen, in which we eat these candlelit suppers, looks a lot better, too: it's as messy as ever, but we don't notice it as much when we sit down in that kindly glow.

I often wish I lived in simpler times. The people of other ages lived by the light of candles because that was all they had. What seems deeply calming to me was probably irritating to them: having to wait until daylight to accomplish things that required lots of light. But then, it wouldn't hurt *us* to have to wait for something once in a while. Our ability to extend the light of day into the night is one of the things that have made us the most efficient people who have ever lived. We ski at night, shop at night, work night shifts.

All of this efficiency does not seem to have made us appreciably happier, though. We live longer and do more than previous generations could have hoped to, but we are not more contented. Probably we are less so. I think of our ancestors sitting by the light of their candles and their oil lamps, talking to each other—even *singing* to each other because they didn't have televisions and radios. It looks good to me.

OCTOBER 8

"Fat, fair and forty..." —JOHN O' KEEFFE

My friend plops herself down in the seat next to mine and announces that all she will have to eat today will be cabbage soup, a honeydew melon, and a salad. Tomorrow she will add a vegetable, which she will choose from a list of approved vegetables. She will add one thing to her menu each day for three or four more days after that, and then, for a whole week, she'll be on liquids only. Then she'll start over at the beginning, with the cabbage soup.

Don't get too thin, I tell her. You're really beautiful now. And she is: vivid-looking, with a deep, rich voice and dramatic clothes that drape well on her. Yet she goes on this cabbage soup diet with some frequency. It sounds awful, I tell her. She says she gets so that she enjoys it. She is a determined woman.

Maybe I don't want her to get thin because I am not. I hope I wouldn't be that shabby, but I know the human heart to be capable of much more. The thing is, I really do think she looks wonderful, and her generous shape is part of that. And I am troubled by whatever it is that makes so many striking women think they're missing something because they don't conform to someone else's standards of beauty. Hardly anyone is immune to that feeling, and it's a bad thing. Comparing ourselves to somebody else uses up energy we can ill afford to lose. All of us have better things on which to focus our energies.

OCTOBER 9

"Art is the most intense mode of individualism that the world has known."
—OSCAR WILDE

An artist friend is having a show of her paintings in her apartment. She's got a big place, and the walls are lined with large and small canvases. Sara is an abstract expressionist, so the paintings are kind of hard to talk about.

But they are easy to feel about. One is called "Hand Full of Water," and sure enough, it's something you can't hold onto. A piece of it you start to see gives way to another piece. All of the pieces appear to bulge out of the canvas together, as if you could put your hands around them and hold them, but it is an illusion. Another painting is called "Valley of the Shadow/Holding." Dark rectangles draw the eye into the painting, through a haze of intricate brush-work kissed with light: you walk through pleasant scenery toward something mysterious and unknown, and you don't have a choice about whether or not to walk there. And that is the way it is in life: we're on our way somewhere, every one of us, and that somewhere is a complete unknown.

What on earth must it be like to be a painter? What is it like to stand in front of a blank canvas and claim it with that first stroke of color? And then to continue, until a dense web of color and meaning replaces the blankness? It's a mystery to me. And my friend who can command a computer seems to me to have another world in his hands. Another friend of mine, a therapist, wades into a group of women incest survivors every day and deals with their tragic shame and anger. I don't have the gift to do that either.

Every talent we have is an art. And everyone who gives herself completely to her work is an artist.

OCTOBER 10

"...The people swarm into the streets, and daily wet to the skin with rain."
—SIR THOMAS MORE

It's raining. Nobody wants to go out in it. People at work make up a giant take-out order so that some poor guy from the deli can slosh over with lunch for everybody. People cancel appointments, or do them over the phone instead.

The street in front of our building is a cobblestone street from the early nineteenth century. The rain falls into pools formed by the uneven settling of the bricks, so that the narrow street is a patchwork of puddles and little streams. In a few places the holes got so bad they've been filled in with modern asphalt, so that there are black circles among the stones.

This old street was, and still is today, the location of the city fish market. It was the largest fish market in the world. The business is run today pretty much as it was run when the street was new: men pushing hand trucks laden with fish to this or that retailer's van. Wagons, I guess, in those days. I imagine the men in the rain and the mud, sliding along the cobblestones with their loads of dead fish. Messy, heavy work to do in the cold rain.

The current occupants of the street look up from their computer terminals to see if it is still raining outside. *I wouldn't go out in this if you paid me,* they say to one another. We are warm and dry in our high-tech cocoons. The fish market people aren't here now; they begin work at two or three in the morning and are all gone by eight or nine, before most of the office workers arrive. But ghosts of their ancestors trundle through the streets, dodging the potholes and cursing the rain.

OCTOBER 11

"Tired nature's sweet restorer, balmy sleep." —EDWARD YOUNG

A half-day today. I walk into the house at 2:30 sharp, instead of nine at night, or whatever. A bonus of three or four hours is all mine to spend as I choose. I usually erect elaborate plans for my free time, pack it full of more tasks and errands than I could do in a week, and then feel rotten about myself when I haven't done them all. Sometimes I make these plans and then completely ignore them, choosing instead to browse through a magazine or take a nap. Afterward I feel even guiltier.

But I also have a certain faith in the wisdom of the organism: maybe we know when we need to goof off. If someone as chronically busy as I am takes a nap, it must be because she needs one. This is the kind of gentle wisdom I try to apply to myself when I haven't moved heaven and earth in a day as I had planned. I apply it to others all the time, soothing inappropriately racked consciences with suggestions about being a little less hard on themselves. How about me? Isn't it okay for me to have the afternoon off as well? I think so.

So I'll get one or two things done with these few extra hours. And then I will do something that is of no use at all except that it's fun—like read a book, or soak in a hot, fragrant bath.

OCTOBER 12

"Your Highnesses have an other world here...." —CHRISTOPHER COLUMBUS

I write this on a glorious autumn day, the kind of a day that is called "Indian summer." What this expression means is that it is not really summer; it just feels as if it were. It is a false summer. It is a revealing expression, "Indian summer": it reveals the remnant of a bigoted belief that Native Americans are liars.

Today is also the anniversary of Christopher Columbus's discovery of the new world. In 1992, on the five hundredth anniversary of that event, Americans were so confused by the differences of opinion about it that observances were very low-key. Everybody knew that European civilization on these shores had brought amazing and world-changing things into being, but everybody also knew that this had been done at the price of an entire ancient culture. At the price, even, of its very memories. Can we commend Columbus's discovery without endorsing genocide?

Generations of Americans have learned about the opening of the Americas to Europe as a benign scientific and religious visit which was to have stupendous power, wealth, and freedom as its ultimate result. We did not hear the voices of those to whom it was an invasion. And now that we *do* hear them, through the angry voices of their descendants, we are confused. Again. Are we the good guys or the bad guys?

Some scholars believe that Christopher Columbus was a *marrano*, a Jew who survived the Spanish Inquisition by publicly converting to Catholicism, the state religion of Spain, while practicing his own religion secretly. If he was, he knew something about oppression before he ever set sail from Spain. If his Judaism had become known, he probably would have been killed.

This doesn't get Columbus off the hook. Or us. But it does remind us that few things in life are simply good or simply bad. Most things are mixed. Columbus was probably neither saint nor devil; he was probably both oppressor and oppressed. Likewise, the bad things we have done as a society are bad. If we're still doing them, we should knock it off. But the good ones are good, and it's okay to rejoice in them. Human society and human motivation are mixed. They were back in 1492, and they still are today.

OCTOBER 13

"Haste makes waste." —POOR RICHARD'S ALMANAC

I am never going to reach this guy, I think as I return yet another call and find him out now instead of me. We've been chasing each other around New York on the telephone for three days now. Voice mail simply will not do. I need to talk with *him.*

I sometimes read books written in the eighteenth century. The intrigues among the characters are often accomplished by means of messengers. Lord So-and-So dispatches a man to Miss Such-and-Such with a tender note. It takes the man an hour or two to ride there. The Such-and-Such servants rub his horse down and give him a meal while he waits for the lady to pen a response. By then it's mid-afternoon; Missy has had a nap and, refreshed, is able to finish her letter. He rides back with it for another two hours.

Life was slow then. It took them forever to get the information they needed to make decisions, and the information they did receive was always out-of-date by the time it reached them.

They didn't have the Hubble telescope or the NASDAQ index. But they did have the most compendious dictionary of the English language ever, all conceived in the mind of one person. They had the most beautiful silver objects the world has seen before or since. They had music we still play, which may not be true of this week's Top Forty when it is two hundred years old.

And this without voice mail. Without fax machines.

Our communications technology would take their breath away. We get a lot done, no doubt about it. Have conversations in minutes which would have taken them years. There's a tremendous volume of stuff going over the air waves all the time.

But two hundred years from now ... whether or not I ever reach the man I am trying to call, who will ever know?

OCTOBER 14

"Some go down to the sea in ships..." —PSALM 107

The gallery on the ground floor of our building contains right now an exhibition of photographs of the seaport. Some of them are very old: there's a platinum print of the Brooklyn Bridge, on loan from a maritime museum, dating back to 1895. The bridge was almost brand-new when it was taken. Many more show deserted places on the New York waterfront today which once teemed with workers and machinery. An empty drydock looks like the fossil of a beached whale. A broken iron fence twists in a lonely curve in front of the deserted water's edge: it's Sheepshead Bay, the place where thousands of seafarers shipped out from New York during World War II. Not a soul around today.

When seafarers and port workers who remember these places the way they were come in and look around, they usually feel sad. New York was the premier port in the world. *We were somebody in those days*, they think. *These places aren't needed anymore. And neither are we*, the old guys say to themselves.

Other pictures show the working ports of today: compared to the pensive black and white of the others, they are in color, vivid shots of ships and water and warehouses and men. Lots of action here, not like the boneyards in the other shots. But the crews are smaller: machines do most of the work these days. A ship which used to take three weeks to unload is here and gone in twelve hours now. And most of the crews are not American guys, but people from poor countries who will work for almost nothing. Two Chinese men haul with all their combined weight on a rope. The old guys look at the picture and say nothing. Once those ropes belonged to them.

"Wait 'til your father gets home."

The two men next to me on the train are talking about the weekend just past. One of them took his kids out to breakfast with his cousin and her kids. Hers behaved miserably and his were angels. *I was embarrassed for her,* he told his friend. *Thought maybe I ought to pinch one of mine or something so hers weren't the only ones crying.* The friend laughed and launched into a story about his son.

It was nice to listen to these guys talking about their kids, having a conversation very like one two women might have had, and it makes me wonder how real the stereotype of the Fifties dad was. The myth is that he was available by appointment only, developing no nurturing skills whatsoever throughout his kids' childhood, until one day, when they were all grown up, he turned around and noticed that they were virtual strangers. The mother, on the other hand, spent twenty-eight hours a day breathing for them and had no life at all that was not connected with their needs and desires.

I doubt if dads forty years ago were as uninvolved in their children's lives as they are remembered today. I know that moms were not anything near that simple. As I listen to these two Nineties dads talking about hanging out with their kids, sounding pretty much like two women would sound, they are not aware of being revolutionary at all. And probably they are not. Moms and dads have always loved their kids. Their division of labor is certainly different now from what it was, which is all to the good. One generation can be quick to judge a previous one, though.

OCTOBER 16

"Be all that you can be."

Some friends and I are attending a luncheon at which the speaker is a famous leader, the first woman to occupy her position, ever. She speaks simply and powerfully about women and leadership. We all agree that we want to go where she is immediately so we can work with her. And we all begin to think about ourselves, to take stock. Am I making the best use of my own talents? Should I be more successful than I am?

I've always been happy in my work. I'm not at the top of it, though. I've never been the big boss of an organization. I've just been what would be called middle management if I worked anywhere but in the church. Should I be trying to become a big boss? Am I a strong enough leader? Have I been the right kind of role model for women in my profession who come after me?

The fact is, though, that I'm not sure that I'd be very well suited to the number one spot. What I really like is hands-on work with people. The big boss doesn't get to do that: he or she is primarily an administrator and spokesperson, leading by inspiring and directing others to do the actual work of the organization. I don't think I would do that very well. I hate meetings. I quit a job once because there were too many meetings. I felt wasted, spending all that time sitting in a closed room.

It's great to be ambitious. But not everyone needs to be the top dog. It takes wisdom and some courage to admit that about oneself. But we work best when we're where we belong, wherever that is.

OCTOBER 17

"Hot lavender...." —SHAKESPEARE, *THE WINTER'S TALE*

I have some special lavender soap and a fancy bottle of lavender bath crystals that I haven't used yet. All day I've been looking forward to drawing a fabulous, good-smelling bath and having a nice long soak. I picture it. The woman in the picture doesn't look that much like me, actually: she is younger and thinner, and she has her curls piled up prettily on her head and tied with a bow. My hair is too short to tie up. And my bathroom isn't as nice as hers, either: she has flowers all around her tub and an ocean view from her large window. I just have the little black and white tiles everyone else in New York has, and my only view is of the roof next door.

But I drop the crystals into the rust-stained tub and watch as they dissolve. The water's a little brown, but it smells great. Feels great, too. I ease myself down into it and settle back.

Ahh.

My usual ablutions are a fast shower in the morning. I mean *really* fast: I'm in and out in less than three minutes. I've got too much going on to linger. And the hot water pounding on me is energizing. But this bath is not for energy. This one's for comfort. Calm. Ease. Reward.

OCTOBER 18

"Open seven days a week."

I am flying in my car along the Long Island Expressway into Manhattan at seven o'clock on a Saturday morning. This is remarkable, as any New Yorker will tell you, because the Long Island Expressway is legendary for its traffic tie-ups during the week. But in the half-light of an early weekend morning there is none of that. Everyone on Long Island is staying put this morning, enjoying one of the last beautiful fall weekends we are likely to have this year.

I'm one of the people who works on weekends when most people don't. I try to grab a day off at some other point in the week, but that doesn't always work, so I really don't get the time off I know I should have. I guess I wish it were different, but I must not really wish for it very hard. I like what I do. I have fun. I do get tired, and wish for more free time on occasion, but I recognize that I could arrange my life differently if I really wanted to. And maybe someday I will. For now, though, my crazy schedule is really very much my own doing.

But a lot of people work two jobs because they couldn't make ends meet if they didn't. Women who raise small children full-time never get a day off, and although there is a certain flexibility to it, it's hard work. Farmers rarely get a holiday, and the majority of farmers in the world are—three guesses— women. Women with children, most of them.

There are more people in the world who work seven days a week than people who don't, and the ones like me, the ones who do so by choice, are definitely in the minority. I'm lucky in the number of choices I have. So here's to the really brave ones, who keep it all together at more than one job because they must.

OCTOBER 19

"Be good to yourself."

This solitaire thing may be getting a little out of hand. I've taken to rewarding myself with a quick game after each completed essay. When I win, the machine celebrates: it displays a wonderful—and infinitely varied—spectacle of playing cards bouncing gracefully off the screen and out into the great beyond, one by one. It's slightly mesmerizing to watch. It's also remarkably generous in spirit, much more so than a human opponent would be: it's as if the computer leapt over the net to shake my hand after I beat it.

Like any other job, writing has its ups and downs. Right now, because of my injury, I can't sit for long, so I usually write lying down, typing my essays with one hand while I support my body with the other arm. This, too, is an uncomfortable position, but if I don't finish this book, who will? So I've taken to luring myself to the keyboard with a quick solitaire game before each essay. At least, that's how it started. Then I wrote one so quickly and so well, in my own opinion, that I decided to reward myself with another game when I finished. That quickly institutionalized itself and became the norm, so now it's a game before and another one after.

And so I'm making progress on this book of days in just the same way we make progress on a year of days: one at a time. You can't live a whole year at one time, and you don't have to. All you have to do and all you can do is get through today.

This is one of the most important things I have learned in my life. What's going to happen next week? Next month? Who knows? And what can we do about next week or next month? Not a thing. By worrying about it before it gets here, you deny yourself whatever joy there is in the present moment.

Not that we shouldn't plan. We have to, with lives as complex as the ones we lead today. But though we plan for tomorrow, we only live for today. When you get through another one, give yourself a little reward. You've earned it. And tomorrow will be here soon enough.

OCTOBER 20

"Get me room service."

I am far away from home on a business trip. I call my grown-up children to let them know where I am in case they need to reach me, but my sense is that they may not even have realized I was gone.

I lie down on my hotel room bed and remember how hard business trips used to be when the kids were little. Hard on me because of the edge of worry about them that got on the plane with me and stayed. Hard on them because they missed me, and because a part of them couldn't quite believe that I wasn't going away because I wanted to. I don't think kids ever completely believe that. We look pretty powerful to them. I'm not sure they believe us when we tell them we *have* to do things. They think we do as we please.

I was a single mother in those days. What if the plane went down and we never saw each other again? What if one of them got sick and I didn't know about it? When they were younger, I would arrange for them to stay with friends, or else someone came to stay while I was gone. Then when Corinna got old enough, they managed the house together. I wasn't worried about wild parties: my kids had their faults, but that wasn't one of them. But what if the furnace broke down? Once one of the cats died while I was in Houston. Another time they ran out of dishwasher soap and didn't know what happens if you substitute dishwashing liquid (don't ever, ever, try that).

I didn't have to go away very often. Just three or four times a year. I would sleep in my strange bed and order room service. I walked on strange streets and bought my girls dumb souvenirs of whatever place I had been. I met new people and learned a lot. I missed the kids, but I was also energized by what I was doing. I was never sorry to get back on the plane and come home, and we were always happy to be together again and all in one piece. It's so easy now that they're on their own. But not being central to someone's daily needs is going to take some getting used to.

OCTOBER 21

"To have and to hold." —THE MARRIAGE OFFICE, THE BOOK OF COMMON PRAYER

A middle-aged couple has come to me, hoping I will officiate at their wedding. We sit together and talk for an hour or so, and I see that they are people of maturity and common sense. Both have been married before, and both their marriages ended in divorce. *I said I'd never get married again,* the woman said. Her husband had left her when their son was only a baby, and she raised him by herself. It is clear that she and her fiancé are devoted to one another, and that they have learned hard lessons from the pain of the past. I cannot think of a single reason why they shouldn't get married.

Both of them are Roman Catholic. All of us are aware that they cannot be married in their own church because they have been divorced. We talk about what that will mean; they are both serious churchgoers. I tell them that these are difficult times for the Church, but that maybe things will be better later on. Maybe someday there will be more agreement between church practice and the way people live than there is now. The man agrees; *I'm sure that things will change for the better someday,* he says.

I'm struck as we talk by the complete absence of bitterness in this couple about this important disagreement with the teachings of their church. I think of all the Catholic school horror stories I've heard people tell for years. A lot of Americans are angry at their Church, and a lot of Americans have left it behind. This couple's quiet patience is impressive. They still love the faith in which they were raised. *Someday we will be married in our own Church,* they say. *Or renew our vows, or something. In the meantime, we'll be faithful and go every Sunday.* That will be good, I say.

OCTOBER 22

"Where love rules, there is no will to power." —CARL JUNG

Anna has to call her doctor, the message on the answering machine says. I am filled with fear when I hear it. Something has come up in one of the tests, I think. I remember our friends whose twenty-year-old died from breast cancer. Unusual in one so young, but it happens.

Of course, *she* is to call, not me. Legally now, her medical affairs are none of my business. But what if she forgets to call the doctor? I tell my husband to make sure she understands how important it is—to add another voice besides Mom's nagging one. *Don't freak out, guys,* Anna says calmly when she finds out about the message. *Why would I forget? I don't want to die.*

Oh. This is actually what I had in mind all these years: a young woman able to take care of herself. But now that this is what she's become, I'm a bit taken aback. What, exactly, am I supposed to be doing now that I no longer direct her life?

Just be there. If she has any questions, she'll ask. If I hover over her as if she were a child, she might not. And that would be bad. Because she still needs her mom.

OCTOBER 23

"One with the earth..."

We are both awake at night, working in our pajamas. I see that Richard is wearing his navy blue wool robe with the red shawl collar. I have a picture of him wearing that robe. It was taken in about 1948, when he was still in college. He is now almost sixty-five. Richard is the kind who never throws anything away.

This is a good way to be. We always have the right kind of screw for any job. We always have little pieces of wood for staking young plants. We always have used plastic bags. Used tin foil. Used boxes. We save all our table scraps and he puts them in the compost pile. It's really disgusting to have a strainer of old lettuce and coffee grounds in the sink, I tell him. *You don't have to touch it*, he says; *just give it to me when it gets too disgusting and I'll take it out to the pile.* He doesn't have to tell me twice. I'm not touching it.

We joke about ending up in the compost pile ourselves when we pass on. Just our ashes, of course. *That wouldn't be half bad*, Richard says, *just as long as whoever lives in this house understands compost. People should die like they live. We could help renew the earth.* We tell the kids about this idea and they look a little uncomfortable; they never know whether we are joking or not. You don't have to put us in the compost if you don't want to, I tell them. But think about it: wouldn't you like us to come back as tomatoes? They think it's the most macabre idea they've ever heard. It is not, I say. It's sensible. Death is part of life. *We'd like to help out to the extent we are able*, says Richard politely. *It's the least we can do.*

Anna forbids us to say another word. Not another word.

OCTOBER 24

"Can you help me out?"

In an exchange common in every city, a poorly dressed young man holds out his open palm and asks me to help him out. I dig in my purse for a few coins and press them into his hand. He says thank you, and tells me to have a nice day.

You know they're just going to use it to buy drugs or booze, a friend says to me, *I don't give them anything anymore.* Other people I know carry apples or individually-wrapped slices of cheese to give out to panhandlers, thereby beating the homeless at their own game, I guess.

Hmmn. I understand the concern behind this practice, but something about it bothers me. I *don't* know what each person who asks me for money plans to do with it. I'm sure some of them will buy booze with it; addiction *is* a major factor in many people's homelessness. But it is not the only one. And it is not always present. Beggars *do* get hungry. But they also need subway tokens, which you can't get with an apple. They need a room. They may need to make a phone call. You can't get those with a slice of cheese.

I tell the young man about a drop-in center that's open twenty-four hours a day and give him directions to get there. He may go. Then again, he may not. But he knows about it, and he has the power to get himself there if he wants to. And he has interacted with a fellow citizen in something other than the anonymity of his usual exchange.

OCTOBER 25

"Gonna find out who's naughty or nice...."

Why is it necessary to run other people down in order to defend one's own choices in life?

I just sat through a radio broadcast of a political convention in which family values were talked to *death*. Some people were edgy about what might really be meant by the term "family values." Single mothers thought they were being singled out for criticism. Full-time homemakers said they weren't going to take it anymore either, that it was about time people stopped criticizing *them*. Gay people were pretty sure they were not included among the acceptable. Widows and widowers were viewed as respectable. Divorced people were a little iffy.

What a strange thing. In the nineteenth century, many women worked outside the home and all women worked within it. So did children. In the eighteenth century, it was common for rich men to have mistresses and maintain them publicly; it was not unheard of for rich women to do the same. In the Middle Ages it was considered wise to send one's children to be raised in another town by another family. There has *always* been more than one model of what families should look like.

So why are people suddenly at each other's throats about it? I always suspect such defensiveness masks insecurity. I guess I just don't think I need the faults of others to certify my own virtues. If I'm good, people will be able to tell. If I'm not, no amount of finger-pointing at other people or groups will change that. Can we change the channel?

"Practice makes perfect."

When I was a child, the standard finger—strengthening exercise for young piano students was a collection in several volumes by one Mr. Hanon. These exercises were the bane of a child's musical life: boring, repetitive, and seemingly infinite in number. One's hour began with the dreary Hanon, starting down in the thunderous lower half of the keyboard and climbing up to the tinkly keys of the upper end. Then back down. Then repeat.

I pictured Hanon as a fat, balding gent in a frock coat and brocade vest. I even drew him that way, and stood the picture up on the music rack so I could stab him with my pencil each time I completed one of his stupid boring exercises. I would play and then attack, play and then stab, until poor Hanon's vest was full of holes. Meanwhile, my fingers were getting stronger and more sure of the keyboard. Even I could see that Hanon was doing me some good.

I don't know what the real Hanon looked like. What do you bet he was young and handsome? But my imaginary martinet, like all stern taskmasters, did me a lot of good. And somewhere along the line I stopped playing those exercises because I had to and started playing because I knew I *needed* to. I even quit stabbing Hanon in the stomach; I'd just play through a few of the exercises to get warmed up and then move on to my sheet music.

When you're a novice—at anything—the rules of the game seem burdensome and unfair. Then you see yourself getting better and better at what you do because of them, and you begin to realize that they are there to help you. You learn to take ownership of the rules of the game, to take pride in your ability to do things the right way.

OCTOBER 27

"This is the way we wash our clothes, so early Monday morning."

I can no longer put off doing the laundry; it must be done today. I drag the clothes hamper out of the bathroom and start down the two flights of stairs with it. This is not as easy with a cane as it used to be without one. Down in the basement I set the water temperature dial and push the button that starts the machine. As I watch the soap dissolve in the steaming water, I think about what it means to do a load of washing in the late twentieth century. Here is what I do: I load the machine and push a button. Then I close the lid. When everything's all washed, I take the clothes out of the washer and put them in the dryer. Then I push another button. That's it.

During the war, my mother used to boil her washing on top of the stove in a large oblong kettle made for that purpose. She would lift the boiler on and off the stove to rinse the clothes. Then she would hang them out to dry. I remember her telling me that her grandmother had given birth to her last child when she was fifty years old and disabled. The laundry project in those days, well before the turn of the century, was also the boiler-on-the-stove kind.

Older than I am now, that woman. Permanently on a cane, instead of temporarily, like me. Washing diapers by the dozens and limping out to the clothesline to hang them in the sun.

And I postpone doing laundry because it makes me tired.

OCTOBER 28

"Take me out to the ball game..." —JACK NORWORTH

A group of parents is here at the church. They are going to start the first Little League in a long time—maybe ever—in Lower Manhattan. An official from the city is here to offer support. There are about a dozen moms and dads. Some of them know a lot about baseball. Some know nothing at all. One guy is talking knowledgeably about equipment they'll need to buy. One of the women has designed an insignia.

These people have been working all day. Some of them are still in their business suits. A few came late, rushing in with their briefcases and newspapers under their arms and taking their seats in the back. There aren't any kids here, so they must have gotten sitters for their children, or left them with older brothers and sisters. Their enthusiasm is obvious, though: they are thrilled with the idea of a Little League team here in the city, of giving their children the same experience they had when they were little.

Many of them grew up in the suburbs. They came to New York as young adults and stayed to raise their children. That is not an easy thing to do. The open spaces of the suburbs, the large school playgrounds, the car pools they remember from their childhoods: you don't have those things here. These parents have to take their children everywhere on public transportation or on foot, and they have to stay with them. It is no longer feasible to send a child outside by himself to play, and it hasn't been for years.

But they want this baseball league for their kids enough to bite the bullet and do whatever it takes to get it. Just finding somewhere to store the bases is a major concern in a place where real estate is measured by the square foot rather than the acre. Maybe they can approach the fancy new high school nearby for room in a closet. Or maybe the office building next door will support the program by setting aside some space. They talk on, about finding businesses which will sponsor teams, about some uniforms one of the dads saw somewhere that looked really cool. They are happy and excited as they plan for their children. I'm impressed.

OCTOBER 29

"I wept that I had no shoes, until I met a man who had no feet."

I have a scar on my leg from this accident. Today a doctor told me it would probably not go away. There is also sort of a dent in the leg where the scar is. That won't go away either.

I've always thought I had terrific legs. Several other figure flaws, but the legs were great. It figures: I can't have a dent in each injured—but ample—hip, where it would do some good. It's got to be on one of my terrific legs. I look down at it and it looks grotesque.

But I go to the rehab clinic in the afternoon, and there I see a young woman: her thin face is ringed with a pink ridge of scar tissue from a skin graft, and one arm is missing. I don't know what kind of accident did this to her, but I do know that my fixation on my own complaints makes me feel ashamed of myself when I see her. I don't feel better because I have seen someone who is much more badly hurt, but it does put my own stuff into perspective.

This progression of thought—from self-pity to compassion for others—is something that can only be done by the sufferer herself. You can't teach it to someone else. Don't say to someone who comes to you with a problem: "You think *you've* got troubles. Just look at So-and-So over there with no legs." That doesn't work; it just makes the person feel doubly downtrodden. *Not only do I have this problem*, she thinks, *but this person to whom I've entrusted my feelings about it doesn't take it seriously.* Just say you're sorry, and leave the moral out. She'll have to figure it out on her own.

OCTOBER 30

"Happy birthday to you."

Anna and I meet on her eighteenth birthday to do some antiquing and then have tea. She falls in love with an Italian couch upholstered in ivory silk. It is so beautiful, she says. So are the Biedermeier lyre-back chairs with blue damask seats. And so is the Meissen china service, white with tiny blue flowers, sufficient for dozens of nineteenth-century diners who consumed dozens of courses: there are gravy boats, fruit bowls, vegetable platters, pots de crème cups, small and large platters, and bowls and plates by the score.

The child has taste. How nice that is, I think as I watch her admiring these beautiful things. They are so expensive: seven thousand dollars for the couch. Fifteen hundred per Biedermeier piece. Five hundred for the smallest of the Meissen tureens. We move on to her favorite clothing store, where she spots her favorite designer's work on a hanger clear across the room. *Good eye,*

Anna, I say: a black velvet ankle-length coatdress with military styling. A steal at six hundred sixty dollars.

We don't buy any of this stuff. We do get a turtleneck at the Gap, and a pair of jeans. Then we go for tea and scones with cream and little sandwiches and large pieces of sweet cake, which neither of us can finish. Our stomachs and hearts are warmed by the hot tea. It has been a pleasant afternoon.

She tells me that she likes liking these things. *I like a lot of things that most of my friends don't like. Or even know about, some of them.* I am given to understand that her folks get some credit for that, for exposing her to things she might otherwise not see. The pleasure was all ours, I say truthfully.

Anna has a ticket to go to the Matisse exhibit at the Metropolitan Museum on Friday with other students at her school, and is debating whether or not she wants to get up at eight o'clock to go to it. *I want to see it, but I never get up before nine,* she says. She hates getting up in the morning. This is because you stay up too late listening to your horrible loud music at your horrible clubs, I tell her, and she smiles. She also likes liking things I don't like. Happy birthday, Anna.

OCTOBER 31

"Ah! The children of the night! Listen to them sing!" —BRAM STOKER, *DRACULA*

I don't remember Halloween taking as long when I was a child as it seems to take now. It was a much more hurried affair: kids used to just grab an old white sheet and go. But now the stores get the masks and pumpkins into the windows by the middle of September.

I also don't remember adults getting into it as much. These days, though, grown men and woman are renting costumes to make themselves into French maids and gorillas and pirates. Last year I rode the subway with a middle-aged Dracula, complete with blood trickling out of one corner of his mouth. I also rode with two men in fluffy pink tutus. I saw two different ends of a camel, in reality husband and wife, walking down the subway stairs hand in hand.

This is a good thing. We shouldn't take ourselves too seriously. To experiment with one's own identity, to try on someone else's, even that of another species—these flights of imagination are a small vacation from the hardness of our day-to-day lives. There's a lot of conformity required of most of us. We have to behave in certain ways or pay a price. We have to look a certain way or pay a price. So go ahead, dress up like Godzilla or Little Bo Peep. It does no harm, and may do some small good.

NOVEMBER 1

"I count myself in nothing else so happy as in a soul remembering my good friends." —*RICHARD II,* ACT II SCENE 3

Every month or so, somebody sees Elvis. He's living in Hawaii now, under a different name. Or he's a garage-station attendant in Ohio, sick of the fame and the drugs and making a fresh start.

Some people are not allowed to die. Marilyn Monroe is one. Jim Morrison of The Doors is another. Adolf Hitler is one, too, so it's not just nice people who live forever in the popular imagination.

Most of us, though, are going to live our threescore and ten and then that will be it, as far as the present world is concerned. There won't be any sightings of us after we've cashed in our chips. So this life, how we live it right now, matters profoundly. We won't be seen anymore; we will only be remembered.

What will you be remembered for? How will people finish the sentence "I really miss her; she was so—!" Sweet? Funny? Kind? Although we spend most of our time in pursuit of excellence and money, those are not the things people will remember about us. Nobody's going to say, "I really miss her; she was so rich!" or "Gosh, I wish she were here; she was such a fabulous housekeeper!" Our colleagues will miss our work skills for a while; they'll say things like, "Now, if she were here, she would have seen this and we wouldn't be in this mess." Someone else will come along, though, to replace our competence.

Generally, though, it will be the quality of our interactions with others that people will miss. It will matter that we're gone if it mattered that we were here. People love you if you love them and show them that love. That's what we miss most when it ends.

NOVEMBER 2

"Coffee, hon?"

I am having my usual cheese omelette in my usual diner. It is seven in the morning, and this is my chosen way to start the day: alone, with someone who doesn't expect me to talk to her serving me delicious hot food. I've got to be available and sympathetic to people all day. This half hour before all that begins is a very peaceful and important time.

For me it is the beginning, a gathering of strength for the day to come. But the diner is right across the street from a hospital, so there are a lot of people in here every morning for whom it is the end of their eleven-p.m.-to-seven-a.m. shift. Their day is over at the time when mine is beginning, and they are tucking into hamburgers and meatloaf platters as I am finishing my orange juice. I don't know when they eat breakfast; probably at about five in the afternoon. Maybe they never eat normal breakfast food at all.

Diners are terrific. All of them are basically the same. They offer a thousand different items on the menu, breakfast available all the time, ridiculously tall cakes displayed temptingly behind glass doors, like a child's view of heaven. Diners are everywhere and serve everyone, modest outposts of welcome and equality in a competitive and hierarchical world. Doctor, lawyer, orderly, or housekeeper: the waitress in a diner calls them all "hon."

Friendliest of all is the fact that most of them are open twenty-four hours a day every day of the year. No matter when you get off work, they are there to pour you a comforting cup of coffee when you finish. Or send you off with a good breakfast under your belt when you start. The diner is sort of like your mother. Comforting. Warm. A little tacky, maybe, but at seven o'clock in the morning, who does one really need to impress?

NOVEMBER 3

"He makes his cook his merit, and the world visits his dinners and not him."
—MOLIÈRE

The Seamen's Church has a weekly potluck supper after its worship service on Saturday nights. *What should I bring,* newcomers invariably ask. *Anything you like,* we answer. *Or nothing at all, if you aren't able. God will provide.*

And God always does. Nobody goes around with a yellow pad checking off who's bringing dessert and who's bringing salad. We just each do what we can do, and the result is almost always a wonderful selection of food. Only once or twice has the fare been skimpy or lopsided. And if, on some Saturday night in the future, everyone ends up bringing a lemon meringue pie, I guess we'll just enjoy coffee and dessert.

You couldn't run a large show this way. But it works perfectly well for our small one. People love the spontaneity of it. A downhome event like this is a rarity in Lower Manhattan, where there is a certain pressure to be chic. But the simple gift of food from each according to his or her ability is an important part of caring for one another. People understand that the responsibility for our common meal falls on all of us, which is a good thing to grasp about a lot of things in life. If everyone does her part, things usually work out pretty well.

People have pictured heaven as a shared banquet, the blessed feasting happily together throughout eternity. Even here on earth, people slow down a little when they eat together, get into long conversations about important things. At the end of the meal, everyone cleans up and goes off, in twos and threes, continuing the pleasant fellowship, walking one another home.

NOVEMBER 4

"For thy sake, Tobacco, I would do anything but die." —CHARLES LAMB

It looks like the damaging effect of secondhand smoke is becoming as accepted an idea as the fact that smoking is bad for the smoker. It turns out that living with a smoker is just about as dangerous as being one, so that people who continue smoking will have to deal with the probability that they are not just annoying but hurting the people they love. This moves the eternal smoking/no smoking debate out of the realm of individual civil rights ("I have the right to do something that's bad for me if I want to; it's my life") into the potentially actionable ("I have the right to hurt you"). Be on the watch for some lawsuits.

I'm an authority on tobacco addiction. I was hooked for years. Tried to stop so many times and failed. Stopped once, only to resume, inexplicably, after six or seven months. It wasn't true that I didn't care about my children, who hated my smoking. Sure, I cared. But I was an addict, so I told myself that this was really a question of my freedom to enjoy myself, that I worked hard and had earned a few pleasures. Pleasures like burning my throat and blackening my lungs. And I was just able to not think about what it might be doing to the girls. Addicts don't think like other people do. Ordinary appeals to reason or goodwill or guilt, therefore, don't work with them.

How did I stop? One year I quit for a day on the Great American Smokeout, and I never went back. I didn't let myself think about never having a smoke again; I just thought about not having one that day. And then the next day, I did the same thing. And the next, and the next.

I don't consider myself cured. I don't think addiction *can* be cured. If I smoked a cigarette today, I'd be back up to a pack a day within a month. Maybe more. I don't even let myself *think* about the act of smoking. Where my mind goes, my body is sure to follow.

I am grateful to have been delivered. I am sorry for those who haven't yet, for those who cannot even find a way to *want* their own deliverance. I didn't want mine, either, for a long time.

NOVEMBER 5

"A common grayness silvers everything." —ROBERT BROWNING

You should color your hair, my friend says when she sees the silver stripe which has lately sprouted at my right temple. *You don't have any gray anywhere else. It'll give you a lift. Why look older than you are?*

I am curious, though, as to how far this gray will go. Am I on my way to a whole headful, or is this it? If I color my hair, I'll never know. And anyway, is it so terrible to look my age? A friend who recently won an age-discrimination suit tells me that gray hair invites the corporate brush-off. Hmmm ... only for women, I think; what about all those silver-maned male CEOs? What about Ralph Lauren? Is gray tired and worn-out on us, only to be distinguished on them? Who's going to put a stop to this imbalance?

A gray-headed man is perceived as dependable and wise, venerable. If we don't buy into the culture's categories, seeing ourselves as worthwhile only if we look young, we women can be perceived as venerable, too. Wisdom comes with the seasoning of years. Young people may be intelligent, but they usually are not wise. I can't imagine wanting to seem younger than I really am. That would be inviting the world to discount my hard-earned wisdom.

I think I'll leave my hair alone. See how it turns out. When I was young, I used to feel sorry for women who were middle-aged, as if the only things I had to offer were my young body and smooth face. I know myself to be richer now that I am middle-aged myself, and I don't feel sorry for me in the least.

NOVEMBER 6

"We are becoming the servants ... of the machine we have created to serve us."
—JOHN KENNETH GALBRAITH

I can't believe what I've done. In a variation on my usual automatic operation of my computer, one that was so minute I still don't know what I did—I have erased this book. All of it—right off the disk. It took about a second. I called Justus, my dear friend and computer guru, to see if maybe it was hiding somewhere in the memory. Together we were able to determine that it isn't. It just plain isn't there any more.

Well, it could be worse. Half of the material is typed in very rough draft form. And all but twenty-five pages or so is backed up on a floppy disk. But twenty-five pages is a lot. These little essays may seem ephemeral, but they actually take me a long time. I'm only good for five or so a day. Maybe not even that many.

Re-doing lost work is awful. Your feeling of achievement is taken from you: you have *done* this already. You're not breaking any new ground; you're just trying to get back to where you've already been once. This kind of loss happens to computer users a lot, which is why my central message for today is this: don't go to lunch. Stay at your desk and back up your hard disk.

And, if it somehow happens to you anyway, or something else does that sends you all the way back to square one, you need some fast serenity. Take a couple of deep, slow breaths. Make a list of five terrible things that haven't happened to you, things that would be a hundred times worse than this. Read each one, and allow yourself to imagine it happening. Allow yourself a feeling of relief when you remind yourself that these things have not occurred. And then go back to square one. You can handle it.

NOVEMBER 7

"I always thought I would go first."

Did you ever get that mammogram?

I only mention it because it's been about three months since we last discussed this, which is more than enough time to put off doing something. It's been so long that now you've probably forgotten all about it.

I spent yesterday with a man who lost his wife to breast cancer several years ago. We were on our way to Washington, DC, for a ceremony in which he was to receive a special medal for his service in the Second World War. Most of the other men had their wives with them. He was alone. She had let her checkups go, and then a lump had appeared in her neck, and by then it was too late. So now he is alone, and the retirement years they had always thought they would spend so happily together are, for him, just time passing.

Her death was a hard one. *She deserved better,* he said quietly, and I know she did. And I know that it came much too soon. A woman in her early sixties is middle-aged today; she should have had twenty more years. Or longer. And one of the hardest things for her husband to handle is the possibility that her death could have been prevented.

So don't do that to the people you love. While it's true that a life that focuses all of its energy on trying not to die becomes a life of fear, and who needs that, you can do what you *can* do to stay well, and you should.

Do it *today.*

NOVEMBER 8

"To have and to hold from this day forward...." —THE MARRIAGE OFFICE,
THE BOOK OF COMMON PRAYER

I find that I must stop myself from showing too much interest in my daughter's new boyfriend. Both my husband and my other daughter warn me to keep my mouth shut, and they are right. Just because he's kind, intelligent, financially secure, and good with kids doesn't mean he's the one. And it's not my call anyway.

But I straighten up the house very carefully if I think she's bringing him over. It's just that I can't help wanting someone to ride up on a white horse and take care of her. Corinna's a single mom. She works so hard. She's a good mother. She doesn't have much money, but she has managed to buy her first home. *She doesn't have to get married,* Anna says. *She's doing fine on her own.*

Well, yes. But people don't get married in order to solve their financial problems or their inability to cope with life. Marriage is pure disaster if those are its only goals. You don't get married because you can't do your life. You get married to get and give spiritual and emotional nourishment, and I long for her to have it. I want her to have a partner whom she can respect and who respects her. Maybe I want it more than she wants it herself. Corinna's been burned once, and she is suspicious of her own choices. *I'm waiting for the other shoe to drop,* she says with a laugh. *We'll just wait and see. I'm not counting on anything.*

This guy seems nuts about her, though, and my husband and I both think that she seems different about him than she has about other admirers. So, in the privacy of prayer, I say something like this: "Thy will be done, of course, but if you'd like my opinion, this one looks pretty good. Amen."

I'm sure God understands.

NOVEMBER 9

"Do not shorten the morning by getting up late." —SCHOPENHAUER

It was my understanding that this meeting was to begin at nine in the morning. Where *is* everybody? In virtuous solitude I sit down on the floor outside the locked conference room door and wait. A custodian comes along and opens the door for me, and I take a seat at the table and wait for someone else to show up. Sure enough, people begin to filter in and pretty soon we are underway.

There are people who are always late for meetings. There are chairpeople who start meetings on time regardless of who is missing, so that latecomers have to slink guiltily into a meeting already in progress. I like to do it that way myself: it allows people to deal with the consequences of not being on time themselves, without my scolding them as if I were their mother.

I couldn't do that anyway, because sometimes *I'm* the one who slinks in long after everyone else. I hate that when it happens. I feel like an irresponsible teenager when I am noticeably late. I look around the table and see people who have to come a longer distance than I do and made it on time. I can't even blame being late on my children like I used to. They've left home. So it's all my fault.

So I am not hard on others when they fail to arrive on time, for I am also one of the guilty. But I still know that it's rude to make other people sit and wait. And I try not to do it. We've got work to do.

NOVEMBER 10

"Blessed are they that mourn: for they shall be comforted." —MATTHEW 5:4

I am planning a memorial service for a man who was killed earlier this year in a car accident. His widow has been unable to bring herself to do anything about this for months, but we are finally talking about what music to have, what should be read and who should speak. This will not be a standard church funeral. *My husband hated all that stuff,* she says. *I'm not even sure how he would feel about my doing this much.* But she wants to have something people can come to and remember him.

They were both teachers in the inner city. They came in the late Sixties, full of idealism, and they just stayed. They taught in the same school, four blocks from their home. They had no children. They just had each other. They lived together and worked together—not a state of affairs you see much today.

It is impossible to describe how I feel, she says. *I was so dependent on him. Not because I'm some little clinging vine, but just because there wasn't anything that we didn't do together. We were so much alike. I never looked ahead and thought about his not being here. Never.*

In years gone by, widows used to wear special clothes signifying their mourning. The woman talks about how useful that would be: the long black veil would hide her red eyes, and everybody would know why she's all but paralyzed without her having to tell and retell the story. *I can't do anything,* she says. *I forget things as soon as I hear them and I get tired from nothing. I haven't gone back to school yet. I know I will. I have to. But not yet.*

She'll go back. When she's ready. The memorial service will help: it puts a definitive ending on the moment of loss, and that needs to happen when somebody dies, whether he was religious or not. And the simple passing of time will do what it always does: make even the most unbearable thing part of history, part of us. "Get over" the loss? Not likely. Not even desirable. Love doesn't end like that. But the loss will be part of a life that is more than just the loss. This widow is more than just a widow; she was, and still is, a person. Though life will never be the same, it can have meaning again. That's it. But that's enough.

NOVEMBER 11

"...at a touch, I yield." —ALFRED LORD TENNYSON

 M y friend, Robin, is a shiatzu practitioner. She's been giving me massages since my accident. Shiatzu massages are not like other massages: they are slow and silent, with Robin carefully placing her hands on certain parts of my body and then leaning on them with all her weight. I can't say they make me groan with pleasure, exactly; all I know is that when we're finished I feel relaxed and very peaceful. Robin tells me that's because my meridians are all lined up.

You may not know about meridians. Neither do I. They are a term from the medical practice of another culture, one with a very different under-standing of the body and the way it works. More religious, I would say, remembering the preference in our healing temples for pills and lots of people in white uniforms and shiny steel machinery: a far cry from Robin's silent hands. Western medicine is truly miraculous in things it can conquer, but it isn't all there is. We're missing a lot if we never turn to the rest of the world.

One thing the East does seem to understand better than the West is the relationship between peace of mind and physical health. That's why a shiatzu session seems more like a prayer service than a massage; Robin and I do not speak, and after she is finished she sits quietly with her hands folded while I lie there in silence. Sometimes an emotion will be opened within me as she works, and tears will come to my eyes. *You're supposed to just let that happen,* she says. *It needed to be released.*

I have no idea what is happening during these sessions, and I don't care. All I know is that I feel better, and the pain that is my constant companion lessens. My doctors put me back together ad mirably when my bones were broken, but they are mystified by my pain. *Well, you're going to have pain,* they say, as if to a cranky child, and they have nothing further to offer except a prescription for addictive pills that will render me unable to work. They've got to see twelve more patients in the coming hour. They can no more spend forty minutes in gentle silence, touching the parts of me that hurt, than they could fly.

NOVEMBER 12

"I call heaven and earth to witness...." —DEUTERONOMY 4:26

There are groups who have, as part of their identity, the belief that the Holocaust did not occur. They think that it was an invention of the Jews, that the careful records kept by the Nazis during the systematic exterminations are forgeries, that the death camps, which can still be visited, are fakes. Yet these events happened only fifty years ago. There are survivors of the camps still alive, with their prisoner numbers still tattooed on their arms. The people who deny the Holocaust think that the people are *lying*. I guess they think they tattooed themselves.

What would make a person so determined to deny history? Aryan Nation and Ku Klux Klan and the others want moral justification for continuing the lifestyle of bigotry they lived before the Holocaust, permission to hate all the people they want to hate. They need to be able to say it's reasonable to hate. That, morally, it's no big deal. So obvious a persecution of the innocent as the Holocaust gets in the way of that. Even Aryan Nation would have a hard time making a case for the incineration of six million men, women, and children. So these hate groups need to believe it just didn't happen.

What's really scary is that there are young people in those groups, people too young to remember, people who must take *any* reports of what happened fifty years ago on faith. What's going to make them believe us instead of Aryan Nation?

NOVEMBER 13

"To everything there is a season." —ECCLESIASTES 3:1

One of my classmates has had to drop out of our program. We are a small group, so the absence of one person is very noticeable. Something came up in her family, and something had to give. Her husband stayed. The children stayed. So did the job. So it was her doctoral program, which meant a great deal to her, that nonetheless had to be given up.

There are lots of women who have had to interrupt their educations because somebody needed them. I was one; it took me eight years to get my bachelor's degree. People do what they have to do, but I remember how painful a thing it was to have to put school on hold. I felt as if people could tell by looking at me that I hadn't finished college. And what if I never were able to go back? I wanted that degree, but I was very aware of how hard it can be to return to school after a few years have gone by. What if one thing just led to another, and I never got it?

But that didn't happen. It required choices and hard work, but I learned that you can do what you want to do if you are willing to make it a priority. It can't be your only priority—at least, not if you've got other people depending on you—but if you cherish it and work toward it, eventually you will get it.

This is a very important thing for every woman to know, for many women have tremendous obstacles in their way. The presence of obstacles ought not to be taken to mean that something is not to be. It doesn't mean that at all. People overcome incredible obstacles to become the people they know they can be.

The novelist and scholar Toni Morrison was asked once if she thought teenaged motherhood was the main thing holding African-American women back. *Not at all,* she said. *Mothers aren't problems. They are tremendous resources. All that's holding teenaged mothers back is that we have given up on their educations.* She's right. You don't stop being a person when you become a mom. Maybe you don't go to college when you're eighteen. Maybe you don't go until you're forty. Pearl Bailey was in her sixties when she went back to school. But make up your mind to do it and you will.

NOVEMBER 14

"Heave ho, my lads! Heave Ho! It's a long, long way to go..."
—OFFICIAL SONG OF THE U.S. MERCHANT MARINE

It is three o'clock on a Saturday afternoon. A crowd of grayhaired men have gathered in the seafarers' club room for a meeting of their organization: the American Association of Merchant Marine Veterans. It has been fifty years since they were part of the merchant fleet that supported Allied forces in the Second World War. It is only recently that the government has recognized these men as veterans of that war. They have always been deeply patriotic, but now they are deeply proud of the honor they have finally received.

Some of the men bring souvenirs: one has a box containing his service ribbons, another a cable from the Secretary of the Navy thanking him for his contribution to the war effort. One man has a set of diagrams of a Liberty ship, the vessel on which they all sailed. They cluster around the old plans, pointing out details of the engine room and the hatches to each other.

More than a few of them had their ships torpedoed out from under them. One man found himself in the water four times. Many of them saw shipmates die. One man says he's never been able to speak of what he saw and he's not going to do it now; *it was terrible*, he says, and tears stand in his eyes. Yet he comes to the meetings.

I never had friendship anything like what I had back then with those guys, says one of the men. I listen to them talk. They *should* be proud to have lived through that, to have worked and sacrificed for a cause that everybody thought was good. I envy them that. We have a hard time pulling together like that today.

NOVEMBER 15

"...childish, but divinely beautiful...." —SCHILLER

After weeks of shapeless hair, I squeeze in a permanent. Dominick has time to perm my hair if I don't need a cut, too, so we agree to wave it today and cut it later, after it's had a chance to calm down a little.

When I was a girl, our neighbor across the street had a beauty parlor in her home: Betty's Beauty Box, it was called. My mother and my grandmother both had their hair done there, and my utilitarian bobs were administered by Betty as well. The Beauty Box was a wonderful place to visit; I used to call upon its proprietor even when nobody in my family was having her hair done. A beautician could get mighty lonely in my little hometown, so Betty was usually pretty good-natured about my visits. My memory is that I was over there all the time, poring over the hairstyle books, having contests in my imagination about which of the models was the most glamorous.

Betty herself was a brassy blonde. She was the only bleached blonde in Forest Hill. Usually she was bright and gay, throwing her head back when she laughed, like Marilyn Monroe. Some days, though, she looked very tired and red-eyed. Once I found her in the Beauty Box, sitting under one of the enormous hair dryers, her eyes streaming with tears. *You go on home* was all she said, and I did. When I told my folks what had happened, my mother and grandmother exchanged glances and said maybe I shouldn't go over there anymore. I think now that Betty had a drinking problem. She later died in a car crash; some people thought that it was suicide. I wouldn't know.

Things are more under control at Dominick's place. It's in a city, and people pop in and out all day to gossip and confer about hair. There are *lots* of bleached blondes here—even some purples and greens on occasion! Poor Betty, born too soon and in the wrong place. She would have loved it here.

NOVEMBER 16

"This dust was once the man." —WALT WHITMAN

A woman who lost her son last year comes often to sit in the memorial garden where his ashes are interred. There is a wooden bench there; she sits on the bench in all kinds of weather. *I go even when it's cold. I just want to be where he is, be in the weather he's in. All my friends want me to feel better to get out and have some good times and all that. And I do get out. I have some good times. But this is my son. I have the right to remember him. I have the right to stay connected to him. If the only way I can do that is to feel sad, then that's what I'll do. I know I make people a little nervous when I sit out here, especially if it's cold. They don't want me to be sad. I really appreciate it, their concern and all. But it helps me to come here. I just stay a little while. Thinking about him hurts, but it helps me.*

We have an instinctive desire to help the people we love avoid pain. We want them to feel better. But pain is a part of life and love; where death has separated the two, it is inevitable. This woman is doing herself more good than her friends would do her if they succeeded in their attempts to sweep her grief under the rug. She loved her son's body throughout his life, from powdering his little bottom to bandaging his scraped knees to pretending not to notice his unneeded first shave. She's his mom, and that's a lifetime job. It doesn't end because he has died. There is so much contact that she can't have now, so much that used to be physical which can now be only in her mind. She's getting on with her life just fine. But she has the right to grieve, and to go to this place which houses what remains of the body she treasured is part of her grieving.

NOVEMBER 17

"All is flux, nothing stays still." —HERACLITUS

It may actually snow a little today, they said on the radio this morning. If it does, it will be our first snow of the season. Pretty early for New York: we don't usually get snow until the end of November. Sometimes not even then.

My memory is that we used to get it earlier. And that we used to get more of it. *Global warming,* we tell each other whenever the subject of mild winters comes up. *Probably not,* say the scientific types, pointing to worldwide averages and cycles and things. *Your area may be having warmer winters, but other places are colder. It averages out.*

I call my dad. *It's about eighty-five out here,* he says, *and we're waiting for the rain.* They've been dry as a bone in California. In Minnesota, where my stepdaughter lives, it's cold as usual, and they've been having snow for a while. They had eight inches just yesterday, so it's about normal out there.

But I still think things have changed. You don't smell burning leaves in the fall like you used to, or burning trash, either. It's against the law to burn stuff now. But that smoky smell in the air is not what I think of when someone mentions pollution. It was an exciting and wonderful smell. And I remember frost on the ground in October ... where the heck is the frost?

It's funny how I want the weather to be the same as it was when I was a little girl. I am so different from what I was then, but I want the world to be the same. When something as large as the weather turns out to be changeable too, it's a little nerve-racking.

NOVEMBER 18

"Strike, but hear me." —THEMISTOCLES

A group of people in a discussion group have been assigned a fifteen-minute discussion about homosexuality. They come from a variety of religious backgrounds: Catholic, Protestant of various types, Episcopalian. They come from different cultural and ethnic backgrounds as well: African-Americans, Caribbean-Americans, Anglo-Americans, Latino.

The discussion is an emotional one. Some people want to talk about homosexuality as if it were a sin, others as if it were a disease. Others are angered by both of these approaches and view it as simply a given for a small portion of the total population. Some worry about gay people as role models for young people, and think they shouldn't teach, or be religious leaders. Others worry more about narrow-minded individuals being role models for our children than about gay ones.

If there are any gay people in this discussion group, they sure aren't talking. So we're missing a piece here: we're talking about people without hearing from them directly. That's a real problem, for nobody knows how it is to be in a situation except the person who is in it. People often don't want to hear from those who represent something about which they feel strongly negative, though, as if they feared being talked into something wrong.

But nobody really talks anybody into anything. People make up their own minds. Sometimes they *change* their minds. But nobody does this *to* them: they do it themselves.

The people in the group are all friends and colleagues. They like each other. You can tell they feel uncomfortable about the vehemence. with which they disagree about this difficult issue. They wish they all felt the same, and that their disagreements didn't make them feel angry. But an hour later, when the discussion has moved on to other things, harmony has been restored. They didn't kill each other after all. They remember that they are friends.

Don't talk about religion or politics, people say. But you should be able to talk with people you care for about things that matter.

NOVEMBER 19

"We don't know how lucky we are."

After spending a couple of weeks watching other people catch the flu, I seem to be coming down with it myself. A sore patch on one side of my throat that won't go away. Oh, no.

One meeting today can't be canceled or postponed. I suffer through it, my throat growing more painful with each minute. Afterward, I talk to a man I haven't seen in a while. *Saw a friend of yours yesterday,* he says, and we talk about our mutual acquaintance. He's worried about him: he's suddenly lost a lot of weight. Oh, I say, and my heart sinks. We both know that our friend's companion died of AIDS. And now it may be his turn, a journey that can end only in death, often heralded by a sudden profound loss of weight.

After the meeting, I go home. I drink lots of orange juice and take some aspirin. I curl up on the couch under a quilt. I feel awful, but I know that I'll be better soon. Maybe tomorrow. Maybe it will take a few days. I think of my friend, who probably also feels awful today and has no such assurance. He is young, younger than I am by at least ten years. He has lost someone he dearly loved and now faces his own mortal illness. He cannot count on his body to mend itself, as I can.

So many people know this sorrow who shouldn't: young people, watching their strong, beautiful bodies waste and weaken. In the terminology of the AIDS epidemic, this phenomenon—the sudden loss of weight and muscle—is called the "wasting syndrome." *Waste* is just the right word: the flower of a generation, young men and women, young children, spent too soon, before they have had a chance to become who they might have been.

I hate having the flu. But I am so lucky to be only temporarily ill.

NOVEMBER 20

"In the midst of life, we are in death." —DIES IRAE

We were sitting at dinner last night when we heard a terrible screech of tires and the even more terrible sound of two cars colliding. Outside, three women, blessedly unhurt, surveyed their crumpled cars and waited for the police. Soon the cops arrived, and the ritual of finding out what happened, and how it happened, got underway. We went out to see what we could do, and what we could do turned out to be letting one of the young women use our telephone.

Mom and I were in an accident, she said into the phone to her sister, and went on to detail the damage to the front end of her car. Her voice was taut with excitement; the crash was a bad thing, for sure, but there was also a celebrity to it, a certain jubilation in having been singled out in such a remarkable way. Right up to the jaws of death they came, she and her mother, close enough to reach out and touch it, and then they were snatched away, safe and sound.

Thank God nobody was badly hurt, she said. True. Amazing, though, how little permanent comfort that thought actually is. One ought to be grateful for being alive, and one certainly is, but the bottom line is that an accident is a royal pain in the neck: after the initial glow of realizing you still have vital signs, you're just irritated. *I don't have time for this,* you think. *Tough,* says life. *Here it is anyway.*

Of course, tomorrow she's going to have to get on the phone with her insurance people and see about getting a new car. It was a small truck, actually, and it sure looked totaled to me. *My brother uses it for work,* she said. *It was full of his carpenter's tools.* Where's his job tomorrow morning, and how's he going to get there? I could see that she and her mother were trying to figure these things out already. So much for celebrity and jubilation and being glad to be alive: irritation is all that will remain of this mishap in the morning.

But in the midst of the irritation, something will remind her: a newspaper story, television coverage of a terrible accident. From time to time, maybe for the rest of her life, she will remember that today could have been the day on which she died. And that, for some reason she can never know, it turned out that it was not.

NOVEMBER 21

"'S wonderful! 'S marvelous!" —IRA GERSHWIN

A friend was talking to her elderly mother, telling her that she was doing some research on Josephine Baker, the African American dancer who was the toast of Paris in the 1920s. "Oh, she loved you!" her mother exclaimed, and it turned out to be the truth: my friend's father was in vaudeville, and one night during Baker's American tour he took his daughter backstage to meet the star, who covered her with kisses and greasepaint.

Abandoned at an early age, Baker began working as a domestic when she was eight. She began hanging around the saloons and bordellos of St. Louis, soaking up the jazz, and started performing in public when she was ten. Her comic style and exotic beauty attracted the attention of bigger and bigger producers. As soon as she was sixteen she worked on Broadway, quickly becoming a star. When she went to France it was love at first sight: she reveled in the freedom of a society that didn't know about Jim Crow. She became rich and poor and rich again and poor again, accumulating and discarding husbands and fame as she lived a life that epitomized *le jazz hot*. During the war she was a spy for the French resistance, using her fame and beauty as bait for unwary German and Italian officials. She adopted twelve children from many different nations, all waifs as she had been. She crossed the Atlantic several times, reeling from the fresh slap of racism each time she returned to America, and then fighting back, integrating lunch counters and rest rooms a full decade before the sit-ins of the 1950s and early 60s. She died after attending a gala in Paris in honor of her remarkable life. The autopsy showed that she died of a cerebral hemorrhage. Those who knew her said no. She simply died of joy.

NOVEMBER 22

"You pays your money, and you takes your choice."

I only just got home. It doesn't happen too often anymore, getting home this late in the evening. It used to happen all the time, and I used to wonder what on earth families were for if they weren't for being with in the evening. I would work all day and into the night and then crawl back home, exhausted. Too tired to do anything but go to bed. Then I would get up the next morning and do it all again. I managed to be affable with my loved ones in those days, but that was about it.

That job was definitely fast track. It looked fabulous on a résumé. Somewhere along the line, though, a person has to decide whether she's living for her résumé or for herself. Whatever is on the other side, we only go around once in this life, so we'd better have the quality of life we choose. We may not get a chance to choose again.

It's important to admit that there is a cost to making that choice, though. If you choose not to go all out for whatever it is that counts for success in your profession, you will not get the rewards that go with it. The people who decided to tough it out on the fast track will. You can't have it both ways—that only happens on TV, I think. You have to be at peace with that, to be able to say to yourself, *yeah, I'm not going to be the most famous or the most important at this, and I can live with that. There are things I value more than being number one.* You'd better come to terms with what's important to you—not to someone else, but to you—and then be sure you're spending as much of your time as you can paying attention to that and not to something else.

"There's nothing like a good, homecooked meal."

Cooking from scratch is not time-consuming. I mean, it doesn't have to be. I, for instance, am making butterflied leg of lamb and ratatouille right at this very moment. The lamb is sitting in a dish of olive oil and a little lemon juice, with garlic poked into its crevices. It can sit there for a couple of hours, and then it cooks very quickly. My eggplant, onions, garlic, and tomatoes meal melt together in a slow oven all afternoon. It's a fabulous meal.

Of course, you do have to be here to get that slow oven started. That is why I can only do this kind of thing on a day off, when I'm home. When my kids were little I was part of the crockpot movement, a generation of women who threw a chuck roast into the pot on their way out the door so that the family could have a homecooked meal that evening. Of course, everything was very well-done when you used that method, and everything somehow looked alike after a long day in the crockpot. My kids got sick of stewed meals pretty quickly. Besides, the pot reminded them that I wasn't there, and they didn't always like that. Now I don't even know where my crockpot is. I see other people's, sometimes, though, at yard sales: tired olive green crockpots from the Seventies, waiting quietly to provide the olfactory illusion of mom in the kitchen in someone else's home.

It's not hard to cook from scratch. I'd love to do it every night, but I don't. We eat out sometimes. We order Chinese food sometimes, and nobody dies when we do. Nobody died from the stuff that came out of the crockpot, either. However much groaning there was around our house about it, it was nice to be greeted by the wonderful smell of dinner all ready to eat when we walked in the door.

NOVEMBER 24

"Come, ye thankful people, come...."

I sprang out of bed today at six-thirty in the morning. It is Thanksgiving; I am a domestic frenzy itching to happen. My husband suggested an alternative to mashed potatoes. Maybe we should have scalloped potatoes this year for a change. No. I am the Great Dictator of Thanksgiving. It has to be the same food every year.

All day I cooked and listened to the radio. Anna made apple sauce and cranberry sauce. Corinna brought a new sweet potato recipe, the only experimentation we seem able to tolerate. The turkey announced its readiness by popping out its plastic bellybutton about three hours before it was time, and one set of guests was forty-five minutes late. *Next year we'll tell them three o'clock*, said Corinna. But when we finally were assembled and seated, it was perfect. *The best Thanksgiving ever,* we all said.

And yet there was not a person there who is not dealing with something difficult in his or her life. A friend and his mother will stop by the nursing home later to take a plate to his dad. Another longs to see the sister he left behind in North Korea forty years ago, a girl of twenty-three who is now a woman of sixty-five. Several at the table quietly wear the scars of divorce. A couple face unemployment at the end of the year. That's just four weeks away.

All these problems will be with us tomorrow. But we can choose the attitude with which we walk through the highs and lows of life. And, since being miserable won't make my troubles end any sooner, I'm going with gratitude for what I've got.

NOVEMBER 25

"When the going gets tough, the tough go shopping." —MODERN PROVERB

The day after Thanksgiving. America's biggest shopping day. Although I know better, I have gone with my daughter and granddaughters to look for a refrigerator for their new home. The traffic is horrendous. We inch along a four-lane highway lined with stores. All the parking lots are full, and we have to follow a man to his car and wait until he leaves to get a parking place.

The appliance store is mobbed. Past rank on rank of televisions (all tuned to the same soap opera), past rows of vacuum cleaners and vaporizers and stoves, we make our way to the back of the refrigerator section, where the cheaper models without icemakers gather in humble rows, like the sarcophagi of third-rate mummies. Corinna is a pit bull when she shops; she never pays full price. Never. It is hard to find a salesperson, but she locates one and begins to deal. I take the kids over to watch the rows of televisions. Thirty or forty images of the same man look longingly at thirty or forty images of the same woman in a satin nightgown. *Why is the lady on TV green, Mamo,* Rosie wants to know. A passing salesman hears her and scowls.

It's funny to be in this temple of consumerism the day after such a lovely Thanksgiving. Yesterday's contentment is the opposite of today's buying frenzy. We'll get a good deal on the refrigerator; Corinna will see to that. But as I look at the hordes of shoppers and their bored children, at the neon signs and the thirty televisions with the thirty identical soap operas, I remember yesterday. *Whew.* Let's strive after yesterday's peace instead. It is pure gold.

NOVEMBER 26

"The thing I fear most is fear." —MONTAIGNE

When a bomb exploded in the World Trade Center in New York City, two classes of kindergartners were among the thousands temporarily trapped in the immense twin towers. I leave it to the imagination of anyone who has parented a five-year-old, or remembers being one, to contemplate getting twenty or thirty of them down 107 flights of stairs in pitch darkness amid clouds of sooty smoke. Friends of mine who made that frightening descent themselves describe being unable to see where they were going, unable to breathe deeply, and uncertain of what lay at the bottom of the stairs. They were terrified, and they were adults.

I read in the paper that the children kept their spirits up by singing as they trudged down those stairs. And that the songs they sang were Thanksgiving songs. Imagine those little voices, singing about turkeys and pilgrims and the richness of this great country, going down and down in the sooty darkness, not knowing where they were going but plugging along anyway. The most daring stunt man in Hollywood is not braver than those children and their teachers.

In ways not nearly so dramatic or so immediately frightening, all of life is something like that terrifying descent: we never know for sure what lies ahead. And the courage to keep on walking comes from singing our songs, the songs that remind us of how wonderful a thing it is to live in this world, how passionately we long to continue living in it. And all of life's victories are something like that last step from the smoke and darkness, finally into the light of day.

NOVEMBER 27

"...tie up thy fears...." —GEORGE HERBERT

In Minnesota where my mother grew up, ice skating is usually possible from November to the end of March, sometimes even longer. They put warming houses up on the lakeshore; there's a woodstove inside, and skaters can come in and escape the sub-zero temperatures.

One day my mother was skating after school. As it grew near to supper-time, she made her way to the warming house to take off her skates, put on her boots, and start for home. But the warming house was crowded, and she was too shy to push her way in, or even to ask. She decided she would just go home and warm up when she got there.

It was farther than she thought. Her feet, already cold from skating, grew colder with every step. They were blocks of ice, it seemed; soon, she couldn't

215

make them obey her. She couldn't walk. She knew how dangerous this was. *I will die from the cold here by the side of the road*, she thought, and began to cry. Her tears froze on her face.

The story had a happy ending: her father came out looking for her. He carried her home and washed her feet over and over with lukewarm water until they began to sting so much that she cried again—*a good sign*, he said. The next day she was as good as new.

I never forgot the story of how my mother almost froze to death when she was little. The part that stayed with me was the picture of her standing uncertainly outside the warming house, not wanting to be a bother to anyone. My mother was an unassuming person, reluctant to ask anything for herself. This is a good thing, but it can be overdone. On that particular day, it could have killed her.

NOVEMBER 28

"Laughter is the best medicine." —PROVERB

It's two in the morning, but I happen to be awake, perhaps because of the flu medicine I took a few hours ago. Its label alleges a side effect of drowsiness, but adds further down in the small print that it may cause excitability or nervousness in some patients, of whom I must be one.

So I thought I'd try to do some work. I have a stunningly boring sociology text to read for school and some business letters to write. If that won't put me to sleep, nothing will.

The lady who presides over my radio station at night has elected to intersperse tonight's offerings with overtures from Gilbert and Sulivan operas. She plays *The Mikado* in its entirety, a 1950s production with Groucho Marx as KoKo. Instead of doing the work I should be doing, I find myself listening to Groucho and laughing out loud. The performance goes on for about an hour and a half. Somewhere in the middle of it, I drift easily into sleep. The alarm wakens me at seven. The sociology book is lying open on my chest.

I didn't read the sociology book, but Groucho and I had an absolutely wonderful time. I didn't read myself to sleep; I laughed myself to sleep. You can't be tense when you laugh, you know; laughter is a muscle relaxant. An enzyme or something is released into the blood; it's what makes us feel weak and floppy after we've laughed a lot. That is not a bad deal: a sleeping potion that you make yourself just by listening to something funny and laughing at it. The human body knows how to get what it needs. Imagine a complex chemical process like that depending on as social a thing as laughter. I'm going to remember that little gift we have the next time I find myself awake at night.

"Do not veil the truth with falsehood..." —THE KORAN

A family is waiting for the train on the same subway platform on which I wait: a man and his wife and two little girls. The father wears an African-style tunic and trousers. The mother and daughters wear the white veil that identifies them as Muslims. They are Muslims American-style: the veils do not cover their faces, only their hair, and they wear western-style dresses. The severity of the white band framing their faces draws attention to their fine features and beautiful dark eyes.

Americans usually think of Muslim women as oppressed. The veil, in particular, seems to Americans to be an obvious symbol of submission to male authority, and you sometimes read articles by American women who have traveled in African or the Near East and returned home longing for their Muslim sisters to be set free.

We need to be aware, though, that Muslim women themselves do not always see veiling in this way. The invitation our brief attire extends to men we don't even know to admire our bodies seems to many Muslim women to be anything but an expression of freedom. Distinctive Muslim dress also signifies pride in their own faith and heritage, a heritage many Muslims correctly believe is not understood or respected by Westerners. We assume everyone would choose to be like us if she had the chance. This is not true. Doubtless many would. But not everyone.

Last year there was an Olympic-style athletic competition for Muslim women. Competition was fierce and professional, Coverage of the games—the judging, and everything needed to support the athletic competition—was done by women. In most events the Iranian women prevailed. Many of them were militia veterans from their country's long war with Iraq. Their costumes were very brief; they relaxed their rules about dress completely in the luxury of their female-only surroundings. A women-only Olympics? This is the last thing most of us would expect to find in the world of Islam, but it happened.

"Darkness is not dark to you..." —PSALM 139

W hat a chic apartment we have. It has gorgeous wood floors and a sophisticated paint job, one which makes the most of the architectural details of this former warehouse. It has a European kitchen with three ovens in it. It has two bathrooms. One of them has an enormous mirror in it, so that two people can admire themselves simultaneously side-by-side. The mirror is surrounded by large round lightbulbs, the kind movie stars have in their dressing rooms. They are very bright.

I lie in bed. Out of the corner of my eye, I can see into the bathroom. My daughter has turned on the movie star lights so that she can put on makeup. They are so bright they hurt my eyes. *I confess*, I yell. *Turn off the interrogation lamp!* I can't quite take those lights in the morning, either. I am unprepared for the way they search out and illumine each crow's-foot.

The garish light of the movie star lamps invades the soft darkness of the room like an unwelcome in-law. Anna obligingly turns them off, and I am alone again in the dark. It feels good to lie down in the dark. I remember a time when I was afraid of it, when familiar furniture seemed large and sinister in the darkness. It is not so now. I feel peace and rest, relief from the artificiality of the various lights through which I move every day. I cuddle under the quilt, and am deliciously warm. My various fractured bones hurt most of the time these days, and they appreciate the chance to be horizontal. Against the dark of the room, the windows show me the night sky, and the blocky buildings which stand against it become lovely.

DECEMBER 1

"Nobly to live, or else nobly to die, befits proud birth." —SOPHOCLES

Mary Fisher is the single mother of two small boys. She is HIV-positive. She was not in any of the high-risk groups. She contracted the virus through her husband, who had used intravenous drugs. Mary's family is wealthy. She knows that her family will love and care for her children if she dies. But she also knows that nobody could love them as she does, and that they will be permanently scarred if AIDS takes her from them before her time. She works hard to stay well, and so far she has managed to do so.

She also works hard at educating the people she meets about the disease. She does not have the luxury of telling herself that AIDS is someone else's problem. So she travels all over the country, asking the powerful people among whom she has moved all her life to stop and listen. She "specializes" in audiences who have not yet come to see AIDS as having anything to do with them or their families. Hers is a compelling prophecy of compassion to those who would rather talk about something else.

I would never have chosen to be HIV-positive, she told the Republican National Conventional. But she took this thing for which she did not ask and made it into something that can only be described as holy, something that joins her to unpopular groups—drug users, gay men, minorities—that society easily dismisses. *I am one with them*, she says. Whatever contribution to the world Mary Fisher might have made if she had not become infected with HIV, it is hard to imagine it being more important to more people than the one she's making now.

DECEMBER 2

"A journey of a thousand miles must begin with a single step." —LAO-TZU

Sixty sit-ups is a lot. There was a time when I did two hundred a day—*I swear* I am not making that up—but sixty is a lot for someone with my injuries. When I lie down on the floor to begin, it seems like an impossible number. I divide them up into groups of twenty. It is my hope that I will get stronger and stronger, and then I'll be able to do them in two groups of thirty. And then maybe all sixty at once, after a while.

Twenty is not so many. You can do sixty easily if you only do them twenty at a time. This is not a bad rule for the rest of life, either. Most of the things which seem so daunting when taken as a whole are quite do-able if you break them into several pieces. You do the beginning. Then you do the middle. Then the end. You don't do any task all in one gulp; you do it a piece at a time.

It is a curious truth that people who consistently do not achieve according to their abilities often have higher standards of what the result of a task should be than other people. Their standards are so high that they are afraid even to begin, fearing that they will never do it perfectly. Or they are afraid to leave one stage of a task and go on to the next; they know they could have done the first better. They are daunted by the enormity of the task, and so they do not attempt it; this would be like my not doing any sit-ups at all because I knew I couldn't do sixty at one time.

High standards are a good thing to have. *Impossible* standards don't do anybody any good. Something is better than nothing, which is what you get if you never begin at all.

DECEMBER 3

"Music hath charms to soothe a savage breast." —WILLIAM CONGREVE

Elevator music is an enormous industry. Stores subscribe to it because they think it makes people buy more, and studies have shown that they are right. Offices use it because they think it makes workers calmer and more productive; in a program of canned music, there are cycles that dictate a movement from slow songs to more up-tempo ones, on the theory that the gradual acceleration is energizing. Offices play such cycles especially in the afternoon, when people tend to get sleepy.

Not every popular song ends up in our nation's elevators. It can't be too rhythmic, and the performers can't be too individualistic: we shouldn't be able to identify them. They should sound generic. Lots of strings. Very little brass.

Christmas music too is introduced according to a strict schedule: so many carols per hour, beginning after Thanksgiving and building slowly to an emotionless peak on Christmas Eve, after which they abruptly disappear.

Stores and businesses wouldn't use this stuff if it didn't work for them. So we're being manipulated by canned music, among other things. That's a little disconcerting. But sometimes our individuality strikes back: sometimes the elevator music turns out to be a song from childhood, something my mother used to sing, and I am suddenly back there. Not a worker. Not a shopper. Not even here—back there.

Hah.

DECEMBER 4

"I know how those in exile feed on dreams of hope." —AESCHYLUS

On the radio this morning, there was a report about a big celebratory party made up entirely of people whose candidate had just lost an election. They had a fabulous band and great food, and about two thousand people attended. A lot of them were young people who had actually worked on the campaign. Of course they hadn't been invited to any of the victory parties, so they decided to have one of their own. *Why not have a good time?* said the young man whose idea it was. *This is politics. You win, you lose. There's always next time.*

That guy's a survivor. There's a widespread tendency to avoid admitting defeat, to reframe losses so they sound like victories. But this is a dangerous thing to do: if you can never admit that you lost or failed, you never get around to figuring out where you went wrong so you can change your strategy and win next time. You just keep doing the same thing again and again, and you keep losing.

I always do something wonderful for myself when I lose, and I lose fairly often. First, treating myself well makes me feel better, and I need that, because I hate losing. Second, some kind of celebratory event provides an AMEN to the loss: I blew it, I've observed the loss in a way that is healing to me, and now it's time to go on with my life. Finally, giving myself a treat when I lose takes the shame out of it and brings the loss out into the open, where I may examine it and grow from it: I don't have to hide anything, don't have to pretend it didn't happen, and this helps me to get honest about what I have to do to avoid another failure.

"Better late than never."

Another major oil spill yesterday, this one off the coast of Spain. As big as the *Exxon Valdez*, maybe. The vessel tried to come into the harbor in rough weather without a pilot, which turned out to be a bad idea. Now the captain is refusing to cooperate with the authorities. He's in deep doo-doo, as they say in Spain.

The captain works for the ship owner. That's why he's not talking: the owner has told him not to. So he can't respond to the flurry of questions which now surround him. This leaves the media no choice but to speculate on what happened. The captain's the visible person in this incident, so the questions and blame focus on him. It's safe to say that it will be a while before he works again.

Probably the full investigation, when it finally happens, will reveal that this thing happened because of his error. But sometimes people are faced with the choice between following a bad order and losing their jobs, and this may be what happened to this guy. The company may have told him to get that ship in yesterday, period. He knows that if he doesn't do what the owner wants him to do, a captain who will can easily be found.

Organizations sometimes become more concerned with their own institutional power arrangements than with whatever it was they set out to do. This can make a worker cynical: your job becomes making your boss and your boss's boss look good and feel good. If you do this, you have succeeded. If you do not, no matter what else you may have accomplished, you have failed. And if things go wrong because of this, you are likely to be the one who takes the heat. As the sea captain sitting in his ship off the oilsoaked coast of Spain is currently finding out.

DECEMBER 6

"Time discovers truth." —SENECA

Red Barber, a famous baseball announcer, died recently in Florida at the age of eighty-four. Right up until his death, he used to talk on the radio on Friday mornings with a younger announcer—a guy half his age. Red would talk about some unforgettable player of the Forties, and Bob would ask him questions about the game and how it has changed over the years. The talk often didn't stay on baseball; Red and Bob would start out talking about Roger Maris's record-breaking homer and end up discussing moral values. Red was gently humorous. He spoke simply. Bob would laugh at his digressions with the combination of amusement and respect you hear in young people's voices when they talk to old people: *This guy's old*, his tone would say, *but damn, he's on the ball*.

It's easy for someone who is still at the busy stage of life to forget about the great gifts of age: wisdom and serenity. Not everybody develops these things, but it looks to me like more do than don't. Old people have seen a lot. They know that things come and go. They've won some things and lost others.

So they are a good antidote to our exaggerated self-importance: about what we're doing, about its outcome, about our own winning and losing. We get so involved in our busy lives and their important goals that it feels as if they were matters of life and death. Old people know that they are not. If this doesn't work, you won't die. You'll just do something else.

Bob did a tribute to Red on the radio a few days after Red died. *Good-bye, old-timer*, he said. He's going to miss their talks. He talked about needing Red's wisdom, about there being so much more he had wanted to ask him. I think I'll call my dad today.

DECEMBER 7

"Comes a pause in the day's occupation that is known as the children's hour."
—HENRY WADSWORTH LONGFELLOW

Having finished another essay, I move the mouse over to the solitaire icon on the computer screen and click it twice. As the cards appear on the screen, shuffled and ready to play, I feel a flutter of anticipation. It's familiar: it's the same feeling I get when I have spread something wonderful out on the table to eat all by myself. Or when I open a letter from someone I haven't heard from in a while. It's the brief feeling of being on vacation. *This is going to be good*, it says.

It is a secret pleasure, this solitaire game I use to reward myself for writing. Nobody else benefits from it but me. And, if the truth were known, I don't benefit all that much. Maybe I sharpen my wits a bit, but not in any way that matters a whole lot. It is only for fun. Part of its pleasure is the secret-ness of it, and that is also what makes me feel a little bit guilty. I hide with it, like an addict taking a liquor bottle into the bathroom where nobody will see her have a drink. When somebody comes into my study and I am relaxing with a quick game, I feel as if I'd been caught goofing off.

You shouldn't need a reward for writing an essay, my inner parent tells my inner child. *You're a writer for heaven's sake. You love to write. Writing essays is what you do. You shouldn't waste your time on a silly game.*

Nonsense, says my inner forty-one-year-old. *Yeah, I'm a writer. Yeah, I love to write. But I need a change of pace, a little rest in between work periods. Everybody needs that. However much you love your work, you can't do it perpetually and continue to do it well. Or continue to enjoy it. You need to vary it.*

222

I slide the mouse over to the games icon and click. An inviting array of cards appears on the screen, ready to play. *Okay, friend, deal me in.*

DECEMBER 8

"The great man is he who does not lose his child's-heart." —MENCIUS

By the time she has paid her mortgage, her childcare, and her grocery bill, Corinna has hardly anything left over. But she always has her Christmas gifts bought before anyone else. She starts combing the stores for bargains early in the fall, and manages to find just the right gift for everyone. They are never expensive, but each is purchased with the recipient's individuality in mind. She is the first to have her Christmas cards done.

She has always loved getting ready for the holidays. I remember her sitting at the kitchen table when she was five, working hard on decorations made of loose pearls from a string that broke and sticks left over from the ice cream bars of summer. Twenty years later they still hang on our tree, lopsided and missing more pearls than they retain, but still beautiful to her mom. So much work for my little girl, so long ago.

I savor her continuing sense of excitement. It's not easy to be excited when you're grown up and life is hard. You become the one responsible for making magic happen, and people who continue to expect it to drop into their laps are disappointed people at this time of year. But it's amazing how many people continue to do that: they go along in their everyday routine until the holidays are upon them, and then feel hurt and angry because the holidays are not special, when they haven't done a thing to make them so.

The holidays we observe at this time of year celebrate miraculous events. Because we know these stories of the miraculous, we long for a miracle in our lives most keenly in these weeks. But we remember that in those stories, people had been looking and hoping and working for the liberation symbolized in the miracles for many years. It was those who were not looking for it who saw nothing. The perception of miracle in your life is up to you. The act of getting ready helps you see it.

DECEMBER 9

"Pluralism lets things really exist..." —WILLIAM JAMES

A string of blinking lights hangs clumsily across the window of the gas station as I pull in for a tankful of regular. The guys have decorated for Christmas, I see: a white plastic reindeer with large, babylike eyes stands in the window next to a display of antifreeze, and they have sprayed the edges of all the windows with fake snow, an act they will regret come February, when they get around to scraping it off the glass.

Some workplaces are chic and shiny and well-designed; at holiday time, a florist comes in with discreet pots of poinsettia and abstract arrangements of tall twigs painted white. Many more are not: the gas stations, the government offices, the taxi stands, the diners. I am always touched to see how people who work there have tried to spruce them up a little for the holidays, how they have twined tinsel garlands around the bulletin board and pinned Christmas cards to the wall.

I guess it has something to do with self definition: this is who I am. And with group definition: this is what we celebrate. That's why this time of year can be awfully hard on people whose religious heritage is something other than Christianity, which is a growing number of Americans. They feel as if they were not part of the "we" the decorations celebrate. It's not that they dislike the Christian faith, or that they don't like to see people have a good time. They usually don't even say anything: why make a fuss? It's only that this particular kind of self-definition is one they can't share. Something to keep in mind when you're deciding how to adorn your office for the holidays.

DECEMBER 10

"The mirth and fun grew fast and furios." —ROBERT BURNS

As the commuter train hurtles through Elizabeth without stopping, we pass the municipal pool. It is empty and deserted, a cold, dark rectangle beside the railroad tracks.

It's so different in the summertime: a bright patch of aqua rippling quietly in the morning sun, full of kids every hot afternoon. We get only snapshots as we zip past: shiny wet bodies bobbing in and out of the water, kids bouncing off the diving board with their arms and legs at crazy angles. I cannot hear their shrieks from the train, but I can see them.

There is more room for fun in the summer than there is in the winter. The dark afternoons of December do not beckon us out into them; we scurry home to dinner and homework. We do not linger. Winter seems endless to kids, an eternity of heavy clothes and lost mittens. It is less endless to us: adults marvel together in December about where the year has gone, marvel at how short each year has become.

The seeming endlessness of time is one of the great gifts of youth. In my memory, the summers of my childhood were long and languid. A year was forever. Winter went on and on. Time was cheap. We spent it like water.

We did not know then how short life would be. Just as well: we might have lived desperately, tried to make every minute educational. We might have taken notes. We might not have thought there was time to stay in the water for just five more minutes, to lie on the rug and stare into the orange embers of a winter fire.

DECEMBER 11

"Silver and gold I have none, but such as I have give I thee."
—ACTS OF THE APOSTLES 3:6

A friend is exploring a vocation to a religious order. When people find out about it, most of them are horrified. It seems to them that she is giving up everything that makes life good: freedom to decide for herself, the right to keep the money she makes and the things it will buy, the possibility of love and marriage and motherhood.

And all those things are good. It will be hard to say good-bye to some of them. *Well, the vowed life is not for everyone,* she says. *It's always been a minority lifestyle.*

Becoming a nun was the last thing she would ever have wanted for herself, she tells me. As a young person, she looked at it as a life of complete deprivation. Now she sees it as a life that says no to some things in order to say yes to others more completely. Empty of some things, it will be full of others.

For several years now, she has been restless. Something has been missing from her life, and she hasn't quite been able to put her finger on it. But the first evening she visited the sisters, the feeling of coming home washed over her in a sweet wave. *It just feels right,* she says, *I can't explain it any better than that.* She is as excited about her new life as any bride is about hers. As any incoming freshman is about hers. As any expectant mother is about hers. As full of dreams, doubts, hopes, and fears as any of them.

DECEMBER 12

"A clear fire, a clean hearth...." —CHARLES LAMB

I don't know how to light a fire. I watch my husband do it all the time: newspapers on bottom, small wood on top of that, and logs on the very top. I duplicate this arrangement and light it. The newspapers blaze briefly, then subside to spend the rest of the evening in a sullen smolder. He comes along, and puts it back together exactly the way I had it; it bursts forth into a blaze right out of Charles Dickens.

My father was also good with a fire. I used to watch him, and attempt to duplicate his fire-laying technique, too. Nothing. It's been fifty or sixty thousand years, I guess, that women have been lighting cooking fires. It's just a good thing they weren't left in my care. None of us would be here today.

But I wish I could light them so they'd stay lit. I'd have one all the time if I could. *It's just as well,* my husband tells me; *it doesn't really heat the house, you know. More heat goes up the chimney than goes out into the room.* I tell him that the psychological effect is worth the cost and that I would wear sweaters.

Words have a special power when they are spoken by firelight. They seem to mean more, as if every remark were a precious confidence not entrusted to just anyone. Firelight makes people feel safe; we are encircled by cold darkness, but the firelight is cheerful and brave. Wild beasts will not come near us. Surrounded as most of us are by wild beasts of some kind, not all of them physical, we draw closer to the brave crackle, and we are safe.

DECEMBER 13

"Sweet dreams."

How long do I have to rest, Rosie asks for the sixth time, and I stifle a scolding reply. You haven't even started yet, I remind her. You've just been wiggling and talking. That's not resting.

Her sister, who is younger, snuggles into her comforter and is asleep within five minutes. But of course: three-year-olds need naps more than six-year-olds do. I've got some nerve, even *trying* to sell a nap to somebody that age.

I remember how mean-spirited adults seemed when they imposed an unwanted nap on me, how utter was their disregard for my inner rhythm, how interminable the afternoon when I was supposed to be napping. *I'll lie down with you for a few minutes,* I tell Rosie, *and we can cuddle. You don't have to sleep, you can just give your body a rest.*

I join the girls on the couches we have pushed together to make a bed in the living room. I awaken forty-five minutes later to the regular breathing of two sleeping sisters. I didn't work while they were sleeping. I *slept* while they were sleeping. That was not my intention. My picture of the afternoon was that I would work efficiently and creatively in the silence of their nap, a benign, industrious presence in the corner of the room. Their loving grandmother, keeping them safe in slumber while doing her important work. A grandmother for the Nineties. But Nineties grandmothers need rest, too, I tell myself, and then I creep carefully out of bed to get some work done before the little girls wake up and it's too late.

DECEMBER 14

"In all abundance there is lack." —HIPPOCRATES

The heat in our building is centrally controlled. I suppose it's a desire to control costs that prompts the heat to go off during the day, but there it is. I suppose most people are out during the day. But I happen to work at home most days, and by ten in the morning it's pretty cold in here. I listen hopefully for the hiss of the radiators, but they are cold and silent, and so am I.

I go into the kitchen and turn on the oven, setting it all the way up to five hundred degrees. I leave the oven door open. I am hoping that this will bring some heat into the apartment. All over the city, people in slum apartments are turning on their ovens, too, hoping for the same thing. Every year there are terrible fires caused by people doing this. Often children are killed in these fires.

This week there was a story in the paper about a nursing home in Bosnia in which a number of elderly people froze to death in their beds. They had run out of fuel of any kind. A photograph showed an old man, bundled up in a coat with a blanket over his head sitting despondently on the edge of his bed. His wife's shrouded body lay on the floor. All that was visible of her were her feet, her sad little feet still in their house slippers. What a terrible thing to happen to an old lady.

I feel sorry for myself because I am cold. But I will not die from the cold, like that tiny old lady. Or like some children will, here in New York this winter. The heat will come on later this afternoon. I am very lucky. It could easily have been another way.

DECEMBER 15

"God rest ye merry...." —ENGLISH CAROL

This is the absolute worst time of year, my friend says grimly as we walk along the sidewalk. Her mixed marriage requires every ounce of diplomatic skill she has: balancing the Christmas present hysteria her kids imbibe from the television and from their friends with her husband's seriousness about their Jewish observance; trying to explain to her parents why he can't join them for their Christmas tree trimming party. *I'm a basket case every year.*

Jewish parents feel swallowed up by Christmas. Wanting their kids to feel easy with their peers but proud of their own heritage, they are assaulted on every side by the allurements of the season. Intermarried couples are even more torn. My friend experiences a double whammy: trying to protect her kids' Jewish heritage but knowing that she herself represents a threat to it in the eyes of many Jews. Another friend says this is a terrific time of year to visit her family in Israel and ditch the whole problem.

Two festivals of deliverance—the Christians' celebration of the Nativity and the Jewish Festival of Light—shouldn't put a good woman like my friend in bondage. This season should be wonderful, not awful. She and her family deserve better.

She's going to have to claim her own turf if she's ever going to get some peace at this time of year. She'll have to do with her kids what she and her husband think is most productive of joy and meaning for them and then close her ears. They'll explain to the relatives once—and then not again.

She can't make twenty relatives happy in her situation. She can only take care of her small part of the family. That's going to have to be enough.

DECEMBER 16

"Sweets grown common lose their dear delight." —SHAKESPEARE, SONNET 102

There is hardly anything we cannot easily obtain today. Raspberries in January are no problem: just a little more expensive. If you're willing to pay, you can have them. You can buy any kind of fruit and any kind of vegetable at any time of the year. We've almost forgotten the concept of something being "in season."

This gives us lots of options, but it's also something of a loss. Waiting for something to come makes you appreciate it when it finally does. The first raspberry. The first sweet corn. The ones that came in on the plane from Ecuador this morning look fabulous, but we didn't have to wait for them. We take them for granted now. And—I think—they no longer taste as wonderful.

I walk along the corridors of a shopping mall. I never come here if I can avoid it; I detest these gleaming temples to our bloated consumerism. I detest their seductions and our passivity in the face of them. But no store along Main Street in my town sells sheets, and that's what I need.

I have six or seven sheet-selling stores from which to choose here in the mall. Every sheet imaginable is here, two or three hundred patterns, easily. After the first twenty or so, I am in full sensory overload. I can't choose. I go home, sheetless.

Some of us are not designed for too many choices. One store with a modest linen department would suit me fine. I'd appreciate what I *could* have much more if I couldn't have everything.

DECEMBER 17

"Everyone helped his neighbor...." —ISAIAH 41:6

All the seats on the #2 train to Brooklyn are taken, and people are standing in the aisles. The door between our car and the next one opens, and a man with no legs rolls through on a skateboard. He stands about two and a half feet tall, including his conveyance; he is just an upper body on wheels. The car swerves and jerks mightily, but he never falls off the board. He braces himself expertly against the floor with his hands as the car lurches sideways, then pushes himself forward again.

Nobody in New York looks at anybody else on the subway, but everybody is looking at him. He works the car, holding out his paper cup for donations. I see a war between suspicion and compassion in some people's faces; compassion wins as they realize that you just can't fake having no legs, not even in New York. The most skeptical straphanger can see that this one's for real. Even people who never give to beggars reach into their pockets. Gracefully, and in complete control of his unique form of locomotion, he is out the door and across the treacherous connection into the next car.

Not long afterward another young man with a paper cup comes through. He is tall and well-made; both his legs work. The man on the skateboard proves an impossible act to follow: nobody reaches for purse or pocket. The young man passes through to the next car, where a similar reception undoubtedly awaits him.

DECEMBER 18

"At Christmas play and make good cheer, for Christmas comes but once a year." —THOMAS TUSSER

I have resisted getting ready for the holidays as I should have this year. I have been dispirited, a bit sorry for myself because my back hurts so much of the time. So I haven't shopped for food, or for presents. I haven't sent out any cards; in fact, I haven't even gotten around to buying any.

Anna is all ready, though. She has shopped slowly and carefully for the last few weeks, thinking hard about a gift for each person on her list. She wants to talk about what we should have for dinner on Christmas day, and what we should serve on New Year's Eve. As we talk about possible menus, I feel myself begin to get interested. My planning gears begin to turn. Before I get to work, I stop to buy some Christmas cards. I begin writing messages on them as I go home on the train. I also do a mental flow chart for the dinner preparations, and a gift list. By the time I get home, I am excited about Christmas.

Instead of falling exhausted into bed as I have done for months now, I dig out some decorations and begin putting them up in the places where they always go. I call Corinna to find out what Santa Claus should bring to our house for her kids and to solicit her contribution to Christmas dinner.

I know that I won't get everything done, and I don't care. I never get *everything* done. I don't have enough money to do everything I'd like to do for the holiday, but then I never do, so that doesn't matter, either. My back hurts like hell, but I no longer care about that, either. It doesn't hurt any more than it did when I was feeling so sorry for myself that I didn't care that Christmas was coming.

DECEMBER 19

"Well begun is half done." —ARISTOTLE

I am envious of those who have everything done for the holidays already. I make such good beginnings: I get my cards out of the drawer, address and mail about half of them. I have such a feeling of accomplishment about having done that that I allow myself to feel as if I'd done the job, when in fact I've only done half of it. The rest slink out the door a day or two after Christmas. Maybe even later.

Christmas Eve, and I find that I haven't gotten enough charming little things for people's stockings. I usually come to this realization after the midnight service, when there's absolutely nothing to be done about it. Throughout December I have thought of this or that appropriate little thing to pick up. But again, thinking about it gives me a feeling of having done it. I never actually get around to picking up the appropriate little things. I unwrap one of my own gifts to see if it would be good for Corinna's stocking, and it is. In it goes. The person who gave it to me will never know. You have to be hard-nosed at times like this.

Well, nobody's perfect. Everybody knows I work hard, I tell myself. And everybody knows that Christmas is a really busy time for priests. But everyone else I know works hard, too. I have no real excuse for not getting everything done except not being perfect. So that will have to do.

I don't kick myself around the block about this. These holidays are not about my perfection—or lack of it. They are about love, not deserving. You don't earn love; it's a gift. We don't buy it from one another. We *give* it.

DECEMBER 20

"Sorrow and sighing shall flee away..." —ISAIAH 35:10

The doctor dashes off a couple of prescriptions. *Take this for pain and this one at night,* he says. *The night one is an antidepressant.* I make a face. *They're muscle relaxants,* he tells me. *And they're not habit-forming, like the sedatives they gave you in the hospital.* Seeing that I am still not sold on taking mood-altering drugs for a bad back, he talks for a while about the pills and what I can expect. Still full of misgivings, I leave. I haven't made up my mind yet if I'm going to take them or not.

My acupressure therapist fixed my back without drugs, says a friend at dinner that evening. *Maybe you should think about that before you start taking those strong drugs.* I cringe at the phrase "strong drugs," picturing myself insensate in a crack house somewhere, or lying on a couch in an opium den. Working with homeless people can make a person skittish about any drug; the

230

wrong stuff in the wrong hands has ruined more lives than you could shake a stick at. What will I become if I take this stuff? But then what if I go to an acu-whatever and end up more seriously injured than before?

Besides, said the doctor, *you are depressed. You've had this accident and everything in your life has changed. Who wouldn't be depressed? This should help.* I'm startled to hear him say this, although I recognize the symptoms myself: disturbed sleep, concentration deficit, a pervasive sorrowful feeling, compulsive eating. In my work I have often encouraged people to take the psychotropic drugs prescribed for them, and have often been impatient at their reluctance to do so. Now I'm dragging *my* feet. I fear a substance that will make me feel different. I don't want to be different. I remember a homeless man telling me the same thing about the anti-psychotic drug he was supposed to be taking and which he desperately needed. *I don't want to be different, I'm me.* I was unsympathetic. And I was right. But now I understand how he felt.

DECEMBER 21

"The proof of the pudding is in the eating." —MIGUEL DE CERVANTES

Every Sunday, either my mother or my grandmother would stay home from church to cook dinner. Almost always, it was roast beef with Yorkshire pudding, the Sunday dinner of my father's Yorkshire childhood. We would walk in the door from church and be greeted by that wonderful smell. To this day, it means Sunday afternoon to me.

When I began to cook, I noticed that the recipes said you shouldn't beat the mixture very much: just enough to blend the ingredients until they were smooth. My mother beat hers to death. Then she'd let it rest and beat it again. And then again. *You don't have to do that,* I pointed out. I made a pudding without beating it, as a demonstration. Sure enough, mine came out light, fluffy, and sky-high, just like hers. *See,* I said, *you don't have to beat it at all. I like to do it this way,* she said. *But it's more work,* I said. *I just like to do it this way,* she insisted. Until she couldn't cook anymore, she did it her way: beat the eggs, milk and flour; let them sit; beat them; and let them sit again. Here is the way she did it:

YORKSHIRE PUDDING MY MOM'S WAY

2 c. milk   2 eggs   1/2 c. white flour   1 tsp. salt

Beat together eggs and milk; add flour and salt and beat well. Let rest at least five minutes. Beat well again; let rest. Beat well again and pour into 9" pie pan, into which you have poured 3 tbsp. of the drippings from the roast. Bake in a preheated 425° oven until puffy and brown, maybe 25 minutes; serve at once, with the roast. *Serves six.*

"They have sought out many inventions." —ECCLESIASTES 7:29

There are any number of folk legends associated with Christmas that probably have their roots in pagan mythology. They were handed down from generation to generation before the missionaries arrived, and then they were given the merest spritz of theological content so they could be told during the new feast of Christmas. The one about the animals talking on Christmas eve is probably one of these. The various tales about St. Nicholas rescuing poor children and providing impoverished girls with dowries may also be older than Christian belief; they may have been ancient pagan stories about a holy man that proved just as useful for the new religion as they had for the old. We know that Christmas trees date from pagan practice in Germany, and mistletoe and holly were sacred to Druid holidays in England before they became associated with the Nativity.

I bring this up because you often hear people complaining at this time of year about how we're getting way from the true meaning of Christmas. It turns out that we've *always* gotten away from the true meaning of Christmas—or, rather, we have always expressed its meaning in ways peculiar to the cultures in which we lived, and we have always taken stories and practices foreign to the religious festival of the Nativity and made them over so they sort of fit. I don't think there's anything so terrible about that.

So Frosty the Snowman comes to life, rather like the animals who suddenly began to talk in the stable at Bethlehem. King Wenceslaus and his page go out on a good errand, and a miracle saves the page from frostbite. Scrooge and the Grinch, each in his own century, repent of their selfishness. And everybody has a wonderful time on Christmas morning.

Religious people should teach their children their religious truths, but they shouldn't lose too much sleep over the many secular aspects of this time of year. Faith that's real isn't weak and spindly; it's pretty tough. Frosty the Snowman poses no threat.

DECEMBER 23

"Bah! Humbug!" —CHARLES DICKENS, *A CHRISTMAS CAROL*

Everyone loves *A Christmas Carol*. But Dickens grew to be downright sick of it by the end of his career; a large portion of his living came from personal appearances at which he read from his works, and no audience would let him leave without at least a sliver of Scrooge and Tiny Tim. Once, when he performed it for an audience of two thousand workers in Birmingham, the grim industrial center of nineteenth-century England, the people were so moved and delighted with Scrooge and Tiny Tim and the Spirit of Christmas Past that they sent over a present for Mrs. Dickens the next day: an elaborate cast-iron plant stand. They were poor people; for them, that was an expensive gift. They recognized Dickens as the tireless champion of the poor that he was, and they were transported by his vision of a Christmas which would change the life of a family that was as poor as their families.

They knew, as Dickens knew, that most human suffering is caused by human selfishness. *A Christmas Carol* holds out the possibility that it is not too late. Scrooge's cold heart melts. Bob Cratchitt will be able to support his family. Tiny Tim will *not* die. It is this hope that makes us love this story more than any other at this time of year.

DECEMBER 24

"One Christmas was so much like another...." —DYLAN THOMAS

Just about everybody who could be discharged has been. The only people in the hospital on Christmas eve are pretty darned sick. As I walk through the corridors on my way to visit a woman who has had a heart attack, I see families visiting loved ones, bringing them poinsettias, even tiny live Christmas trees. It is hard to be here at such a time. In some of the rooms I pass, a tense hush prevails: people wait in an anguished little cluster for someone they love to die.

What a terrible time of year for a tragedy like this, people say. And it certainly is. All of our longings for life to be perfect are especially keen in these last weeks of the year. We feel the places where love falls short in our lives very acutely right now. It is easy for us to feel as if everybody else were living the happy life we are denied.

And yet the times in life when we are shaken profoundly by tragedy are also the times when we experience the most profound spiritual growth. We immediately sort out the important from the unimportant when sorrow comes to us, and we are wiser for having done so. The Christmas you lost someone you loved will be the Christmas you never forget. It will be hard to get upset on a Christmas years hence because you have run out of wrapping paper or forgotten to buy special Christmas postage stamps. *That's nothing*, you'll tell yourself, and you'll be right. There is no better time of the year than these holidays for a person to come to understand that love is what they are all about, and that love must never be taken for granted.

DECEMBER 25

"There's no place like home for the holidays."

I talk on the phone with a divorced friend: she is suffering through the annual who-goes-where-for-Christmas agony. The next day I have breakfast with one of her daughters, who talks about how hard it is on the kids. *I didn't cause this divorce,* she says. *So why do I have to spend my Christmas break traveling around to implement it?*

She does, though. The children work out a plan for time with each parent, and they have a good time in each place. But it's hard: the pain everyone in the family feels about the divorce is worse at this time of year, when we all have Norman Rockwell images of family life dancing in our heads. Generally they are brave about it, carefully feeling their way through this transition from being one kind of family to being another. But my friend cries, sometimes, when she is alone. She used to make Christmas really beautiful for her children when they were little. She longs to be able to do that now.

I'm seriously thinking about doing Christmas myself next year, says one of the daughters. *Have a dinner in my apartment and invite everyone to come to me. Start making traditions of my own.* I think she's onto something. *New occasions teach new duties,* says the old hymn, and it's true. They can't resuscitate the family into being the way it was ten years ago for a few ornamental days at Christmas. A changed family can't do the holidays the same way it did before; that only makes the losses more painfully obvious. So maybe this is the answer for her family, Maybe this family's home is where the children are now, not where the parents are. Each family member should search her heart—or his— and discover what's the most important and loving thing to do now.

DECEMBER 26

"Health and intellect are the two blessings of life." —MENANDER

The leg that looked and felt like a piece of wood six months ago looks pretty much like a leg again. It is no longer swollen; I have an ankle now. Except for a purple scar at the very point of impact, it is the same color as the other leg, so I even have a matched set, just like I used to. The scar itself is no longer a dent; just a scar. It may well fade away altogether, the doctor says. Although it can take a while to fade—maybe a couple of years.

I have been impatient throughout this slow healing process. I still am, comparing my abilities with what I used to be able to do before my accident, rather than with the extent to which I was disabled immediately afterward. That's the wrong approach: all it does is make me feel depressed. I can't run, like I could before. But I can walk, which was something I couldn't do six months ago. I can't sit for any length of time without pain. But I can sleep through the night without being wakened by pain or taking a drug. That wasn't true six months ago.

Except for some special exercises, I haven't done anything that has made me better. There has been no surgery. My body has done it all on its own. My only contribution has been to give it the time it needs, and all I had to do to accomplish that was to lie down more. I imagine this process going on inside my horizontal body, patiently continuing day and night, cell by cell, starting from a few seconds after the accident and going on 'til today, and for as long as necessary. What a remarkable machine the body is.

And yet I found it so hard. I've had a hard year, I tell a friend, and it feels as if it were true. Why is it "hard" to rest more? It ought to be *easy*. Why have I not done what I've always joked about doing if I were ever laid up: rent all the movies I've never seen and enjoy myself? I didn't relax and enjoy it. What I did was limp back to work too soon. It's not that lying down is hard. What's hard is losing the major part of myself, the part that defines herself by what she does.

DECEMBER 27

"Thank God for tea!" —SYDNEY SMITH

You're not supposed to eat your big meal of the day in the evening, I am told. Everything that you put into your mouth then turns into fat unless you do some kind of vigorous exercise. I'm usually so exhausted at dinnertime that my only exercise is a trip from table to bed.

But lunchtime is no good, either. There was a time when I could pack away a fabulous lunch, even a glass or two of wine, and still go back to work and be productive in the afternoon. Now I will just go back to work and fall asleep if I eat heavily. Maybe that's middle age.

They say it's best to have a big breakfast, and eat light for the rest of the day. But if I run for the seven o'clock train, I don't have time for a princely breakfast. Maybe I'll grab a cup of coffee and an inferior muffin after I get to work, but that is not a Good Meal. I'd love to have one of my wonderful diner breakfasts, but often there is no time.

So there is not time in my day for a large and relaxing meal. Instead, I eat in the undisciplined, pressured way associated with people who use food as if it were a drug.

My father is English. He has tea every day at around four o'clock. This is not just a cup of tea; it is a small meal, with a slice of toast or two, a cookie, a piece of cheese or fruit. He's retired, of course, and his days are not like mine. But millions of English men and women who are *not* retired find time for this civilized interlude before the close of the business day, and don't return home with a day's ravenousness to unleash at the dinner table.

Just an idea.

DECEMBER 28

"...a memory without pain..." —SOPHOCLES

I am halfway through my fourth day without any pain in my back at all. I can hardly believe it when I wake up in the morning. I almost don't want to tell anybody for fear the God of Pain will hear me and notice his mistake. But it's true. *Four days.*

Perhaps it's the dry weather, and it will return again when it gets damp. I don't even care if it does. These four days have shown that I will one clay be free. I won't spend the rest of my life the way I've spent these many months. I've become so accustomed to having pain all the time that it has become part of my life. It's not the end of the world to have pain. I could handle it for my whole life if I had to have it. I could.

But now it looks like I won't have to. *It's terrible that this accident happened to you,* my friend says. And it is. It came out of nowhere for no reason. But now I see signs that its effects will have an end—signs that many other people who have other terrible injuries never get. That doesn't make any sense, either. I didn't deserve the injury and I don't deserve the healing. Which is why we should cultivate the joy of every good thing that happens to us. Might as well milk it for all it's worth. We usually don't control the comings and goings of these things. They are ordinarily not the result of our good or bad behavior. So we can't predict when the next wallop will come.

Or the next bouquet.

DECEMBER 29

"When Herod saw that he had been tricked ... he became infuriated...."
—MATTHEW 2:16

Today is the day in the Christian calendar called the Feast of the Holy Innocents. It commemorates the story of King Herod's order that all male children under the age of two be killed, in the hope that he would kill the infant Jesus and thus eliminate a rival for his throne. Like the similar tale about Moses in the Old Testament, this story turns the tables on an unjust king, and the baby escapes unharmed.

In both stories, though, we are faced with the large-scale slaughter of children. The artists of the Middle Ages often depicted such slaughter of the innocents. The sacking of cities and the ruthless murder of their inhabitants were features of medieval warfare, so it may well be that the scenes of massacre which these artists depicted were things they had actually witnessed. In any case, they dwelt on the horrors with deep sensitivity to the sorrow of it: in one painting at the Basilica of San Francesco in Assisi, a mother holds her bloodied child and nuzzles him as if to wake him, unable to believe that he is dead.

This is such a child-centered time of year. A news item about a child's suffering seems even sadder during this time of year than it does at other times. We know that all children should be happy, all the time, and yet we also know that many are not. Having just spent more than we intended to, perhaps, on our own kids, we are keenly aware of the many youngsters who are not as lucky. *Thank God we can do this much*, we say to ourselves. And a voice inside every mom or dad says, softly, *but what about the others?*

DECEMBER 30

"To think is to say no." —EMILE AUGUSTE CHARTIER

A thirtyish mother of two small children is annoyed: her friend has again asked her to watch her children on a school holiday that is not a work holiday. This is the third time in two months. *I feel badly about it, because I know how hard these holidays are for her and I sympathize. But I feel undervalued, as if my time is not worth anything because I don't punch a clock. I like having her kids come—they all get along well and have a good time. And I like to help out. I guess I just don't want her to assume that I will. I do have a life, you know.*

We're so chained to the dollar bill and the clock that it's hard for us to imagine time except in terms of work. We figure up the cost of everything we do as if we were being paid: *this is worth my time, that isn't. I'll have someone else do it.* It is easy to make the unconscious equation, *"work = remuneration,"* a part of our lives without even recognizing it. But when we do this, the person who does not earn money becomes less worthy, easier to interrupt. *You can do that*, someone says, *you're home all day*. WRONG—buy that line, and you lose all claim on your own time and skill. You may be home all day, but you're still responsible for the productive use of your time. You won't be productive if you don't make decisions about how to spend it. You'll just be frazzled and angry and too polite to say so.

So *say* so. Get yourself a bottom line and stick to it. It's wonderful to help out a friend on a school holiday; tell her in advance that you need many days' notice because you're busy. And if you don't get that notice, just say no.

DECEMBER 31

"Hope springs eternal in the human breast." —ALEXANDER POPE

At the end of 1989, the Berlin Wall came down. The Soviet empire imploded, collapsed upon itself, a system which could no longer endure. The possibility of self-determination became real for the millions of people who had lived under its oppressive weight for decades.

Leonard Bernstein journeyed to Berlin to conduct a special New Year's concert at the Wall. An enormous chorus joined the Berlin Philharmonic in the fourth movement of Beethoven's Ninth Symphony, the famous musical setting of the German poet Schiller's "Ode to Joy." Only Bernstein took some liberty with the tsext: instead of the German word "Freude", which means "joy," he substituted the word "Freiheit." It means "freedom." The huge crowd went wild. My husband and I were listening to it on the radio with a friend. We went wild, too. It was wonderful to be alive during a moment in history like that. The Nineties were going to be a decade of peace. At last, the Cold War was over.

It's been a few years. The Nineties are far from being a decade of peace. Human history is like that: one problem always replaces another. Your life is like that and so is mine. At last, we say to ourselves when we've climbed a mountain. And then we look up, and there's another one. But that's okay. Something in us continues to struggle on. We continue to hope. We keep on trying. We find things to laugh at, even if sometimes we must laugh through tears.

We have a New Year's Eve party every year. Old friends and neighbors come. One woman is undergoing chemotherapy for a recurrence of cancer. Several people have married off sons and daughters and several have had grandchildren. One man lost his wife. Two people have lost their jobs, and two others have retired.

Another woman's divorce just became final. A mixture of good and bad news, the year just past, just like all the other years. And we accept the bad things, somehow, and rejoice in the good. And clink our glasses to another year, not knowing what it holds. We are magnificent.

If you liked this book, Morehouse also publishes these others by Barbara Crafton...

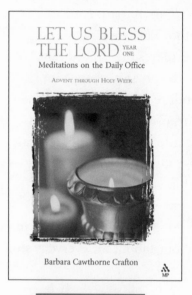

LET US BLESS
THE LORD YEAR ONE
Meditations on the Daily Office

ADVENT THROUGH HOLY WEEK

Barbara Cawthorne Crafton

MP

**Coming in
Fall 2004**

Let Us Bless the Lord

*Year One, Volume One: Advent
through Holy Week
Meditations on the Daily Office*

Barbara Crafton brings her trademark
humor, pathos, and marvelous story-
telling ability to the Daily Offices,
where her writings complement
perfectly the morning, noon, evening
and nighttime prayers.

Let Us Bless the Lord will be published
in four volumes. The first, covering
Year One: Advent through Holy Week,
will be available in Fall 2004.

Some Things You Just Have to Live With
Musings on Middle Age

In Some Things You Just Have to Live With, author Barbara Cawthorne Crafton explores the "spilled milk" of our lives, the physical changes our bodies endure, and the new and energizing purpose we can discover by plunging into the middle of life in a deeper—and sometimes mystifying— relationship with God.

". . . enormously well written ... so good, you feel as though you're in her home and that she's a good friend gabbing about the everyday stuff of life." —*The Dallas Morning News*

". . . a group of little essays so readable, so full of charm and subtle theology, one might read it in one sitting." —*Diolog* (Episcopal Diocese of Atlanta)

Also available as an audiobook, read by the author, on CD or cassette.

Meditations on the Psalms
For Every Day of the Year

A wonderful way to start or end
each day.

"Crafton writes with a combination of
toughness and compassion; her stories
are funny and tragic, and her observations about everyday life are well
stated." —*Library Journal*

"Crafton has a good eye for mystical
moments and for the ways we can see
God's presence in the midst of everyday
life." —*Spirituality & Health*

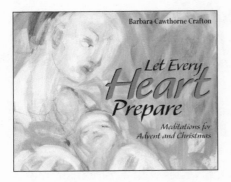
Barbara Cawthorne Crafton

Let Every Heart Prepare

Meditations for Advent and Christmas

Deepen your experience of Advent and Christmas with Barbara Crafton's meditations, keyed to the hymns of the season.

"Lots of personal family stories and a warm narrative voice make this little book most appealing." —*The Living Church*

"… a sort of grownup Advent calendar of meditations for each day of Advent and Christmastide … I can't think of a better way to observe the season." —*The Interim* (Episcopal Diocese of Missiouri)

"I hope that you find yourself humming familiar tunes as your read, and that the condition persists for the rest of the day." —Barbara Crafton

Living Lent
Meditations for These Forty Days

"Claim some minutes for quiet reflection every day. Just do it ... We're allowed to enjoy things in Lent now, as long as we don't make too much noise."
—Barbara Crafton

Spend a few minutes each day during Lent with one of today's favorite voices, Barbara Crafton.

"We want our Jesus to have been a superman of some sort, to have been unnaturally good and bright as a child, to have lived life in a superhuman way. The church has not taught this. Jesus was not superman. His death was not a megadeath. It was a human death, like ours, soaked in sorrow and betrayal and defeat. Truly human, he tasted our despair. Truly God, he redeems it." —from *Living Lent*

The Sewing Room
Uncommon Reflections on Life, Love and Work

"To read this book is to contemplate the meaning of all the small moments and major events that make a life worthwhile ... Weaving together threads of the lovely and the ugly, Crafton shows the richness of life." —*American Reporter*

"Through honesty, humor, openness and real vulnerability, this writer reflects on life, love and work, and invites readers to enter her 'sewing room' and do the same." —*Horizons*

"a book that can touch the heart" —*Healing Ministry*